SALES SECRETS
you don't know

SALES SECRETS THAT CAN HELP YOU
EARN MORE ROCK HARD COIN!

TRACEY PRESTON COOK

Date of Publication: January 2022
p: 320
ISBN: 978-1-943573-04-2

Cover design and illustrations by author.
Edited by Amy Beth Cook.

IMMERSIVE
PUBLICATIONS

Thank you to my wife Amy
and our four sons
for your love and support.

These are icons you'll see throughout this book.

 A sales secret you don't know.

 An example of what's being discussed.

 An analogy or analogical example.

 Sidebar commentary or additional information.

 Example phone messaging.

 A story or example of a sales story.

 A persuasive strategy.

 A tactical approach.

 Utility tips.

 Cool. Check it out.

SECTION 1

ROCK HARD COIN

"I'll sell the *new* torches up at the caves. I'm better looking and subtle. You're way too 'Ooga! Ooga!' but that may be what it takes to sell those 'refurbished' torches hut-to-hut."

"Product value without an emotional appeal is like an extension cord that wraps around in a loop and plugs into itself. The cord has value but doesn't have power."—ImmersiveSelling.com

CHAPTER 1

The Quad Close

You will have to ask for the sale. Everyone in sales must. Why do we feel anxious about asking? It's a question we even get paid to ask—and it's just one question.

Just one.

SALES SECRET #1:
The Quad Close

When you ask for the sale, that one question requires four decisions to be made.

There are four decisions to be made from the one question because before buying, the decision maker (DM) must decide:

- If they trust you/the product.
- If they emotionally want the result you are offering.
- If they can logically rationalize buying and doing so from you.
- If they can or will financially pay for the product.

You have an immense amount of influence over these decisions (which is why you have a career in persuasive sales) and on some level you already know this. That's precisely why you may feel apprehension about asking for the sale. You may not be sure if there are sufficient levels of trust, emotion, and logic to allow the mind of the key decision maker (KDM) to pay you. What if the notion that you are "afraid to ask for the sale" is actually intuitive wisdom telling you that the KDM isn't ready to pay for it? That would explain the past apprehensive feelings. The hesitation may not have been because you're fearful, but because you're intuitive.

From the very onset of your sales situations (especially those in virtual and video) you will be working on these four components of the sales close which is why I call it the "Quad Close." Asking one question to close your sale, will require four...not one...four decisions to be made. Each part is a component of the whole, or a "component sale" of the Quad Close. The four component sales are:

- The **TRUST** component sale.
- The **EMOTIONAL** component sale.
- The **LOGICAL** component sale.
- The **FINANCIAL** component sale.

These component sales that make up the Quad Close are occurring simultaneously.

SALES SECRET #2:
The True Buying Motives

Decision makers buy what they emotionally want from whom they trust. When they can logically validate their decision they will financially pay for it.

What you'll notice as you observe future sales situations (both yours and others) is that the first three component sales of the Quad Close ***must close*** before the Financial Sale ***will*** close. In the past when you were using that one question to close your sale, you were asking for the Financial Sale—the fourth component sale in the Quad Close.

Those sellers who *are* aware of this will likely become proficient at closing and earn a larger pile of Rock Hard Coin. Once you know this secret, you can start progressing each of the component sales right from the onset of the first sales situation. What follows are descriptions of what occurs when one of the component sales hasn't closed but you ask for the Financial Sale anyway.

The Trust Sale Not Closing

When you ask for the sale (*the Financial Sale*), if the decision makers don't trust you (*the Trust Sale does not close*), even if they want the product (*the Emotional Sale does close*) and can logically support the purchase (*the Logical Sale does close*) and have the capital to pay for it—they won't. At least not from you. The decision makers (DMs) may find a seller they *do* trust and you've done all the work for someone else by "selling the product" (*instead of selling the result*). This is a down side of favoring "product-centric" selling.

The Emotional Sale Not Closing

When you ask for the sale (*the Financial Sale*), if the decision makers don't want what you are selling (*the Emotional Sale does not close*), even if they support the purchase with logic (*the Logical Sale does close*), trust you (*the Trust Sale does close*), and have the financial means to pay for it, they won't. You've probably seen this wherein every logical reason ***not to buy*** was eliminated and every logical reason ***to buy*** was illuminated, yet the decision makers just wouldn't buy. Emotional want is the primary buying motive.

The Logical Sale Not Closing

When you ask for the sale (*the Financial Sale*), if the decision makers can not logically rationalize or support the decision (*the Logical Sale does not close*), although they may trust you (*the Trust Sale does close*), and want what you are selling (*the Emotional Sale does close*), and have the capital to pay for it, they won't. The inability to support or logically rationalize the decision to buy could be due to the timing, lack of proof, priorities, ROI, etc. The logical validation could be either to themselves or others.

Whether you're remote selling, in person, on video, in social or within a virtual showroom the Quad Close is the fundamental construct of your sale. In high value complex B2B sales with multiple decision makers in a consensus buying committee situation, those four components add even more intensity to the decision they will make. Whether the price is $100 or $100B, ***the higher the price and value of your sale, the more the Quad Close matters.*** Once you understand what it is, the Quad Close is not an obstacle. It is an advantage. You'll also realize that your efforts invested in honest selling and truthful approaches are being rewarded by contributing to both the Trust Sale and the Emotional Sale. This makes it easier for the decision makers to rationalize reasons to buy. Your honesty supports the Logical Sale.

The Quad Close is a tool. To utilize it, you must pique curiosity because you need engagement or you cannot begin the sale. For that you need a tool that I call an **"Emotive Gatekey."**

Inspiration for the Quad Close

Aristotle [384 BC - 322 BC] posited that there are three basic appeals in persuasive rhetoric (sales):

- **Ethos** (*an ethical appeal*) —which is "**trust.**"
- **Pathos** (*a pathological appeal*) —which is "**emotion.**"
- **Logos** (*a logical appeal*) —which is "**logical proof.**"

The primary forms of persuasive appeals have been largely accepted for thousands of years.

Gorgias [483 BC - 375 BC] (whom I personally consider to be a foundational framer of sales) was a sophist who introduced persuasive arrangements (what he called "Kairos") that allow sellers to modify their message to fit proper timing and audience receptivity.

As a starting point for my work and developing the Quad Close, I took inspiration from Aristotle, Gorgias and the many sophists, philosophers, and rhetoricians that have contributed to the foundation of sales.

"Defeatist advice is a warped assessment of you from toxic people. The advice and assessment both function like curved funhouse mirrors. Just because the distorted images have some familiarity, does not mean that you should believe them."—ImmersiveSelling.com

Chapter 2

The Emotive Gatekey

"Blonde...name's Blonde," is what his smooth, practiced swagger suggested he could say when I introduced myself, but I didn't get his name. So in my mind, "Blonde" it was.

TRACEY: **"I got a call last night that you needed help with a large enrollment. I just arrived, where would you like me to set up?"**
BLONDE: **"Yo. Dude you can put ye'r stuff down there at the end. I'll be there in awhile," he said in a dismissive tone that matched up perfectly with the swagger.**

> **I had received many months' worth of rejection in one day.**

He waved me in the direction of a line of tables each with an insurance agent setting up a laptop or arranging brochures. It was an annual enrollment back in the early 2000s and he had invested years into cultivating a team of insurance agents he called his "Supreme Team." We were enrolling the employees of a large entertainment-type complex which included hotels, golf courses, shops, casinos, and conference centers. Blonde was the primary agent on the account.

Because the benefit premiums were paid by the employees, each one had to visit with an agent and there were only 10 days allotted for the enrollment of our insurance products. The employees could opt into (buy) any policy (accident, sickness, dental, life, etc.), or opt out entirely.

I was unsure how I made it onto Blonde's Supreme Team, especially since I was a fairly new agent. Agents could earn six months' worth of commissions in just 10 days, so every agent licensed for that state wanted to be on the Supreme Team. I intended to do what I could to prove myself—I was nearly flat broke and hadn't even earned that month's rent back home.

Everything about Blonde said, "surfer dude posing in a business suit." He (supposedly) spent most of the year in Fiji (which he referred to as "My Island") and said he came back only for this enrollment. With a 30% share of every commission paid from agents on his account and 100% commission on his own sales, it was easy to see why that 10 days could potentially fund his year. I'd gone to the end table and had been setting up for a few minutes when he walked over and cleared up any confusion as to how I got on his team.

BLONDE: "Dude, you see that corner way over there?" he asked, sneering a bit as he pointed to the opposite corner of the conference room.
TRACEY: "I do, but I have a question—" I tried to respond.
BLONDE: "Look dude! Over there. Don't look at me, look where I'm pointing."
TRACEY: "The corner with the rickety little table and—"

The rickety table had what looked like a plastic kindergarten chair and a few bent-over fake plants that had collapsed under the weight of someone's frustration.

BLONDE: "Dude. You listening, noob?"
TRACEY: "Yes. I'm listening."
BLONDE: "Way over there in the QC is where you are. You're not here. Over there is you. Here's not you. Any questions?" he asked, pointing again to the Kindergarten Corner.
TRACEY: "Well—" I tried.
BLONDE: "Look again. See it? The QC?"

I took another look and decided that the only thing missing from the sad ensemble was a "dunce hat."

TRACEY: "Well, so, what's the QC?"
BLONDE: "The 'Quitters' Corner.' You're today's 'Waiver Dude.' So that's what we call you. 'Waiver Dude.' We could go with 'Waiver Noob' if you like that better?"

He used air quotes to bracket and underscore the important parts, which, you know, helped me to keep up. But I already knew exactly what the "waiver dude" would get to do. Fill out waivers.

State law required waivers to be signed by everyone who opted out of coverage. This prevented anyone from claiming, after an injury, that they'd "meant to enroll" but were denied or negligently overlooked at the time of enrollment. Waivers were pure overhead and paid absolutely nothing but they proved every employee had the opportunity to enroll. Each waiver had to be filled out by hand, by a licensed agent, which took three minutes on a 3-part carbonless form and then signed by the employee/decision maker before returning to their job.

Blonde used the prestige of the Supreme Team to lure in new agents trying to prove themselves. The rate of attrition for the noob position in the QC was high, thus the name. Each new agent probably had the same thought I did. Stick around a bit and hope for a shot at selling.

> This company is a stellar insurance provider with impressive products that I would highly recommend. The company is perhaps one of the very best insurance companies in the world with awesome management and stellar customer service—every company has a small blemish (all it takes is one blonde apple in the bunch).

TRACEY: "Am I permitted to sell?" I asked in a measured tone.
BLONDE: "To the 'nopers'?"
TRACEY: "Yes. May I sell to people opting out?"
BLONDE: "Listen Waiver Dude, if you think you can eke out a commission after we've already done a 'sit,' you just go right ahead and knock yourself out. Just so you know, you won't be the first to try that...and no one, and I mean no one has ever closed a single sale sitting in the QC. It can't be done Dude, but you just get on over there and try."

Blonde was right about people saying "no" outright. ***I had received many months' worth of rejection in one day.*** He was also right about closing. I didn't even come close to being able to talk about a single solitary product, let alone close a sale. Every decision maker had just heard "the pitch" from one of the best agents in the company and had no desire to hear any of it again. "All I wanna do is sign the waiver 'n' get back to work," was the objection du jour.

So. It didn't go well. At some point I stopped trying to sell and started asking more questions and taking mental and written notes (after they left I'd jot down on an index card anything they mentioned that could be helpful later). I asked all about their job, why they didn't buy, why they had considered it but then declined (in a very unassuming and consultative tone). I did a lot of listening. A lot.

What I heard was at least a dozen different variants of the same objection, "Can't afford it. Not enough in my paycheck as it is... 'n you guys think I should be deductin' more?" Later that evening on my way out, I assured Blonde that I'd be back the following morning. He burst out laughing.

TRACEY: "No. Really. I'll be here in the morning." I was completely serious.
BLONDE: "You're trying to get me to call off the invite for the next noob—you won't show and I'll be left high-n-dry and we'll all have to fill out our own waivers. Do you think I'm stupid?"
TRACEY: "Not at all. But I'll be the first one in. Ready to fill out waivers. Same spot. The QC's mine."
BLONDE: "Mmmkay whatever, Waiver Dude."
TRACEY: "The QC is mine."

I knew that the next day when the new, uninformed agent showed up, Blonde would give that agent the one open spot at the end of the row that I had tried to set up at. He'd do it just to spite me (which he did). So, I intended to find a way before the next morning to actually sell from the QC.

But how? It feels impossible.

The best agents had already presented amazing products by the time I got to visit with the decision makers (DMs). Everyone I had access to had already emphatically said "no," and came from all walks and all levels of the organization.

There were no observable patterns such as "management are all choosing to opt out" or "maintenance buys accident policies but housekeeping opts out." There didn't seem to be a behavioral pattern (visible at that point) and everyone signing a waiver was protecting their paycheck and had their decision set-in-stone.

After checking into my hotel room (I was spending my rent money on a hotel), I got right to work and set up a hotel-wall-version of what I call a "Wall of Wisdom" (W.O.W.) [*see Strati-Tactical #3*]. It consisted of the day's index cards and many new ones completed that night. What I denoted on the cards were: facts, thoughts, observations, objections, resolutions, motives, data, mannerisms, replies, statements and opinions. I then organized them into four categories mirroring the Quad Close. After a long work session, I realized I had not defined the real problem that I was trying to solve. This is very common in sales and business. The real problem is often unknown—but many *think* they know.

My real problems were:

1. They didn't emotionally care. There was no emotive engagement.
2. All people have what I call internal "mental gatekeepers" (MGKs). These function similarly to those that guard the front ends of corporations except the MGKs guard the time of the DM by making mental decisions to engage or avoid engagement. They guard against anything irrelevant to the persons' priorities, which was the conclusion reached by the MGKs (my product had been reviewed and was irrelevant) of the DMs I had access to.

My problem seemed like the other agents had already presented the products, received a "no," followed by my attempts to persuade. While this was true, it was the symptom, not the core challenge (which was they didn't care, weren't engaging, due to irrelevance).

My solution was to build some kind of emotional engagement tool that would pique curiosity and make the DMs care so the MGKs would let me have access to their minds' attention. This would result in engagement. I decided to call the tool I needed to make, an "Emotive Gatekey."

SALES SECRET #3:
Emotive Gatekeys

An Emotive Gatekey can probably be developed for every product being sold. If it's currently selling (even with poor-to-moderate results)**, then it's highly likely a gatekey could be developed for sales support.**

Just as the sun was rising I looked across the Wall of Wisdom taped up all over the room (I used temporary drafting tape for the cards to avoid damaging the walls). A pattern within the decision makers' mindsets emerged.

What is everyone's primary motive for NOT buying? They live paycheck-to-paycheck...meaning they are emotionally cranked about their paycheck and don't want to lose any more of it. So. They certainly don't want to lose ALL of it either. It's the paychecks...

I had downloaded the technical copies of all of the policies, which I was then rifling through searching for anything related to paychecks, earnings, or replacement. The policy name holding my Emotive Gatekey was called something unwieldy like, "The Personal Short Term Employment Accidental Injury Compensation Policy for Employees" (which just rolls right off the tongue, huh?). That may not have been the exact name (I either can't remember, or I'm maintaining the company's anonymity) but basically it was a form of insurance for injuries leading to loss of work. The policy defined "unable to work" as sustaining any injury, on or off the job, that would prevent someone from fulfilling 100% of their on-the-job duties as written in their job description.

SALES SECRET #4:
Emotive Gatekeys Are Sometimes in the Details

Details are important. Very often, you will find the basis for your Emotive Gatekey in the finest of fine details.

For example, a maintenance professional who broke their leg skiing would not be able to climb ladders or work on slippery floor surfaces, or ascend to the roof for maintenance, and as such, would be considered eligible. Once the injuries were confirmed by a medical professional, the injured employee could collect cash benefits that would replace most of their paycheck (until they healed and returned to work as directed by a medical professional).

The policies state this is insuring against injury and an inability to work, but it's not the person being insured. It's the paycheck. It's paycheck insurance. That even sounds snappy. I can't call it "paycheck insurance" officially but I can reorient the perception of what the policy protects. It's paycheck assurance. An assurance they will keep getting paid should anything happen.

I also learned that the policy (that no one was selling—but I would) paid a commission almost three times higher than the core products Blonde's Supreme Team members were selling. It involved a lot of paperwork and wage information so the other agents avoided selling it.

SALES SECRET #5:
Consensus Trance Assessment

The reason some challenges are so difficult is the true underlying problem may not be clearly defined or known. There's a sort of consensus trance that accepts a group assessment or "the way we've always done it" as the accurate diagnosis of a problem. Trying to solve that diagnosis will yield answers that solve the peripheral symptoms. Emotive Gatekeys solve core challenges.

I grabbed only an hour of sleep (which feels worse than staying up) to ensure I would arrive first. I was a blur of activity and made friends with the maintenance department. They either liked me, or disliked Blonde (or both) so they provided me with all new furniture so I could convert the QC into the "Question Center."

Throughout that second day, I had just three minutes with each decision maker while I filled out the waivers. After some small talk, I would then just casually ask, "Do you have any way to insure against the loss of your paycheck?" The reactions were pretty consistent, starting with the first employee that morning who was opting out. She looked surprised and intrigued. "What's that?" she asked, leaning forward, "I've never even heard of that. Like what is it?" I explained that a savings account was obvious insurance against paycheck interruption. I also shared the reality that most cannot save enough to cover up to a twelve-month recovery from an injury, but that our policy does insure against interruption of their paycheck. I then shared some thinking on how people insure their boats, cars, homes, and even themselves with life insurance—but the one thing central to paying for all of that is left unprotected...their paycheck.

SALES SECRET #6:
An Emotive Gatekey Can Be a Question

Questions are too often overlooked as viable tools of persuasion but are some of the most effective in your kit.

By the end of the enrollment I had earned a very respectable pile of Rock Hard Coin. An Emotive Gatekey literally uses something of incredible emotional relevance (so you have to first figure that out) and reframes a perception to make a key (then you develop that) to unlock resistance in the mind using an emotional appeal. An Emotive Gatekey makes its appeal where the sale is actually located because **your sale is in the mind.**

Sales Secrets in This Book

A portion of the sales secrets in this book are featured as those numbered up to #116. The rest are all located within the text, tools, analogies, stories and sidebar commentary. When you read something you find valuable that you didn't know, you have found one of the many others.

"Your spoken words are transmitted like Wi-Fi into the minds of decision makers and are interpreted as holographic ideas. The DMs imagine whatever scenario you suggest."—ImmersiveSelling.com

Chapter 3

Your Sale Is in the Mind

Your sales are physically located within the minds of the decision makers you are appealing to. You should see that your income is controlled 100% by those minds. Your ability to influence the mind is what will produce a larger or smaller pile of Rock Hard Coin. Your mind set, skill set, sales tool set and efforts will modulate the size and accumulation rate of your pile.

> **"While you are selling, stay focused on where your sales are located; the mind is where your sale actually is.**

The sale is not in a manila file folder. It's not in your CRM. It's not in the sales pipeline (the pipe). Your sale is not somewhere in your office. It's not located in the proposal you just completed. ***While you are selling, stay focused on where your sales are located; the mind is where your sale actually is.***

Many sellers invest far too much time and effort into the physical environment of their sales and not enough into the mental environment of the decision makers. What is happening in the room or on the screens, matters far less than what is occurring in the minds of decision makers.

Where'd the Sale Go?

Let's assume you're on week five of working an important sale and it's going exceptionally well. It shows all of the indicators typical of sales you've closed in the past.

The KDM, "Diane," even speaks of the various components of your sale in the context of an eventuality. For example, "Well, actually we can work out the finer details of scheduling the training next month when we get an installation date set." Diane probably wants to buy, trusts you, and can logically support the purchase and installation decision. You both agree to meet again in a few weeks to allow her schedule to lighten up.

What you don't know, and neither does Diane, is that the company is being acquired and the new investors are replacing Diane with their own "Diane" whom you've never met. When you arrive weeks later for your meeting, there's a predictable conversation with the gatekeeper (GK):

GK: "Oh...um, oh no. No one called you?"
YOU: "No. Why?"
GK: "Diane is no longer with the company."
YOU: "What? How did tha—when did this happen?"
GK: "I can't disclose that information but her calls and meetings are being taken by 'Marissa.' Someone should have contacted you. Marissa will be taking all of Diane's meetings."

So where is the sale? At that specific moment your sale is no longer in the building because it's in the mind of Diane. Your sale went out the door when Diane packed up her box of things from her office.

Your thinking may be of the let-well-enough-alone variety, followed by, *"If seller 'A' and seller 'B' both go into separate complex B2B sales situations and one believes the sale is located in the mind, while the other seller believes the sale is located in the pipeline or a file folder, what difference does that even make?"*

SALES SECRET #7:
The Lone KDM

Working with just one KDM may carry the same risk as working on a business document on a laptop with just one copy of the file on the hard drive. You should establish a backup option.

Technically it shouldn't matter if the actions, decisions, investments-of-time, resources, and appeals created by both sellers are nearly identical and everything goes "text book" perfect. But very few sales progress according to plan.

SALES SECRET #8:
Your Focal Point of Relevance

When you focus on the mind of the KDM, don't focus on yourself, your product, your company, or interests. Focus on the KDMs'. That focal point will probably increase your chances of receiving a "yes."

If seller "B" believes the sale is located in the file folder, CRM, or the pipeline (pipe), their efforts will probably be reactionary and directed toward product-focused appeals. If seller "A" believes that the sale is in the mind, the focus will be less on the seller and more on the minds of the DMs and KDMs. Seller "A" will engage in consultative strategies, open-ended questions and various levels of discovery. All of these differences will lead to thinking tactically when your strategy is focused on the decision makers. Understanding your end point goal is an important aspect of tactical way-point thinking.

Why Call Money "Rock Hard Coin"?

We have direct deposit, check cashing by smartphone image, and electronic transfers that convert our perception of income to just digits and balances. Expenditures don't feel as real either, with automatic withdrawals, debit cards, auto deductions, and scanned transactions. The associative meaning of money has lost some of its weight. "Rock Hard Coin" is a phrase that counters the objectification of earnings. The reason casinos convert visitors' cash into plastic chips is so that gamblers have a lowered regard for their money. "Rock Hard Coin" reverses those processes in your mind and adds weight to the perception you have of your sales earnings. This sets up an exchange rate within your mind between efforts and results.

Starting back in the early 1990s, I would take one full commission earned, and cash it at the bank. I would bring in a set of leather pouch-type sacks and request the check be cashed into coin. I got the idea from period films that featured the type of oil-skinned pouches you might see dropped down upon a pirate's table in the old world or carried about in the Highlands of Scotland. The resounding "thud" of a sack of coin is unmistakable and stays with you so I wanted to recreate that. It's an advantage to remember the heavy clink sound (muted slightly by the leather sack), and think of that every time you wish to quit your sales endeavors (especially prospecting).

When you want to quit at 4:00 PM and grant yourself a "well-deserved early quit time," you'll think of that resounding thud of a sack of Rock Hard Coin and equate quitting early to potentially missing out on a new sack. The phrase "Rock Hard Coin" adds real weight to the meaning of sales commissions (and it also sounds cool).

"It is more effective to use logic to help someone ***buy from you*** rather than using logic to ***sell to them***."—ImmersiveSelling.com

CHAPTER 4

Tactical Way-Point Thinking

Becoming lost in the wilderness while backpacking induces both disorientation and intense panic. This is especially true when the "genre of lost" is not remedied by simply backtracking to find where the trail became a bit fuzzy or discovering where you sort of wandered off the path a bit. That's not lost—that's getting a little turned around. In that scenario you get to just walk back, do the "aha" thing with a sigh of relief, get back on the trail and all is well.

> **"Forward thinking develops product. Reverse thinking sells it.**

"Actually lost" induces intensified panic and a core dump of adrenaline when you realize you'll be spending the night wherever you happen to be when it gets dark.

That's "actually lost."

Everyone in sales has become actually lost within a sales situation at some point in their career. Everyone. In the wilderness when we get lost we tend to panic and run (usually in the wrong direction) back where we came from to try and regain the trail. The compulsion insists we return to what is familiar to stop the panic. We run because we just want it to be over.

Almost invariably, of the 360 directions we could run, with only one direction being correct, the chances are slim the right direction is selected in a state of panic. The same is true in sales situations. When we become lost we run to what is familiar. Like the familiar trail being sought once again in the wilderness, we run to logic in our sales situations. Logic is familiar and feels like it is the way out. It's a default mode to return to, which is why I call it "default logical sales mode" (DLSM).

SALES SECRET #9:
Default Logical Sales Mode (DLSM)

When a sales situation isn't going well, it is a natural reaction to seek out a strategy that will work. Often sellers will fall back on what they know, which usually consists of logical proof, data, facts, downloads, and marketing collateral. The problem is the sales situations become dominated by the Logical Sale, which may or may not be the actual causation (a lack of proof) **for the sales situation sliding into the weeds. Running to logic is a mental state or mode that becomes a default fall-back position.**

Being lost in a sales situation means there is a disconnect between you and where the sale actually is, in the mind of the DM. So being lost in the situation means you don't know *where they are*. Even if you know *where you are*, your position in the sales situation isn't relevant to earning Rock Hard Coin until you know where they are. We have to find out where the DMs and KDMs actually are in their thinking because that's going to be the way out. Discovery questions are perhaps the most effective tool [*see section 5, chapter 16*].

In the wilderness you regain your orientation by climbing a tree or mountain to establish an overview. In sales we can use open-ended questions to establish that overview. In the wilderness we would be searching for anything human made like a road, power line, or a radio tower on the horizon. If humans built it, they will need to maintain it. This means there will be a road from the radio tower back to civilization. In sales we seek out "the radio tower" which will represent our goal—usually a closed sale or the close of your incremental "mini sale" which would be the next commitment you are seeking.

From the tree top or mountain top perspective we could plot a path from the radio tower all the way back to where we are. We could accomplish this by plotting tactical way-points based on prominent landmarks such as a tall tree, bluff, mountain, stream, or unique outcropping. Even if zig-zagging, we would need to follow each way-point to the next to reach the radio tower and not become re-lost.

SALES SECRET #10:
Reorient a Sales Situation with Questions

It's not that logical proof can't work. It can. It's more powerful, however, when combined with the other appeals of emotion and trust. Try to explore the sales situation with discovery questions to learn where decision makers are in their thinking.

Once you've learned the DM's true position in a sale, you'll want to join them there. This lets you see the radio tower from their vantage point and how they are thinking. That reveals the tactical way-points you can plot backward to where you are. Then moving forward in the sales situation is intuitive and definitive. ***Forward thinking develops product. Reverse thinking sells it.***

SALES SECRET #11:
Incremental Smaller Commitments

It's more effective to seek smaller commitments incrementally (such as scheduling a follow-up meeting) **within your sales situations, than going for bigger commitments. Smaller commitments are like "mini sales" and often have many of the same components as larger sales. In this way you're also helping them grow accustomed to agreement.**

Using discovery questions, intuitive logic, emotional intelligence, and learned mental sales diagnostics, you'll probably become proficient at plotting tactical way-points in real time. This requires reverse thinking, but to do that you'll need to see an overview of where you are (the tall tree or mountain top). To illuminate this and the thinking that follows in the next example is one of a somewhat straight-forward sale (to keep the variables somewhat limited).

Tactical Way-Point Thinking—Mental Reversal

Imagine a business owner who believes a stained lobby carpet must be replaced. This would be disruptive to their business. A professional carpet cleaning service can probably remove the stain. Because the business owner has formed an opinion, a sales situation may require tactical way-point thinking to illuminate the solution—first for the sales professional's mind in reverse, and then for the DM in forward motion. To demonstrate this the tactical way-points in the next example are plotted in reverse.

6. **Radio Tower Way-Point:** agreement that the lobby carpet can be cleaned and not replaced.
5. **Mountain Way-Point:** final questions and answering session.
4. **Cliff Face Way-Point:** outline of possible solutions/video demonstration of proof or carpet cleaning company's corporate video. Reduction of the perceived risk of paying for cleaning.
3. **Crooked Tree Way-Point:** observation of the problem in their mind/full understanding of their perception.
2. **Tall Old Growth Tree Way-Point:** observation of actual problem at facility/metaphorically standing beside DMs and seeing from their vantage point.
1. **Where You Are:** open-ended questions to learn of the situation—such as how they feel about the stain (is it a crisis or merely a nuisance?) and what caused it. How it happened, what's occurred since, and when did it occur?

Seeing your sale from multiple vantage points encourages a strategic approach using tactical way-point thinking. This thinking process also applies to your own personal production goals (and exceeding quota). Many sales professionals feel their quota is too high. Instead of offering resistance, you could respond with a new tool set that accelerates your sales production because it includes the use of **analogies.**

SECTION 2

ANALOGIES

If you don't know how to build an analogy,
you can still use those in existence
if they apply to your purpose and have relevance.

If you would like to build your own analogies,
there is a Strati-Tactical in section 8 to help you.

"When speaking about technology, an analogy is worth a thousand nerds."

—ImmersiveSelling.com

Chapter 5

Analogies at Work

Analogies utilize a short story or scenario format to compare two things. The two things being compared are unrelated but share at least one thing in common. The premise or first thing being compared in the analogy is familiar to the person you are trying to influence. The second part of the analogy is a thing or opinion that is unfamiliar or not yet believed. It's this second part that you are introducing to the decision makers (DMs) and key decision maker (KDM) by using the analogy and the familiar premise to do so.

> **The mind responds well to analogies because they use what's already in the mind as a self-evident premise.**

Analogies offer you the story-based approach to accomplish persuasion. Analogies are engaging because the mind feels like it's "in on the process." That's actually what's occurring.

For an example subject (one you know well), let's take a look at something in our industry—social selling. We've been pounded with the misfocused advisement to engage in "social selling only!" for years. Most in sales have either attached value to social, ascribed fear, or adopted a strong opinion about social selling. Many are already on board and see it positively (as do I).

What about those who aren't utilizing it? What about those who may buy into the "only!" part of "social selling only!"? How would you convince a seller that social should be added to a current tool set and not replace a traditional one? A blizzard of data would not likely work as well as analogies.

"You Need Two Wrenches"
(Illustrates traditional selling + social selling)

Imagine you need to remove a bicycle tire to repair a flat. Placing a wrench on one side of the axle works great until you need to remove the nut from the other side. You need two wrenches, one on each side of the axle so they can work together to remove both nuts in opposing directions. That's how social selling works with traditional sales tools. Having tooling on either side of the axle pivot point in the sale often prevents either side from slipping unnecessarily.

There are many different analogical structures. These four are my "go-to" favorites which could be labeled as:

1. Analogous Statement
2. Very Short Story Analogy
3. Scenario Analogy
4. Story Length Analogy

When deciding which type to develop and deploy, assess the intensity of the challenge, importance of the outcome, and the receptivity of the decision makers. Using a story length analogy to explain why a company might want to add a small additional item to a purchase order would be overuse of persuasion and would annoy the receivers.

Using a story length analogy to illuminate why buying this year as opposed to waiting until next year's budget is complete, would be warranted and useful. The same is true for shorter analogies. Using an analogous statement to convey the complexity of cold fusion may not suffice (it's probably too short). But using it to suggest an upsell would probably be effective. What follows are examples of these four analogical structures.

Example 1:
Analogous Statement
"Push a Rope"

Ropes derive their strength from being pulled. Not pushed. When you try to push a rope, the curved result you see is a limp "S" shape. That is similar to how a KDM mentally reacts to being pushed into buying instead of pulled.

43 words with a 12 second spoken delivery time.

Very short analogies will usually serve you well for persuasive support, and there's much to be said for brevity.

Example 2:
Very Short Story Analogy
"Stranger on the Street"

If someone you encountered on the street was unfamiliar, you might not interact with them. You may even avoid an interaction. You aren't passing any type of judgment—they just aren't typically within your usual social circle. You might be into sports or baking and they're carrying a giant cello case. You may assume you have nothing in common.

If a close friend of yours arrived at that moment who knew both you and the cellist, and introduced you to that person, what would occur? In a very short period of time you would be comfortable and might visit and adopt a new opinion of someone you assumed you'd have nothing in common with.

An analogy's familiar premise is like that close friend. The idea or point you are making that is not yet believed is like the cellist who is unfamiliar.

142 words with a 44 second spoken delivery time.

Example 3:
Scenario Analogy
"Storage Room Light, Pull String"

If you enter a long and narrow storage room in a building you are unfamiliar with you'd need to stop and work out where the light switch is. Perhaps you are searching for a few bulk items like glass cleaner and some cleaning supplies.

After opening the door to the room, you discover that where the light switch should be located is just a smooth wall. You do that feel-around-on-the-wall thing hoping to run into a switch, but the switch discovery collision never happens.

A voice from somewhere behind you says, "They're putting new lights in there. There's a temporary pull string light hanging from the ceiling a few feet further in. Just find the string hanging down." You say, "Thanks," as you begin that shuffle walk forward one-inch-at-a-time waving your hands around in the air similar to what happens when you've just walked through a spider web—the effort, in total, will merely turn on a light to illuminate a room. It's becoming a lot of work for not a lot of situational value.

You might even begin feeling frustrated. Especially if others outside the door are asking you questions to see if you found the cleaner? Found the light yet? Found the right shelf? That is how decision makers may feel answering a bunch of questions as they grope around in the dark hoping to hit the pull-string-of-understanding (your many questions devoid of an overview) **all while asking, "Where is this all going?"**

256 words with a 1:19 second spoken delivery time.

Another reason the analogy works (and sometimes works wonders) is it feels like a very logical process to the receiver. It's structured. It has a framework. It makes the abstract more concrete. The analogy is compartmentalized and it is packaged in a story format. When someone talks at you about the importance of developing a question plan prior to engaging important decision makers in an ideal account—you might agree, "That's a good idea—thanks," but continue doing what you've always done. The analogy, like the "pull string" scenario, lets you feel the actual frustration the DMs and KDM are feeling. You feel newly motivated to reexamine a questioning strategy and plan.

SALES SECRET #12:
Analogies Persuade Entrenched Opinions

Analogies are especially effective when an opinion is entrenched or involves elevated emotions. When people are particularly passionate about a topic, an effective analogy can do what typical approaches probably won't.

Talking informs a listener whereas analogies encourage them to mentally become a participant. When you hear an analogy you experientially feel the point. ***The mind responds well to analogies because they use what's already in the mind as a self-evident premise.***

SALES SECRET #13:
Mental Pictures

Analogies provide mental picture associations for unknown and abstract objects, processes, concepts, ideas, opinions, and invisible things by comparing them to what's already concrete in the mind. They use the pictures we already have in the mind, to make new ones we don't.

The possible range of subjects are also nearly infinite as you develop and use analogies. Everyone knows what a water pipe is. The second thing being introduced may not be well understood or believed but no one is going to ask, "What's a water pipe?" If you're trying to demonstrate capacity, flow, or volume of something, you could use a water pipe and compare it to a drinking straw.

To demonstrate the story-length analogy [*next example*], we'll accomplish two tasks with one tool by illustrating how sales management can greatly benefit when investing in their sales professionals by offering their mentoring and guidance—while also encouraging the individual sales professional.

Example 4:
Story Length Analogy
"The Tactical Landing Zone"

A military training facility that trains special forces will strive to improve the skills of those applying to be in their program. The people being prepared who wish to become members of a special forces team will be pushed, trained, and tested. There are a number of disciplines and skills where coaching is required and the performance of those in the program greatly depends on how that coaching is given.

When you share skills, knowledge and experience, no matter how serious the subject, when the transfer of that experience succeeds everyone wins. A bond of trust is strengthened and an additional dollop of respect is earned by the instructor/mentor/coach (sales manager). The more difficult the tasks and tests, the easier it is to see who is struggling and which individuals are excelling. There is a vetting process imbued in the training and coaching procedures within the special forces applications. It's like an advanced boot camp. So, assume that one of those difficult skills to acquire is night-parachuting to simulate being dropped behind enemy lines to a predetermined location that will then be called a tactical landing zone (TLZ). This location is precise and must be hit within a certain distance by all would-be special forces paratroopers.

Landing in the TLZ is when a special forces paratrooper is most vulnerable and the more "messing around" that's required on the ground, post-landing, the more the team's safety is compromised. Mistakes make it far less likely the mission will succeed. There's a far greater chance of detection the more movement and processes that are required on the ground—such as moving a long distance on foot to the TLZ after missing it with the parachute.

A percentage of those parachuting from planes in the dark are going to consistently nail their landing right on top of the assigned TLZ. The average performers will come within a couple of hundred feet of the TLZ, scoop up their chute, cords and gear and rush to the TLZ quickly and regroup—which is absolutely acceptable. This requires very little effort and a couple of hundred feet off of the mark won't put anyone's safety at risk.

The bottom performers however, might be a half-a-click off. One click = one kilometer which is equivalent to 0.62 miles. So they might be landing 0.31 miles off course. That third of a mile off of the mark is more than enough to blow a mission, get captured, and put the whole team at risk. It's probably not acceptable. Everyone's allowed a misstep here and there, especially during training and try-outs, but consistently missing the mark of the TLZ means something needs to be done while preparing that person for special forces.

Before cutting the prospective special forces member from the team (phasing a seller out and off of the team) due to (consistently) landing 1/2 click off of the TLZ (not closing sales), it's prudent for the team leader to assess what else will be lost when the underperforming paratrooper is cut. What other skills does the paratrooper have? How serious is the shortcoming in performance? Can it be fixed? With how much effort? How much coaching will be required? How receptive is the trainee?

In both sales and special forces, the corrective adjustments required are often far less than what you may expect. Both missing the TLZ and missing closed sales, can often be remedied easily. In special forces, missing the TLZ feels to the team leaders and trainers like a really big mistake. But is it? The assumption is that because the walking distance on the ground is so long (by parachuting-mission-standards), that the fix for the mistake and corrective training would also be vast. That seems true when measured against the walking distance. Long walking distance to the TLZ = long training period to fix lag in performance. In sales the assumption is, missing many sales closing opportunities = long coaching period and much guidance required. Often an all new approach is considered.

But in reality the corrective techniques for both scenarios, sales, and special forces may involve small and simple changes. Adjustments. When parachuting, free-falling for an additional five seconds

before pulling the cord, (take a few extra seconds to think about a sales situation before speaking) **and then once deployed, reviewing the basics in canopy piloting skills** (asking questions) **would more than make up a third of a mile or a "half-a-click" on the ground** (prevent objections, set a correct tactical way-point strategy to reach the close).

Situational awareness upon deploying the chute (asking a few additional questions in the sales situation) **as the landing nears could put a former under-performer right on the tactical landing zone more often. These adjustments might involve very small tugs of just a few inches on the steering cords controlling the parachute—not vast and involved new parachute types, TLZ locations, or different deployment altitudes** (an all-new sales approach isn't always the answer).

The understanding imbued in both the paratrooper-to-be and the special forces trainer/coach is that assessing all skill sets is important. While massively missing the TLZ feels like a big problem, the solution is micro adjustments in the approach (strategic thinking within a sales situation) **that have far reaching positive effects on the ground** (at the time of the sales close).

When sales managers see their position as an opportunity to give an individual gift to a sales professional, that guidance, however small, can have profound effects that ripple through the career of that seller and profits of the company. Could the challenges be solved with micro adjustments to steering cords and situational awareness?

955 words with a 4:54 minute spoken delivery time.

An analogy can decrease negative emotions within a challenge. Because you're talking about the analogical premise, not the problem directly, it softens the critique. The listener is an active participant, which is helpful for **analogies for comprehension.**

"It's nearly impossible for scientists and physicists to discuss quantum mechanics (even amongst themselves) without using analogies. The subject is complex. Analogies make comprehension possible."—ImmersiveSelling.com

CHAPTER 6

Analogies for Comprehension

Scientists use analogies to explain complex concepts and findings to other scientists. Even though everyone conferring with the scientists can well understand the technical jargon without the use of analogies, the analogical model and approach saves time and actually rearranges the thinking of scientific contributors. What that means is using analogies can actually facilitate the creation of solutions.

> **"If a decision maker does not fully comprehend a problem, they won't want to solve it.**

A good analogy can even self-explain what is being observed. A prime environment where complete comprehension can be achieved is within your own mind. Why then would you even need an analogy? It reframes a situation you are analyzing so that even you can see your own position more clearly or see if it needs an adjustment.

SALES SECRET #14:
Universality

Analogies have a universality to their understanding. You can communicate complex concepts to those with even just rudimentary understanding of a concept.

Analogy, Metaphor, Simile: What Are the Differences?

An Analogy: makes a comparison between two things or ideas and it's ***the comparison*** that is of utility. The premise is familiar and already known. The second thing is the unfamiliar component being taught or shown which is used for persuasion.

A Metaphor: represents one thing with another to make a point. For example, "The city streets that are our office cubicles" or "David's mixing-bowl coffee cup." The office cubicles are arranged in blocks that resemble city streets. David's preference for a huge coffee cup is illustrated by the metaphor of a mixing bowl. It's ***the representation*** that drives a metaphor. Although a metaphor and an analogy are very similar, the difference is important.

A Simile: may seem similar to those first two but differs in that it makes ***the direct comparison*** literally. For example: "His hands *were like* a dry, sandy desert." You can detect a simile by listening for the words "*like*" or "*as*."

Analogies can simplify and communicate complex and technical concepts using a familiar premise and analogical parallel comparison.

"The Sports Car & the Internet"

Back around 2006, my technical team had been hired to repair an e-commerce site and discovered their payment center wasn't encrypted. I was trying to explain the importance of encryption for e-commerce to my client. My client understood their online store "just wasn't running right" but didn't know why.

To fix the coding and send them on their way would have been unethical after we found they had no encryption. One form of internet encryption is called "SSL" which stands for "secure socket layer." Often SSL will assist in securing credit card transactions.

Because they didn't understand the technology, I used an analogy. The analogy explained that their e-commerce site was similar to a high end sports car—it would attract a lot of attention once it ran.

I explained that without SSL encryption, the sports car would be sitting in a publicly-accessible parking ramp (the internet) with its doors unlocked (no SSL). The only reason the sports car (e-commerce site) hadn't been tampered with or stolen (hacked) up to that point was the engine didn't run right (customers weren't putting credit cards into the e-commerce site. It wasn't taking their card numbers). Once the sports car's engine ran again (checkout page and coding issues fixed by us), its distinctive exhaust signature (their advertising) would roll out across the city (internet) and many would come looking to see if it was secure. Without SSL encryption, the sports car would be sitting there running in the parking ramp with the keys in the ignition and the doors wide open. That got their attention and they understood SSL encryption for credit cards.

You will want to keep your subjects, comparisons and analogical construction choices applicable to a wide receivership. Some sports analogies do that quite well whereas many tend to be a bit overused. Some are used so often they have become a cliche' and this can retrogress your sale. The whole point is progress. The subject of sports is tempting because it feels like business lines up with the whole point of sports. To win. The parallels seem perfectly aligned: we collaborate as a team, the manager is like a coach, you're scoring, lone wolves have some drawbacks, etc. Being fixated on the subject however limits your mind during ideation to come up with other more accessible (and maybe even more effective) comparisons outside of sports.

An oversight can be made by those using sports analogies with an assumption that all hearing the analogy are interested in the sport being cited. Do all listeners know all the rules of the game? Is the challenge they are experiencing based on strategic problems, motivational challenges, or coordination issues common to many sports teams' challenges? Perhaps a potential client is a perfect fit for the approach but much of the time, if the topic isn't handled with a freshness and some originality, it may be received with less enthusiasm than you may think (people are often patient because they're being polite). Some sellers have the personality type to pull off humor. Some can pull off a sports analogy. Here are a few things to strive for when you use a sports analogy.

1. Pick a sport that's easily recognized. Most understand footballs are oblong and some passing and kicking happens to try and get the ball to the goal on the opposite side.

2. Explain the basic rules involved required to follow the specific analogical application: e.g., avoid something like making a reference to "passing a football behind the line of scrimmage" without explaining that rule. You can do this by simply stating, "As you probably know, football has a line of scrimmage where...etc."

3. Use a very short analogical statement first to see if everyone receiving the analogy cares about sports. If you sense they don't, move onto another analogical option you've developed to make the same point.

4. Bring enthusiasm to an existing sports analogy or add something new.

Example of Two Analogical Topics: One exploration, the other sports. Both solve the same problem.

On the facing page of Strati-Tactical #1 there is a reference to illustration Fig 1.1 and how to think about and utilize the diagram and its various "zones." Even though it's explained thoroughly, comprehension of the sales concepts is involved. It's advanced material and many readers may become fixated and focused on "the progression of numbers" as a way to simplify the material. This is not what the diagram is intending and the numbered zones are for referential purposes. To help the mind receive it, I used an analogy, (reprinted here) entitled, "Tactics: Search Zones Approach." An alternate sports analogy example follows that here that I could have used if I were going to use a sports analogy.

Tactics (excerpted from facing page of Strati-Tactical #1)
"Zoned Search for Sunken Treasure"

The "zones" in diagram Fig 1.1 (in Strati-Tactical #1) won't necessarily be followed in numerical order. This is similar to deep sea exploration for sunken ships. Their search grid consists of columns and rows laid out on the ocean floor and they follow a process. If, however, the explorers see a barnacle-laden 1600's era cannon shape protruding from the sand outside of their current zone, they will move outside of their planned search. They will then establish and work on a new zone around the opportunity while still simultaneously progressing on the former zone. Their search area zones may increase to a third and even a fourth. Their numbered progressive search plan by zone can be modified by the situation similar to new opportunities that arise in your sales situations. You can work multiple zones in Fig 1.1 and not necessarily in numerical order.

If the audience was a consensus buying committee made up of non-sports-enthusiasts, I would opt for the analogy you just read. I could have used the sports analogy below to make the same point.

Tactics (for Strati-Tactical #1):
"Basketball Zone Play & Defense"

The "zones" in the diagram Fig 1.1 are similar to those in basketball where progression of the ball moves where there are openings and opportunities irregardless of the zones on the court. Various zones are worth one to three points depending on game play. The same is true in sales as it relates to Fig 1.1. Follow opportunities within the sales situations irrespective of the numerical zone progression.

If a decision maker doesn't fully comprehend a problem *(or your solution)*, ***they won't want to solve it.*** An analogy's power is derived from self-evident proof. Because it's generated from within the mind, it also means you can utilize **analogies for idea acceptance.**

Info on Chapter 7:
Why So Many Quad Close Examples?

In chapter 7 you and I will need to utilize an idea using analogies for persuasive purposes. To accomplish this, we will need a topic we are both familiar with. We've already discussed the Quad Close. You are familiar with that, so it will be our topic. This allows you to see the power of analogical persuasion without being distracted by a new topic. A similar approach is used extensively in graphic design called "Lorem Ipsum."

When presenting a graphic design to a client, designers substitute English text in the design layout with Latin because it looks like English. This text simulation is to prevent the mind from reading for content (almost no one knows Latin) and focus solely on design and structural layout. The client can still see what text will actually look like in the design (with no temptation to read for content which would be a distraction from the assessment of the design).

This is why you will be seeing multiple examples of Quad Close analogies. The subject is not being driven home; multiple analogical approaches are being demonstrated using one subject.

You can develop multiple analogies addressing the same subject, opinion, idea, or topic you'd like to influence. You can pull out whichever analogy will be the most appropriate for the receiver, industry, or decision maker. This also gives you option "B" to say something a different way.

"Logic encourages reason. Analogies encourage belief."

—ImmersiveSelling.com

Chapter 7

Analogies for Idea Acceptance

Ideas are perhaps one of the more challenging components of persuasion. This is because they are so closely related to beliefs. Prior to the adoption of a belief it will first be an idea, then an experience. If both are accepted by the mind, it may become a belief.

> "Analogies can 'film' a vantage point for the mind like no other tool of persuasion.

An effective way to start working on an idea is to simply get that idea clearly defined, if even just for yourself. When you engage the mind of the decision maker using the analogy, you help them see an idea differently. ***Analogies can "film" a vantage point for the mind like no other tool of persuasion.*** If done successfully, that shift in perspective is permanent or nearly so.

The lack of adoption and wide use of analogies is likely due to the complexity of the tool's development [*see Strati-Tactical #5*]. Developing analogies is involved. Avoiding the use of analogies simply because you might have to work at the development is like avoiding parallel parking your car because you want to avoid learning how. You can totally do that, but you'll have to walk further. Avoiding analogies can equate to more persuasive work required to accomplish the same task.

The Quadromat

Imagine sitting in a laundromat waiting for your laundry to be done when in walks a couple carrying a basket of laundry. You have assumed that they washed their basket of clothes at home because they are heading right for the dryers instead of the washers. *Maybe their dryer is broken?* This theory is proven incorrect though when you notice that the clothes are already dry...and are also all dirty.

You can visually confirm they are dirty because the couple takes turns sniffing a washcloth and then a towel. They both dramatically recoil from the smell, with wrinkled noses. They also point out several stains and dirt on the clothing. That's enough proof for you and now you are riveted by the couple's mannerisms as they shrug, and then proceed to fling dirty laundry into a dryer. *Could it be...that they are actually going to dry dirty clothes?*

Sure enough, you watch as they coin the thing up and smack the go button. Round and round it goes. Hot-baking-heat, setting those stains. They skipped the first three steps of the four components of laundering clothes. They are asking one machine to do the work of the rest. The steps they skipped or didn't ensure were complete were:

Step 1. Sort laundry by color and type.

Step 2. Wash the clothing using soap and water in a machine.

Step 3. Ensure the machine will drain and spin the soap from the clothes then rinse and spin again.

They skipped to this step:

Step 4. Dry the clothes in a dryer.

This couple literally jumped right to the fourth step and are attempting to launder clothes without the first three steps completed. Jumping to the fourth step in laundering clothes does not work any better than jumping to the fourth component sale in the Quad Close by asking for the Financial Sale.

Trying to simply explain to anyone that the Quad Close happens to the seller whether they believe it or not, *tells them* about closing prematurely. It doesn't *show* them.

The Quadromat *shows you* what it looks like and the analogy uses a parallel comparison so the concept doesn't feel like critique. The absurdity is self evident and attaches a scene to a sales concept that is readily accessible to the minds of sellers. The same is true in appealing to the minds of your decision makers. Also noteworthy is the complete absence of proof, data, logical reason, etc. What's utilized is what's already in the mind.

What your mind may gravitate toward next is the question, "What about when sales have closed in the past and I was unaware of the Quad Close?" The answer to that question is revealed in the next analogy.

Counting to Eight, Nine, Tennis

If you and a friend were practicing tennis on public courts but you didn't know or understand the rules of tennis you might just practice hitting the ball back and forth.

If two other people who *do* know the rules of tennis joined you and added some structure to what you were all doing, but you continued to intuitively just try and return the tennis ball when hit to you, you're going to score some points even though you don't know the underlying structural rules. This is why the opinion, "I've been selling this way for years and *I* close sales," may be true, but no one knows how many points (sales closes) **were *actually* available. When those points are Rock Hard Coin, then it matters.**

It's common to hear high performing sellers respond to the questions, "How do you do what you do?" and "What are you doing differently than everyone else?" with an answer like, "I don't really know how I specifically do it."

Colleagues of high performers in sales may explain the high performance with any number of cliches such as, "He's born to sell," or "She's a natural sales person," or "They are probably working harder than everyone else." Most high performers earning more Rock Hard Coin aren't working harder than everyone else, they're working more effectively.

SALES SECRET #15:
Analogies Save You from Heavy Lifting

Using strictly informational presentation sales approaches, while useful, can sometimes be like the home improvement shows that "stage" homes for sale. They bring in a bunch of rented furniture from warehouses that they have to carry in. Using analogical sales approaches is like utilizing the furniture already in the home and rearranging it to feature new ideas and spatial associations without having to do heavy lifting.

Proficient selling focuses the mind not on the product but on the result. The result you are selling becomes more vivid in the mind when you utilize analogies for idea acceptance. This is because a portion of the persuasion that occurs over the course of a sale, develops in the mind after the sales professional is no longer in the presence of the DMs or KDM.

SALES SECRET #16:
People Appreciate Simplicity

Analogies break down complexity into basic conceptual shapes that are simple and fit together.

They recall, review and remember meetings they've had with us and what we've said. Analogies provide a leave-in-mind for **retelling in your absence.**

"What's even more powerful than a leave-behind as you exit a sales situation is a 'leave-in-mind,' otherwise known as an analogy."—ImmersiveSelling.com

Chapter 8

Retelling in Your Absence

When a KDM says, "I need to think about it," they will often proceed to do just that. That leaves your influence on that sales situation suspended for a time. Consensus buying situations with multiple decision makers and team selling often have periods of contact, questions, listening, and collaborative discussions followed by periods of time where little or no contact is convenient or possible between the sellers and the DMs. This can be frustrating, especially when you're deeply invested in the sales efforts.

> **"A major benefit of the analogy is the solidified concreteness of how DMs feel while you're influencing their opinion.**

This can be a time that requires patience from the sellers involved and you can be more confident in what you left behind if it included an analogy. This is especially true in situations where the sellers were required to adhere to a vigorously-controlled buying process, usually involving an RFP (request for proposal).

There aren't many sales situations more frustrating than having limited or no contact with a prospective KDM or a consensus buying committee. This is especially true when you must submit a proposal blind (not the most effective way to sell). Many corporations (perhaps unwisely) insist on it as their buying process and miss out on your consultative value.

SALES SECRET #17:
Failure by RFP

A request for proposal isn't always optimal for the seller to gain new business. Some companies use the RFP as a buying method. An analogy can help you differentiate yourself from the competition especially in the form of an analogous story.

Your analogy often continues working for you even after your sales situation has concluded. If your analogy is effective and engaging, people will remember it far into their future. Because the analogy is story based, it can differentiate you as well.

Sand in the Wind

Imagine being paid to pile up sand in a windy and flat area using a hand held shovel. You only get paid for completed five foot high piles of sand still standing at the end of the week. Each day at sundown you must leave the piles but can return the following day to add to whatever piles are still standing—but much of the sand will have blown away during the night (that's how it often feels in sales when time elapses between meetings).

Using an analogy in sales is like using a full-size tour bus in the windy flat area to block the wind from taking sand away from your piles overnight. The bus blocks the wind. The analogy blocks doubt and erosion of belief over time. The story keeps the pile together just as the bus keeps the pile of sand together. To stop the wind from blowing beneath the bus you could use sheets of plywood leaned up against the bus. Within the analogy the plywood is like using relevant details and personalization.

Do you think DMs have discussions amongst themselves about your sales performance? Your solution? The result you sold? What will they be talking about during deliberations? Any seller who has had the privilege to be a KDM prior to selling will know that the discussions are fascinating from the standpoint of comments on "what stood out" to the DMs in the consensus buying committee.

SALES SECRET #18:
Avoid Saying, "I Think"

Stating something plainly is more powerful than prefacing statements with the qualifying expression, "I think." For example, "I think that there is a greater risk for a system overload if we go with approach B." Inclusion of "I think," immediately encourages the receivers' minds to review your education status, expertise, qualifications and position. Your credentials. Even if only subconsciously, the qualifier "I think," invites critique and weakens the statement. Unless you have incredibly impressive credentials, a much stronger statement is, "There is a greater risk for a system overload if we go with approach B."

Highlights of these discussions are outstanding qualities of the sellers and solutions. For you, if you are using analogies, these story-based tools of persuasion will be remembered. ***A major benefit of the analogy is the solidified concreteness of how DMs feel while you're influencing their opinion.*** This will probably be associated with you and will almost definitely differentiate you from competitors.

SALES SECRET #19:
Analogies Repeated and Retold

When you share an analogy, it will likely be reshared and retold in your absence in their own voice. That's indicative of an impression left in their mind. Decision makers will recall what made the deepest impression and that is often your analogy.

Analogies can, and often do, carry the same weight as a product demonstration because the story took place in the mind. Effective analogies can be remembered, sometimes for a lifetime.

SALES SECRET #20:
Analogies Can Be as Effective as Some Product Demos

When you give a product demonstration, and then it ends, where is the product demonstration residing? In the mind of the observer of the demonstration, stored in a core memory. These are very similar to the visual holograms people create (in their minds) **while experiencing an analogy—because they participated in the parallel comparison it actually qualifies as an experience.**

The centuries-old adage, "Give people a fish and you feed them for a day. Teach people to fish and you'll feed them for a lifetime," is both an analogy and a metaphor. You aren't literally going to give the person a fish to eat (though you could), but the fish represents a financial hand out. The lesson being you can prevent poverty by teaching a skill that would provide self-sufficiency and break a cycle of dependency on others. It will reside in the mind for decades or often even a lifetime and the same is true of **sales stories.**

SECTION 3

SALES STORIES

The advancement of technology has somewhat distorted the importance of relationship selling due to the perceived ease with which leads and prospects can be replaced.

Relationships are even more important now. Who do you reach out to when things are rough? It's going to get even more challenging out there and your professional network is a major asset that will help you traverse brutal economic terrain in the future (what's coming is going to be a challenge).

"In just three minutes you can influence and often even change a decision maker's opinion or perception using a Three Minute Center Punch. That's faster than a bowl of cereal trying to solve breakfast."—ImmersiveSelling.com

Chapter 9

Your Sales Story

The Three Minute Center Punch (3MCP)

There is a stigma attached to sales. Some industries' sellers have to endure a more intense stigma while others just have the default "unfavorable" status. You may have encountered decision makers reluctant to meet who have advanced what I call the "Go Objection" (G.O.) [*see chapter 20*]. The decision makers at your video sales situation or in-person meeting may appear disengaged, stressed, or uninterested. Perhaps they're distracted with other work off-screen/elsewhere. They may advance the Go Objection and mention their schedule is pushing them around, so they want you to get right to the point of the meeting.

> **"Build your Three Minute Center Punch directly from a core frustration sitting on the decision maker's desk.**

At the onset of a sales situation as you transition out of the small talk and pleasantries, the next three minutes that follow can be a persuasive opportunity. This is especially true when the G.O. has been advanced. What you do in that next three minutes will greatly affect the quality of the answers you'll receive from the open-ended discovery questions that actually want to get to. Using what I call the "Three Minute Center Punch" (3MCP) you can reframe their perception of you and your product, in just three minutes. There is almost no other investment you could make in that next three minutes that would accomplish the same result.

While selling advertising, marketing, and creative services back in the years surrounding 2005, I realized I needed a tool to answer the Go Objection I often received. Being perceived as an "ad sales rep," I might as well have been trying to sell used cars to corporations. I had stiff competition since the other ad agencies and marketing firms all hired former models, newscasters, and reporters as their account executives (I'm a middle-aged bald guy). Many of my friends and colleagues urged me to fight fire with fire. My answer instead, was to develop new tooling. This is where the Three Minute Center Punch originated. My then-current 3MCP is what follows. Assume that the small talk and chitchat has occurred and the decision makers have advanced the Go Objection with, "What have you got for us?" This was my response.

Example Sales Story: Three Minute Center Punch

Business owners, executives, and leaders of industry like yourselves are often quietly frustrated with the state of their advertising and marketing. When the advertising doesn't produce an ROI, the volume on that quiet frustration gets amplified because we all know advertising is essential to growth. We also all know that great ad campaigns do exist and most of us have a favorite ad. When we come across ads that are engaging, we pay attention. You may even be thinking of an example right now. So you know that if it's possible for others to have ads that are popular and effective, it's possible for you to have the same.

You can probably recall hearing or repeating the age-old saying, "I know that only 50% of my advertising works. I just don't know which 50%."—[*John Wanamaker* (*1838-1922*)]. John Wanamaker said that in the late 1800s. When he said it, he was in a similar position that you may be in and some 13 decades later the problem still hasn't been solved. Why?

Your question to my industry has probably been to ask why it can't be closer to 60/40? Why not 65%? Why not see 70% of your advertising work? Why can't most of your ads work? What will make

yours work?

Are you ready to do something different than what your competitors typically do? Have you noticed that nearly every advertisement you see or hear points at the company the advertisement is for? That sounds logical until you consider what the effect on the ad would be if you removed the advertiser's name and logo and inserted their direct competitor's. No one would probably even notice because they're almost all the same. They drone on with, "For all your blah blah blah needs, we do everything from this-to-that and everything in-between." Ad copy is nauseatingly boring. The results those ads produce is disengagement.

When your favorite ads come on however, you stop and watch, listen, or read them don't you? They are memorable because they affect you. They stay with you. That's because they are about you...not the advertiser's company. Those ads you like spoke to you, the customer, because they were about you the customer and showed you something about yourself that you responded to because it was all about you. Not the business paying for the ad. So you engaged the ad.

The ads that work are immersive because you get to participate. You put details into them that aren't actually there. It's why great writing works in books. What is spoken or written provides imagery which then become holographic scenes (in the mind) if the mind engages. The engagement then allows the scenes to play out in the mind. Engagement is required for advertising to be persuasive and your advertising should be produced to accomplish this. That's the performance result level you could demand from your creative agency. Your ads could utilize engagement and actually be an event within the minds of your prospective customers. Have you ever asked a creative team to do *that* for you? Would you like to?

522 words or a 2.7 minute verbal delivery time.

The primary difference between a standard "sales pitch" and a Center Punch is that the pitch is about the seller and the seller's company. The Center Punch is about the decision maker. It dials right into the core challenges (pain points) and treats the delivery like a highly effective and entertaining advertising experience. Did you notice just how few words within my 3MCP were dedicated to my team's abilities? How nothing was said about how passionate we were about ad production? Did you notice nothing was even said about how many years of combined experience my team had or degrees they held or the client roster we had? Those questions will obviously come up later as they consider making the next commitments (such as agreeing to the next meeting). The 3MCP serves to earn trust and dials into their emotions while encouraging them to become immersed in an approach that features them.

The 3MCP is itself a three-minute ad. The 3MCP literally center punches the mind with relevance because you can ***build your Three Minute Center Punch directly from a core frustration sitting on the decision maker's desk.***

What was the result? I would often receive the G.O., and would deliver my Three Minute Center Punch, and by the fourth minute of most of the sales, the DMs and KDMs who just moments before were viewing me as an ad rep pushing column inches, saw me and the team I described in the 3MCP as consultative experts. That's because the story is also literally imbued with answers to the objections they were likely sitting there thinking. It addressed what was on their mind. It spoke to what was on their desk. What was in their past. What was in their emotional fears. What was in their future thinking.

SALES SECRET #21:
Listen before Talking—Ask before Assuming

The Three Minute Center Punch is not suggesting you abandon discovery and listening. In just three minutes you can reorient their motivation to give you answers that are actually very useful. They become intrinsically motivated to help you help them.

That 3MCP came directly off of my Wall of Wisdom (W.O.W.) [*see also Strati-Tactical #3, "How to Build a Wall of Wisdom"*]. When you develop this tool for yourself, you can deliver it as if it were a live ad (because it is) and it works as a perception-changer. When done effectively it should feel conversational, engaging, confident and be immersive.

Six Ways to Utilize the Three Minute Center Punch

1. As a direct response to the Go Objection.
2. As a sales story.
3. As a source for persuasive appeals. You can pull snippets from the story to support the component sales.
4. As conversational elements. At the end of this chapter you're shown how to convert your 3MCP into conversational elements.
5. As a tactical sales tool when your strategy requires you play "catch up" coming into a sales situation late and there are established competitors.
6. As a unifier so your entire sales team is at least drawing some water from the same wellspring of persuasion.

SALES SECRET #22:
The Center Punch Can Feature DMs' Moment of Frustration
(of their problem)

The core of the Center Punch should feature the DMs' and KDMs' moment of frustration that your product solves, and illuminates the result they experience.

Once you've produced your 3MCP sales story, you can pull pieces out and use them when needed. For example in my 3MCP I could use the introduction to show empathy that I understand corporate leaders might be frustrated with advertising results, but leave the rest of the story for another time.

SALES SECRET #23:
Lead with Your Advantage up Front

If you've been able to identify an advantage (your unfair competitive advantage) **that you have over your competition, resist the temptation to "save it for a grand finale" approach. Move it right up front and put your very best in the front window of your sale.**

If you've memorized the material to the point where you can deliver it in an extemporaneous style (so it sounds natural, fresh and not memorized), the material from your 3MCP can be utilized in various ways without a lot of thought.

Most people in business are pitch-fatigued and don't want to hear another one. So you may be thinking that the 3MCP isn't worth the time to develop if you're only going to utilize it in a single-use application after receiving the G.O. Your perception may be that your current pitch is serving your needs. **The 3MCP is not a pitch.** Here is a demonstration of another way to utilize this story conversationally.

The 3MCP Delivered Conversationally

Assume we are dropping into the middle of a conversation within a sales situation that did not begin with the 3MCP nor was the G.O. advanced. The 3MCP at the beginning of this chapter will be parsed and used conversationally here, but representing the same time period of a few years surrounding 2005 for continuity of the material. It's also assumed that in this application, discovery questions have already been asked, listening has already occurred, some challenges are already known, etc.

KDM: "...and that's another reason why the project was marginalized."
TRACEY: "So it was budgeted, but then the market shifted at about the same time."
KDM: "Exactly."
TRACEY: "So the focus now is on the release of Product X?"
KDM: "Well, that won't even be ready for another year. We can talk about that when we get closer to that time."
TRACEY: "For a major product launch to go smoothly you should avoid waiting until just a few months before it's revealed to the public."
KDM: "A full year in advance?"
TRACEY: "There are packaging, product logos, advance release videos, montage teasers, distribution, marketing, advertising, legal research, market research, pricing, effective advertising and many other considerations. You can't even produce ad concepts until legal is done and they need to be involved as we advance product name generation—which is deceptively involved. Many people are actually

pretty unaware of what makes a cohesive product campaign work. Ask around and see what kind of answers you get when you ask others, 'What makes an ad campaign work?' or 'What makes a great ad?' The chances are good they don't really know."
KDM: "Does anyone actually ever really know that? Do you?"
TRACEY: "Yes. Your question actually reflects what many in business struggle with. You can probably recall hearing or repeating the age-old saying, "I know that only 50% of my advertising works. I just don't know which 50%." John Wanamaker, a business person back in the late 1800s, said that and it's still true. It still hasn't been solved. I can't help but wonder why the percentage is so low. Fifty percent? Why not sixty? Sixty-five? Online metrics help tremendously with web advertising, but what about the rest?"
KDM: "So what makes an ad work?"
TRACEY: "The question encourages another question that I've found myself wondering aloud."
KDM: "Answering a question with a question?"
TRACEY: "Well it's a pivotal question that lets the answer stand upon something foundational. Without the second question, there's nothing to support the answ—."
KDM: "The question is price?"
TRACEY: "The question is, 'Why pay an agency to produce the same type of advertising your competition has been endlessly using?' That just becomes an expensive battle of ad impressions. Who can run their ads more often and in more channels?
slight pause
So *that* price could be asked but it's not the priority question. The more important question is, 'Who is the focus of the ad?' It should be about the decision maker, not the company running the ad. Your advertising should speak to the needs and wants of the receivers and feature the moment that your result fits their life or experience. The secondary question that drives that is to ask whether or not a company paying for the ad campaign is willing to make the ads about the customer instead of about the company?"
KDM: "Do you have an example?"
TRACEY: "You've no doubt seen those roadside assistance type ads or ones for reliable tires, or the various towing service ads or the security response type businesses that feature the cold rainy night at the exact moment of need (*specific ads could be mentioned in conversations but not here in print due to copyright and trademark concerns*)**. Or the pinnacle of human achievement type ads that then transfer that accomplishment over to the mind of the customer so they see them-**

selves in that place, winning, wearing a company's product or using the advertised equipment that got them to that achievement. Humor, entertainment, and clever situational themes all add relevance to the viewers' experience."
KDM: "Product features?"
TRACEY: "Not exactly. Unless they are about the customer."
KDM: "Advantages then."
TRACEY: "Perhaps, but great advertising is about the customer. Not you. Them. It's very difficult to get people who are approving the advertising thematic approach and conceptual direction to let the ad be about something other than the very company paying for the creative production."
KDM: "Why?"
TRACEY: "It feels counter intuitive. The ad seems like it should be about you, for you, and about what you do for others."
KDM: "Well yeah."
TRACEY: "Except that produces ads that aren't great ads. They end up sounding like everyone else... 'We do everything from this-to-that and everything in-between. We have blah blah blah for all your blah blah blah needs.' It disorients the listeners and viewers and turns them off for the very same reason you don't like sales pitches, pop-up ads online, junk mail, flyers on your windshield, etc."
KDM: "Yeah I hate those things."
TRACEY: "We all do."
KDM: "I had to sit through one just last week..." **story of enduring sales pitch**
TRACEY: "Yes. So why did you dislike the pitch?"
KDM: "It was pitchy. Pushy. Pretentious. Insincere. I could go on."
TRACEY: "Well, we all could. That's the point. Their pitch wasn't about you. It was about them. What is spoken or written starts the imagery that then becomes holographic scenes, like a version of virtual reality that can take place in the mind of your customers."

All of the impactful components from the 3MCP were, or could easily be, worked into the conversation wherever needed and it wouldn't (and didn't) sound like a pitch. The 3MCP focuses your relevance and center punches the exact moment of need or want. You may be thinking that these two variants of the 3MCP were lacking intrigue. To the average reader, that's true. It was written for them (that's the whole point) not us. The DMs and KDMs of business would become visibly engaged at about the point of the "50/50" quote. That 3MCP produces intrigue by saying what they were thinking—and engagement resulted using the very objections they already held. That is intriguing to a KDM in business. The immersive effect stories have on the mind is why **stories can solve industry-wide objections.**

The name "Center Punch" is based on an analogy of a drill press tool from a metal workshop. When you try to drill through a metal block using a hardened steel drill bit with a drill press, the bit "walks" around in elliptical circles. This begins once it makes contact with the metal block. The drill bit will wear a divot into the surface and eventually drill the hole. You end up with a scratched surface on the work and an oblong hole that isn't clean or precisely located.

The answer to drilling holes in steel is to use a "center punch" so the hole is precise and accurate. A center punch is a type of awl that when hit with a hammer creates a precise divot in the metal that acts as a starting hole (divot) for the bit. Usually soap stone is used to draw an "X" in the exact spot where you want the hole.

The analogous translation of a center punch is:

- The drill press is your sales department.
- The motor is your effort.
- The drill bit is your sales approach.
- The spinning action of the drill is your communication.
- The act of lowering the spinning bit down to the metal is your engagement within a sales situation.
- The metal is your qualified prospective buyer's opinion.
- The "X" is the subject requiring a change in perception.
- The hole in the solid steel is a changed perception and opinion.

If you're in a down economy trying to figure out how to charge full price (or due to the economic conditions you have to agree to discounts), **your approach will need to be to develop an Emotive Gatekey for every sticking point in your sales cycle. You'll need to position every reason to proceed with you to the next commitment as a result for the decision makers and you'll need an emotional appeal to get that done. Consider their position in the economy. If it's not going well, treat every point of objection and contention they raise as a separate sale for your next prospect; e.g., use the next few, or several sales situations to mine their minds for the emotive gates so you can develop keys** (build your W.O.W. and various tools in the Strati-Tacticals). **Everything you do in this economy matters more and every requirement is more intense. Do not lose sight of their pain, their problems, and their outcomes. Those are your clarity of purpose. Position yourself as an economic solution, way to save time, or be effective. To solve your problems, you must focus on theirs. Build new tools and put in the time** [*see also chapter 32*].

"Experiencing the same sales challenge as everyone else in your company perhaps feels less lonely, but that does not reduce your net loss, or your need for a tool to solve it."—ImmersiveSelling.com

Chapter 10

Stories Can Solve Industry-Wide Objections

Almost every industry that relies on sales to thrive also experiences a challenge or objection that the entire industry must deal with. Sometimes it's more tightly focused to "company-wide" and affects an entire sales team. The point being that it's often a perception challenge, technical challenge, aversion to a type of sale (or type of sales professional), or an economy-based challenge. The wide reach of the objection could also be due to the type of product. The objection isn't personal or directed at you, but you still have to contend with it.

> "A sales story can often nearly eliminate a sales objection experienced company-wide or across an entire industry.

Back in the early 2000s, I experienced an industry-wide sales objection while selling employee-paid benefits (insurance) to corporations. Even after securing a meeting with the employers to get permission to speak with their employees (who were the actual decision makers for the purchase), the employer would resist. They would often adopt the role of a gatekeeper (GK) and disallow my access to their employees. This would occur even after it was clear to them that their employees qualified for benefits, needed the benefits, and could afford them. Still, the employers I was talking to made the decision for their employees without the employees even knowing I'd been there.

These employers were non-stakeholders as they either wouldn't qualify for benefits themselves (especially in S-Corps) or didn't need them because they had amazing health care (especially in C-Corps). So it was of no benefit to them personally to allow the employees to learn about what was available. If the employees never had face time with me, they would never know what they were missing (and never hold it against their employer) so there was literally no downside for the employers to say "no."

Even more frustrating was the fact that the employers paid nothing for the benefits. The employer had almost nothing to do with the sale other than signing one document and agreeing to allow payroll/accounting to mail in a check for premiums withheld from the paychecks of those employees whom I sold to. All that money withheld? It would be able to sit in the company bank account for 30 days earning interest. Though not much interest would be earned, it certainly wasn't a liability or hardship to the employers.

Within the companies I did enroll where the employer let me through, they noticed an increase in morale on their team. The employees felt appreciative for getting more benefits (that the employers weren't even paying for). There was no downside and only upsides—yet most employers refused to allow enrollment because avoiding even just a little bit of paperwork was easier.

The answer was "no" so often it was even widely discussed at insurance agent off-site training sessions and motivational events. It was the number one topic and not one of the hundreds of agents in attendance seemed to have an answer. There wasn't a magic wand, silver bullet, or open sesame statement and there also wasn't a name for the objection so I called it the "employer won't let me through" objection.

The objection plagued my sales efforts until I encountered a particularly frustrated employer ("Alissa"). She and I had a discussion about the challenges on her production floor. She sighed, almost imperceptibly, and became quiet for a moment after I asked her what the challenges were. I had earned her trust and so she shared. A lot.

ALISSA: "I've been having to cover shifts, move people around. I'm trying to train new people in various positions to cover being short-staffed."
TRACEY: "That's always a challenge, so what happened? How did you become so short-staffed?"
ALISSA: "Oh, you know. A key employee is out, another had to move. You know... stuff."
TRACEY: "That's tough. How pivotal is that key employee to your operations?"
ALISSA: "Pretty important. You know..."
TRACEY: "When is he or she coming back?"
ALISSA: "Not sure. 'Gary' has been out a couple of months."
TRACEY: "Months?"
ALISSA: "Six actually. He ran the 'Auto923x machine' line (name of machines changed to fictitious names). **It takes like a year to master that monster. You never really do know-it-all on that beast."**
TRACEY: "That would be an interesting machine to see sometime. A licensed position?"
ALISSA: "No, but, involved. A lot of training."
TRACEY: "Team-attained knowledge?"
ALISSA: "Yes. Yes, exactly. You get it."
TRACEY: "So...what happened to Gary?"
ALISSA: "Well, sadly, he got into a car accident. He had never even so much as called in sick in 23 years—then one Monday morning he just didn't show up for work."
TRACEY: "Wow. I'll bet that had you worried."
ALISSA: "Exactly. I tracked him down soon enough but I had literally found him in an area hospital and he hasn't been back to work since."
TRACEY: "Will he? Is he going to be alright?"
ALISSA: "I don't know. He's at home now but, well, it's doubtful. I'm training 'Lisa' and 'Jon' on the Auto923x now so that I can stop covering the shifts and running it."
TRACEY: "And after 23 years you feel a lot of responsibility to hold the position open for him?"
ALISSA: "Yes. I mean, after 23 years I just feel like I owe him, you know? He helped me build this business. So what am I supposed to do? I feel obligated to...I just can't stop. I can't just cut him off. He has to feed his family."

My curiosity was piqued: "*Wait. I definitely missed something there. What is she talking about? Obligated? Cut him off? Of what? It's more than just holding his job open for him. There was a lot of guilt in that vocal tone.*

You don't describe a position as being 'cut off' nor do you describe an employee termination or layoff as being 'cut off'—so what's being 'cut off'?"

TRACEY: "I think I missed something. Obligated? You mean to hold his position open?"
ALISSA: "I guess I have to just keep helping him out—he has family living with him. An aging mother I think. Maybe the government programs will get approved soon, you know?"
TRACEY: "Are you...? Do you mean you're sort of...?"
ALISSA: "Making his house payments? Yeah. Food. Car payments. Next will be medical bills. I'm actually...I mean. I feel guilty saying it, but..." *sigh* "I mean he helped me build this business. Twenty three years of his life. Not one day did he call in sick. Not one. You know?"
TRACEY: "Alissa...the payments you're making to Gary? The cash out of your pocket—*that* is precisely the result my product provides."

After that day with Alissa, the employers I met with would still advance the "employer won't let me through" objection. There were several variants such as: "Now's not the right time" or "I just don't think my employees would care for something like this" or "I just don't see the benefit to my company, sorry." I had this story as a response.

Story for Industry-Wide/Company-Wide Objection:
Response to the
"employer-won't-let-me-through" objection

It's understandable that you feel the benefit to your employees may not outweigh the investment of the time it takes to enroll. Even though the time is minimal, everything must have a return on investment so I'll share with you what your investment can provide besides just the coverage we've discussed. The benefit is for you personally as well as your employees. This benefit unfortunately wasn't in place in time for another client of mine.

Like you, she really cared about her employees, several in particular who helped her build her business. Her key employee whom I'll call "Gary" had been with her for 23 years when one Sunday night was

unfortunately in a severe car accident that put him in the ICU.

Even after returning home his recovery was slow and months later his employer whom I'll call "Alissa" found herself feeling very obligated to make Gary's house payments. He helped her build the business. She felt like she owed him. Next she found herself on a slippery slope and had to buy his family food, pay his car payments and cover his out-of-pocket costs. He couldn't work, and for 23 years he'd never once called in sick...Alissa felt like she had no choice. She felt stuck.

Almost every employer has a "Gary" who's invested their life to build the company alongside founders and leaders just like you. Those employees are incredibly loyal. They're valuable. They're also going to put you in a tough spot if they become injured and can't work.

Even if you find another solution or don't support a key employee after an accident (which you're not legally obligated to do)**—the expectation from your other employees is that you will. You're going to feel obligated. And... even if you elect not to pay their bills, why put yourself in the position to have to make that difficult choice? Even if you refuse to pay their bills, you had to endure the anguish of making that decision.**

My solution gives you 100% deniability and you will never even feel that obligation should someone become injured in a car accident or any other way because I have this insurance policy that covers that. It pays them the majority of their gross wages, which as you know is close to their net.

If they refuse enrollment, you can rest-assured you allowed it to be offered to them. You will have no obligation and feel no guilt should something ever happen to any employee...especially the key employees that helped you build your business.

429 words with a 2 minute and 14 second delivery time.

Mentioning the emotive reality they would feel allowed them to deduce their own then-future result. The employers could see that all of their employees would take careful note of what they, as the employer, would or wouldn't do in response to a loyal teammate stumbling in life.

The employers all knew that their decision to help or not help an injured employee would speak volumes to the others.

It's a severe employee morale liability. One that may not happen but if it did, it could tear a team apart and the employers knew that as I laid out the sales story. What I did mention was how Gary would have been protected by my product (that I thought of as "paycheck insurance") because it covered most injuries occurring on or off the job. What this story did was literally act like an ice breaker in a frozen harbor. I seldom ever heard the "employer won't let me through" objection again after telling this sales story.

SALES SECRET #24:
Emotional Switches Are Transferable to Other Sales

When you find an emotional switch within a DM or KDM, you've found a gem that's transferable to many other sales. It's very likely other DMs and KDMs will have similar emotional switches. Add what you've learned to your Wall of Wisdom. When you find a switch you might be able to develop an Emotive Gatekey with it as well.

A sales story can often nearly eliminate a sales objection experienced company-wide or across an entire industry. Using a story will probably provide you with the freedom to sell instead of the other activities (like handling objections) that are "overhead" and not central to what you probably would rather be doing. Sales stories derive their power from engaging the mind and it's that initial power of engagement that you can tap into with **your 15 Second Segue.**

"It requires the same amount of imagination to develop objections as it takes to visualize buying. Either way, the decision maker is investing mental effort—maybe just redirect the effort?"—ImmersiveSelling.com

Chapter 11

Your 15 Second Segue
A Replacement for the "Elevator Pitch"

When sellers hear the words "sales story" they often mentally recoil. A sales story sounds long. Boring. Unwanted by decision makers. The risk of embarrassment and apprehension builds in the mind of a seller over time to the point where they may nod externally in tentative agreement when the effectiveness of a sales story comes up in discussion, but internally some eschew the idea.

> "The 15 Second Segue can provide a bridge to the next commitment.

The seller may imagine the wrinkled forehead of confusion from the EVPs as they ask, "Um, what exactly is it we're doing here? Should I get my warm milk and cookies?" This is a comment that would be imagined to be loaded with an obvious edge of condescension.

The problem is the word "story." It's associated, broadly, with every sequential verbal and written description of events. However engaging, and many stories are, the mind can render the tool inept with the simple logic of, "Well, many things and subjects are highly engaging that have no place in a business meeting." The story's deep childhood association with fairy tales, adventures in far off lands, and bedtime stories renders it inappropriate for business. Agreed. That association with stories-as-a-subject isn't for business which is why business stories should never, ever, start with "Once upon a time."

Imagine removing every story, analogy, and sequential example from this book. What if I had just told you about this powerful sales tool called an "Emotive Gatekey" and described it as a short statement or question that piques curiosity? Showing you with a story was more effective than telling.

Now consider trying to tell someone about the result they will receive after buying from you. Wouldn't it be better to show them? Just how do you go about that devoid of actual ownership of what you are selling? A product demo does wonders for process, how-to, capabilities, features and benefits which support sales effectively, but what about the experience of ownership? The result? The downstream effects that are positive from owning and could be negative for not owning the solution? Those realities can happen within a story.

The "15 Second Segue" dispels one of the myths surrounding the use of stories to sell—that stories are long. It's 15 seconds long. Exceptional story telling starts a sequence of events on the page or in the spoken words and the scene is completed by the receiver in the mind. When asked what I do for a living I use the following 15 Second Segue.

A 15 Second Segue Example (Tracey's)

"Sales professionals ask for their sale using one question, but there are four decisions buyers make. Not one decision. Four. Buyers use emotion to buy and logic to support their decision to pay someone they trust. I coach sellers to organize their sale around these four components: emotion, logic, trust, and finance so they close more sales."

57 words with a 17 second delivery time

So what's in that 15 (okay, 17) seconds? In Fig 6.1 in Strati-Tactical #6, the diagram shows the elements of a story as being: setting/time, piqued interest, development, events, complication, twist, turning point, and resolution. All of those components are contained (or implied) within the 15 Second Segue above. What follows is a breakdown of the individual parts of the segue story you just read.

Setting	Within a sales situation.
Time	At the sales close.
Location	Assumed a decision maker's office/on video.
Main Character	Seller.
Interest	Unknown aspect of asking one question with four decisions needing to be made.
Development	Buyers using emotion to decide.
Events	Buyers using logic to support their purchase.
Complication	Buyers won't make the purchase (the fourth component sale) unless the other three have closed (emotion, logic, trust).
Twist	I coach sellers to organize their sales situations around those elements.
Turning Point	When the sellers reorganize...
Resolution	...they close more sales.

Your 15 Second Segue does not need to be epic, it needs to be effective and work. What you see above is effective, but probably not epic. Don't over-work your story or become unnecessarily frustrated during development [*see also Strati-Tactical #6*].

SALES SECRET #25:
Difference between a 15 Second Segue and a Pitch

The difference between a 15 Second Segue and an elevator pitch is the segue is about the listener. The decision maker. Elevator pitches often talk at the listener and are generally all about the seller, the product, the company, the features, and the options. A "pitch" is thrown out (like a baseball). **A segue is a bridge to a longer conversation or the first commitment such as a scheduled meeting or video call.**

Some elevator pitches may even include information about industry awards, leadership claims, how the company is ranked number one in the industry, assurances of being passionate about what they do, how the founders started in a barn or garage and built the company up brick by brick over some number of decades, etc. No one cares. Because it's about the company instead of the focus being on the DMs and KDM.

You may be wondering, "Does the 15 Second Segue replace an Emotive Gatekey?" They can and should work together. One can follow the other and there are no rules. When someone asks you what you do for a living or where you work or what industry you work in, you need a concise answer. Especially if you are at a networking event or being introduced in a video conference call. What they want to know, and what the "elevator pitch" once tried to accomplish, was answering the following questions that they are really asking you:

1. **"Who are you?"**
2. **"What do you provide?"**
3. **"Why should I care?"**
4. **"How does it help me?"**
5. **"What will be my result?"**

They are representing all five with the one verbal question, "What do you do for a living?" or "So what do you do?" The result you are seeking when you answer those five questions is to transition the situation over to a commitment for a meeting. Or you may wish to pique their interest enough to ask for more information. Or you may be seeking a referral or introduction to someone who *could* use what you offer.

At the very least you will want to segue from a state of being unknown with no knowledge of what you do or provide, over to a situation where they know and understand the answers to those five questions. Then they will perhaps see their potential result from you, because it's about them. ***The 15 Second Segue can provide a bridge to the next commitment.***

You should be focused on answering those five questions (four questions, if they already know your name, etc.). So how does my 15 Second Segue answer the five questions? Using N.E.D.A. [*see facing page*].

Using "N.E.D.A.": Nested Elements Development Approach

Using what I call N.E.D.A., you can develop most any tool from an organized bulleted list of information. The following example reverse-engineers my 15 Second Segue to demonstrate how I developed it from the list of requirements (which is also not required to be developed in numerical order).

1. **"Who are you?"** I'm Tracey Cook (usually this is taken care of by an introduction that has already occurred).
2. **"What do you provide?"** I coach sales professionals.
3. **"Why should I care?"** Sellers ask for their sale using one question, but there are four decisions buyers make. Not one decision. Four [that's a challenge/problem in sales].
4. **"How does it help me?"** [you will] organize your sale around the four components.
5. **"What will be my result?"** [a reorganized approach using] emotion, logic, trust, and finance will help you close more sales.

The segmented breakdown/insertion of the segue into the five questions above is actually how I develop most segues. Write out the five questions. Answer them. Then take out the questions and smooth out the sentences containing the answers. Bridging sentences that connect the answer sentences should be short.

The commitment may just be a recommendation for who might want what you do, or a referral/warm lead. Once you've secured a video meeting, in-person meeting, conference call or a virtual sales situation, then you can use that situation to accomplish more. Infusing your sales situations with stories can help with even the most difficult of sales challenges, such as price. Migrating the mind to seek out value and worth for a stellar result instead of seeking the lowest price is a challenge and **stories help sell full price.**

You should always know your numbers.
When you know the valuation of your product, depreciation, resell value, structured expenses, return on investment, operating costs, maintenance, projected efficiency improvement for the customers, etc., you can avoid objections and earn trust and confidence.

Revealing the hidden costs of not opting for your solution can also be compelling.
None of the numbers will have as much impact if they aren't tethered to a relevant situational construct that can be experienced vicariously. An effective way to accomplish that is to feature a few select numbers in a story.

"It's inspiring to see a consummate sales professional persuade decision makers to actually want to pay full price. It literally pays to learn how to do that."—ImmersiveSelling.com

Chapter 12

Stories Help Sell Full Price

You and I have to sell the result to gain commitments. It may help to address full price as another tactical way-point "mini sale." A sales story that sells full price will expedite persuasion when a KDM or DM (or consensus buying committee) reacts to your full price. Assuming your full price is fair, worth it, and in keeping with the deliverables and competitive quality, you can hold your price in most situations.

> **"Your rationalization for selling full price begins all the way back at the onset of your sale.**

Back around 2010 I had a prospective client considering my advertising and marketing team but was nearly insistent upon getting a discount. There was a retainer agreement in the purchase agreement and a fairly sizable year-long commitment for an advertising package that would probably more than deliver what they were seeking to accomplish. The KDM just wouldn't budge and insisted on a discount. A sizable one. What was revealed by using questions was that, for him, offering a discount was like part of the concierge service you might see in a five-star hotel. He was investing a sizable amount with us and he viewed it as part of the white glove service. How I responded to his strong insistence on a discount was with a story to help sell full price.

Sales Story That Helps Sell Full Price

Last year I had a client whom I'll call "XtraFrugal People Inc. (XFPI)" in a similar situation to the one you're experiencing. They were seeking some advertising guidance and an ad campaign for a new product rollout. They realized just as you have, that their investment with retaining my team was more than they had budgeted for so they went with one of our discount competitors.

After their product rollout hit a few snags and the advertising they had to use was not well received, their sales suffered. My team had identified the snags, had forecasted those consequences, and suggested work-arounds in the sales situations prior to XFPI's decision to go the discount route. XFPI's former opinion that "marketing is marketing" and "ads are ads" and "most of the creative teams are all the same" faded further when they realized they had to replace the ad campaign, absorb the lost creative investment and suffer through another quarter of lower sales revenue on the new product.

The total discount price "saved" did not offset their losses. Not even close. Little of what was developed was usable (their customers' opinions, not ours) and XFPI had to reinvest at the full price anyway.

SALES SECRET #26:
Stories Save Them Rock Hard Coin

When you develop a story to sell full price, the story becomes a hologram in their mind and so they experience the costs involved with not buying without actually sustaining the losses. They also experience ownership of the result you are offering. The story makes it almost as real as a past experience. This provides you with sales support which often translates to earning more Rock Hard Coin.

Your rationalization for selling full price begins all the way back at the onset of your sale. This can provide story-support with logic and emotion.

SECTION 4

LOGIC & EMOTION

Have you ever watched someone try and logically prove they were the best candidate? Prove they have the best product? Prove they are the best choice for something?

What happens next?

A competitor sashays onto the scene and in one job interview, one sales meeting, or one conversation, they attain the pole position. They achieve this seemingly effortlessly because they aren't trying to prove their way to the position. They are selling that position (if even unknowingly or unintentionally) **by using the same components you should, to successfully sell the result of your product.**

You shouldn't be eager or needy
(no one wants to buy from someone who needs a sale).
You should be a consultative resource, engaged, and relevant.

"When you 'Sell value, not price!' you are actually selling both and merely leading with value."—ImmersiveSelling.com

CHAPTER 13

Value Is a Logical Appeal?

We often hear we should "Sell value, not price!" Sometimes that's a good approach, but we should understand what we're doing before we deploy that strategy. When using it, keep in mind that what you're doing is using logical appeals because unless you modify the approach, the default state of value is a logical appeal.

> **Value cannot be readily assessed without knowing the price.**

The frequently given advice of "Sell value, not price!" may actually be encouraging the decision makers (DMs) and key decision makers (KDMs) to see your sales and services as commodities if they are not accompanied by emotional appeals. Those appeals should be from a sales professional they trust. So ensure your appeals are balanced and include the component sales of the Quad Close. Being commoditized is a challenge in sales that can become intensified within virtual and video sales situations.

To assess value, DMs will have to be able to clearly see the difference between what they are getting as the customer and what they will pay. Which strongly suggests that ***value cannot be readily assessed without knowing the price.*** The sales industry tends to largely agree that the difference between what is included with the product and what it will cost, is the perceived value.

While that's true, what this perception may actually be doing is prompting the potential buyer making the assessment of the value to ask, "For how much?" This question may only take place in their minds but you may also hear it verbalized. Either way, it's probably occurring. They are thinking (and often later asking) about the price and may raise price objections once they know if you haven't preemptively anticipated their expectations. To illustrate the relationship between value and price, we'll take a look at a simplified sales scenario featuring a transactional sale (the complexity of B2B sales would obscure the point).

Analogical Scenario: Box of Office Supplies

Selling the value often leads to the question, "For how much?" You could show someone an entire box of brand new assorted office supplies and let them know the box and its contents are for sale.

Selling the box would then lead you to talk about the value of that box and its many contents and ask questions about their needs and wants.

You'd soon be discussing the value of the staplers, the value of pens for accomplishing "this thing," and the value of the highlighters for underscoring "that other thing." You would then outline what the tools can do for a person, how the button functions on a calculator can provide advantages, and explore the multiple functions of various rulers or dividers.

All of the value, features and benefits would be clearly provable. Demonstrations would further illuminate the value as you stapled paper together permanently or temporarily with a paper clip.

In whatever way you spread it out on the table, piecemeal the presentation, divide or sub-divide it, the running question in the mind of the key decision maker is, "Sounds great. I could use all of that, but for how much?"

"For how much?" is the question that bubbles beneath the surface discussion. Every value proposition, feature, benefit, and description adds to the intensity of the question.

You may be selling high value sales worth $900M each and wonder what you're doing reading about a $50 box of office supplies, right? You can explain the complex math of planetary rotation and gravitational forces with foam balls, a toy marble, some tin foil, wire and string far easier than loading up the algorithmic expanses of mathematical expressions of spatial fields, voids and heavenly bodies on a computer model that proves the math. I'm using a $50 box of office supplies in the way a physicist might use a foam ball model to represent planetary behavior. To "prove the math" we can flip the sales example 180°.

Intentionally Sell the Price?
(analogical scenario flipped 180°)

Flip the box of office supplies sale around 180° and put the price up front and see if your mind doesn't seek out the value. "Would you like to buy a box of office supplies for $50.00?" Now you're "selling price." The first questions anyone would ask are, "What's in the box, and how much is in there?" You probably can't assess the $50 price without knowing the value of what's in the box. Price leads to value and value leads to price.

To test if value and price are inextricably linked, imagine your sales manager absurdly urged you to adhere to the opposite of the frequently given advice and instead insisted you "Sell price, not value!" Trying to sell price and staying off the topic of value would be impossible, wouldn't it? How do you sell the price without knowing the value? Flipping it back around to "Sell value, not price!" produces a similar feeling within the seller, doesn't it? How do you sell value without knowing the price?

When you "Sell value, not price!" you are actually selling both and merely leading with value. You'll either be talking about price very soon thereafter, or the KDM will be thinking about it. So what do you do about that? Does this render "value" ineffective? Of course not. It just needs to be understood so you can see where it fits—and it fits almost everywhere. It's a big part of the Logical Sale, encourages the Emotional Sale, and when proven it helps greatly with the Trust Sale. When used solo however it stands squarely in the Logical Sale and points directly at the

Financial Sale while largely hopping right over the other two—leading to commoditization and price objections. Use emotion to persuade the decision makers to want to buy and buy from you so you get paid for doing so. Use discovery questions after you've earned a little trust, and find out what result they may need or want (and they may not even know that yet) or where a result would actually come out well for them.

An impediment to accomplishing this is the fear-driven compulsion of many in sales to "get to the product demo" or "handle objections" which often puts their sales situations deeper into the weeds. To stay up on the road, make your sale all about them. Avoid using proof to show something is logically better before they emotionally care about a problem or challenge.

SALES SECRET #27:
Sell Value or Sell Price?

Use value to support the decision—not make it. To make the decision, use emotional appeals and the trust that you've earned, and then ask for full price because you've demonstrated value worth their time and sold the result.

It's important to help DMs use logic to validate buying instead of using it to try and sell. Sell the result and this will help you to avoid being commoditized. This doesn't line up with what many in sales have always done (they often sell features, benefits, and options). Selling the result aligns the relevance of your product with the challenges of the buyer's stressors. Once they want the result (or understand it), features, benefits and options will then help them rationalize to themselves and others why the logic is of value. Explaining this to yourself now, however, leaves "worth" dangling in a way. This will prompt the questions, "Then what is driving worth?" and **"Worth is an emotional appeal?"**

"If 'time' really 'is money' as Ben Franklin penned, then when you ask for meeting time, you're asking for a loan. Repay it when you arrive with something worth their time."—ImmersiveSelling.com

Chapter 14

Worth Is an Emotional Appeal?

If you offer something worth their time that is relevant and useful, decision makers will readily engage. You can illuminate what is to come right at the top of the first meeting by offering them a brief overview of what you have planned for the meeting—or also ask them what they would like to gain or accomplish. Sometimes, leading with discovery questions is also a great way to give the sales situation some momentum. However, you should read the DMs because in some industries that's an ineffective approach. People don't want to divulge such information as earnings, profit, challenges, inefficiencies, etc., until they trust you. So be prepared to bring value worth their time (or use your Three Minute Center Punch) [*see also chapter 9*].

> **"When a decision maker engages a sales situation, they are paying you in the currency of time.**

If and when you do lead with discovery questions, avoid an undertone of, "I don't know what to do as the seller so I'm looking for your guidance as the buyer." You should advance initial overview questions from the position of, "I have a lot to offer here that is worth your time and I'd like to discover what would be relevant and helpful for you." *Then* proceed to discovery questions, or deliver the value you bring.

Just as the difference between what someone receives and what they paid to receive it illuminates the value...the difference between what someone receives or learns in a sales situation is counter-weighted by how much time it took to get it. This will determine how the decision maker feels about the receipt of your value.

SALES SECRET #28:
Ask-and-Listen or Show-and-Tell?

Sellers sometimes "rush to the product demo" so they'll relax (because they are familiar with the product). **When you are also well-practiced in the interrogative components of your sale, you'll actually find you are just as motivated to get to the questions and listening instead of just rushing to the product demo. This is because you will feel just as prepared to ask-and-listen as you were to show-and-tell.**

That observation represents the worth. That's the reason people express worth assessment in terms of, "That's not worth my time," or "It's worth the time to find that answer," because worth is an emotional appeal. It's felt. Worth is often expressed in temporal terms because people think of worth in terms of time. Their time.

SALES SECRET #29:
Prequalification

If you don't prequalify your prospects, at least to some extent, you may invest a lot of time pursuing leads that don't yield results. When you receive high levels of rejection from one genre of business, that may be a sign they aren't qualified to buy (investing too much time in qualifying can be just as counter-productive).

There are multiple mentions in this book of "being likable" and just how do you do that? Especially within the restrictive environments of video and virtual sales situations? Delivering worth and being a consultative expert are going to encourage affinity. People like people who are on top of their value and make it worth the time of those they meet with.

People don't like the unprepared. We use the word "worth" far more than we may even realize and seldom is it ever referencing a translation of something directly to monetary value—which is only one of several definitions of "worth." Sometimes "worth" is directly related to money—"What's my used car 'worth'?"

When a decision maker engages a sales situation, they are paying you in the currency of time. That is a personal cost that is later expressed in terms of whether it was worth it or not to have attended. The DMs and KDMs all assess whether it's worth their time to meet you either virtually, in a video call, in-person, or through static means such as written or texting exchanges.

SALES SECRET #30:
Bring the Worth

You are charging full price for the meeting (their time) **and may be under-delivering the implied promise**—(which is you/their result) **if you "wing it." Video sales situations will illuminate unpreparedness more readily than in-person sales situations, so ensure you are prepared to bring the value worth their time.**

Remember that DMs and KDMs have a plan for their day, so you should have a plan for your **questions and listening.**

"Sounds like a Soaring-Eagle-Motivational-Poster! How can I listen to *this*? Huh? What if being miserable and *not* improving my sales *is* what makes me happy?!"

SECTION 5

QUESTIONS & LISTENING

You communicate a lot of information by the questions you ask. Knowing what you wish to know and where your sales situations are going, means you have clarity of purpose. The initial questions could be centered around learning what they actually do, how they do it, and why they do it.

A few quick examples are: "Many of the companies we've assisted use the XYZ approach and process, but I noticed you are using the 123 method. That's interesting. What are the advantages?" "I'd like to learn about that, would you share your thoughts?" "Do others do that as well or just your company?" "Are there challenges to doing it that way?"

You need this information because not only will it help drive your own clarity of purpose, it will help you create and communicate one for the buyer. Buyers need a clarity of purpose to buy, as much as you need one to sell.

"There's a sort of mental brightness that illuminates your sales situations with competence when you have clarity of purpose. Decision makers sense that. They pick up on your preparedness."—ImmersiveSelling.com

CHAPTER 15

Clarity of Purpose

Clarity of purpose (C.O.P.) describes what it is you should be striving for at any given point in your sales situations. Your goal. At almost any point whether video, remote selling, virtual, in-person, social, or telephonic sales situations, you should know what your clarity of purpose is.

> "Is what I'm doing right now contributing to a purpose?

So if you're in the midst of an objection, you may ask yourself if you know why it was advanced, and where your situation is now headed. If you're within discovery questions, are you learning what you wish to know? If you are in chitchat city, should you be in discovery? We are so accustomed to asking decision makers questions that we often overlook the ability and responsibility to ask ourselves what is currently happening and where we should be going in our sale. That requires a certain sense of knowing. This is something you can only know if you have an overview of the situation or perception based on experience, or a plan for the meeting. That should be based on a defined C.O.P.

What if you realize within a sales situation that your C.O.P. is to convince the DM that other decision makers who aren't present should attend the next meeting? You may be talking about, or listening to, many different subjects but your true C.O.P. would be to get that accomplished.

SALES SECRET #31:
Open-Ended Question Camouflage

It can be a temptation to arrive at a sales situation unprepared and compensate with strong, open-ended questions because they "get the DM talking." Open-ended questions are powerful (and valuable)**. Use them, but not in lieu of preparation.**

Your C.O.P. is often the "next way-point" of the way-points you've plotted either in your mind, in real time, or prior to the meeting. It's what your priority is or should be.

SALES SECRET #32:
Question Preparation

Searching your own frustration in sales will help you determine how and what to prepare. What do you want to know? What don't you know?

To ensure your sales situations are staying on track, you can spot-check your own focal point strategy with questions like:

1. ***Is what I'm doing right now contributing to a purpose?*** **If so, what specifically?**
2. **What just occurred? What is currently happening?**
3. **What is the next tactical way-point?**
4. **What should I be preparing or doing to reach that way-point?**

Ideally, your efforts in question #1 above should be pointing toward the answer to question #4. When you see the effectiveness of how questions can guide your own decisions and actions, it will reinforce the effectiveness of questions. While posing questions to decision makers you should experiment with some of the more effective **question types.**

"When a question redirects the sales situation in a new direction, that question just got work done."—ImmersiveSelling.com

Chapter 16

Question Types

Of the dozens of types of questions that have existed for centuries within sales, you'll probably be using a half dozen or so. The following five are the primary question types that get the most work done:

1. **Open-ended discovery questions**
2. **Focus questions**
3. **Leading** (persuasive) **questions**
4. **Follow-up questions/magnification questions**
5. **Closed-ended questions**

Here is an expanded look at each type and how they may apply to what you're doing:

---

1. Open-Ended Discovery Questions

While seeking to understand the operations and challenges of a business, any question that seeks out information is probably going to be a discovery question. These offer the seller new information while using subtext.

The way you can do that is to ensure your questions are relevant, helpful in your understanding of their situation, considerate, and intelligent. Yes, there is such a thing as a misfocused question. Ask intelligent ones and they will see what you are seeking to learn by the questions you ask. By asking questions that are misfocused you may inaccurately communicate that you don't care, are incompetent, unprepared, inconsiderate, or pushy. "Winging-it" is almost always a misfocused strategy (but the one advanced in many sales situations).

SALES SECRET #33: Question Strategy

When you use open-ended questions "to get them talking" that is effective for discovery but without an over-arching strategy, you risk losing directional control over your sales situations.

Here are a few examples of open-ended discovery questions (this is not a comprehensive list). What you should note here are not the exact words or phrases, but the approaches taken.

- When your department (or company) encounters challenges in this area, what process do you use to solve them?
- So when you took over the department last year how did you go about solving the challenges you mentioned about [the subject being discussed]?
- What has worked well in the past when you've sought ways to [leverage opportunities] or [act on some opportunity]?
- When your preparations and plans work out, what will be the result?
- What is your thinking on [the subject being discussed]?
- How would you improve your former solution? If you could do it all over again, what would you change?
- What worked well? Why do you think it succeeded?
- What has been your experience over the past year with your current system?
- You mentioned you haven't seen an ROI. Why haven't you seen the return on investment you were hoping for?
- How have you coordinated joint-responsibility between departments up until now?

SALES SECRET #34:
A Question Is a Sales Diagnostic Tool

While you are learning about their operation and challenges, your questions can help them see their own challenges. Questions can be a powerful diagnostic tool.

Open-ended questions seek answers but they also reveal, for better or worse, your vantage point and priorities. For example, the answers to the following open-ended questions will benefit you, and the DMs will know that. This doesn't suggest you shouldn't ask these questions, you should. Just know you are revealing your priorities.

- **Who are the decision makers?**
- **How are decisions made?**
- **Where are you in your buying process?**

If you are seeking to understand how to help them, then the following kinds of open-ended questions will benefit *them*:

- **How are you approaching your competition this year and does that differ from last year's approach?**
- **What challenges have you found to be more difficult in this economic environment?**
- **How has the state of current commerce benefitted you or hindered your progress as a company?**
- **What would you be at liberty to share about your current pursuit of new business in that area?**

Decision makers appreciate and respect solid questions that you've obviously thought through. Remember to not lose sight of your clarity of purpose. Often that requires listening to your intuition. It's just as important to listen to your intuition as it is to hear the DMs.

---

2. Focus Questions

Focus questions can help you dial into a specific area and stay on a topic you suspect will lead to the next way-point. Without the focus question as an interrogative tool, the DM may have moved onto the next subject.

The construct of "asking" keeps them involved in a topic longer because people naturally like to answer intelligent questions and share what they know. This provides a deeper focus on a topic or a way to underscore something.

Another use for focus questions is to phrase a potentially touchy subject as a focus question. This facilitates a gentle approach and lets you say, "Hey, look at this." You can call attention to something otherwise not highlighted. This is especially helpful when asking about challenges and problems you see that your result would solve.

> **"Have you ever wondered, or looked into, whether or not that** [insert relevant thing or situation] **has been underutilized as a source of future profit?"**

---

3. Leading (persuasive) **Questions**

Use questions to lead the mind to a conclusion or way-point. This approach should be consultative, helpful and very understated. You're leading them to a place in the conversation that will give you more information.

> **SALES SECRET #35:**
> **Depth of Field**
>
> **You've seen photos or illustrations where the foreground is in tight focus and the background is blurry. This is done to add interest and highlight a subject. The principle is called "depth of field." You can use questions to focus and lead a situation in the same way. Bring the topic you wish for the decision makers to see into the foreground, and then focus their attention using leading questions.**

For example, at a time when a key decision maker may not feel it's a priority to consider a solution, you could lead them to focus on their division or company challenges (that your result would fix) by asking leading questions.

> **"We've been focusing our discussion on your goals for generating revenue. What are some of your thoughts on reducing costs over the next year** [will likely lead to how your product saves them operating costs (if that's what it does)]**?" or "How do you envision next year's operations?" or "Could you share your thinking on how each quarter next year could improve over the preceding?"**

---

4. Follow-up Questions/Magnification Questions (they are similar but different)

A follow-up question seeks more linear information about the same topic or referencing the same question whereas a magnification question zooms into a topic for a closer look at details or conditions. It's going to be a challenge to just guess or assume what stressors are affecting a business. They aren't going to be motivated to share the depth of detail you may need to acquire enough information for diagnostics until they trust you.

Follow the Action, or Zoom In?

When action photographers and videographers are shooting events they may follow the ball, pan a crowd or otherwise move their cameras in a horizontal motion to capture more of the scene. When they see an opportunity to capture more detail or an exciting moment, they zoom in on the detail.

This is similar to a magnification question. This is following the action, similar to how a follow-up question continues on a subject path. You and I use questions the way photographers use cameras. We follow the subject with questions and zoom into our sales situations using magnification questions. This provides detail about situations, and finer detail about components and people.

When delivered in a consultative tone, you can actually use magnification questions to earn trust. When the DMs can see you're really trying to help them, and they sense you could (if you had the information), they will be more inclined to share.

An Example of a Follow-up Question:

"Were the three generally all in agreement moving forward with that departmental transition plan you mentioned was under consideration last year?"

Example Magnification Questions:

"You mentioned there was an alternate idea to the one implemented. What did the alternate idea offer? Was it well received by all? Why wasn't it used as part of the transition? What detail did most people seem to focus on?"

---

5. Closed-Ended Questions

This question type is generally seeking (or can be answered with) a "yes or no" answer or from a short list of options such as "small," medium," or "large." You can use the closed-ended question to help someone arrive at a conclusion. This pulls them forward into a mental position of some conclusive state. For example, if your system has a far better warranty and you're in need of logical appeals, you could ask if they've reviewed their current warranty. That's a "yes or no" closed-ended question but asks a larger question without asking it, *"I wonder if our current warranty is sufficient? I wonder what the other vendors' warranties cover?"*

Closed-Ended Questions (more examples):
"Who typically decides which system to install when replacing this? When were you thinking of acquiring a new solution? Is your decision making process nearly complete?"

Most of the question types can be worked into various delivery methods and will serve you well. Do your sales ever go **off-road? In the weeds? Ask your way out.**

"Questions are powerful 'tactical support' that can illuminate the direction to your next way-point like a compass reading."—ImmersiveSelling.com

CHAPTER 17

Off-Road? In the Weeds? Ask Your Way Out

Back in the early 2010s I was selling advertising. It was the fifth time I'd met with the DMs and each time it was a different configuration of decision makers. I had attempted to get them all in the same room at the same time, but I had somewhat ignored my own clarity of purpose (C.O.P.) because I had earned the trust of the KDM and placed too much confidence in that accomplishment.

> **"Once the right questions had been asked, he softened his resistance.**

This fifth meeting was supposed to be the signing of the purchase agreement so it was the sales close and as I later recommend in the closing section, I made a concerted effort not to elevate the sales close to an event-level-status. I'd already asked the KDM for the sale at the fourth meeting and got an affirmative confirmation. This meeting was intended for the signing of the purchase agreement.

Things were going fine with the KDM ("Mitch") until one of the EVPs and principle investor in the company ("Kyle") stopped in to contribute to the final decision. I had met with Kyle in the former sales situations but he didn't assert himself at that time (even though I sensed something was a bit "off" in his enthusiasm). I only needed one signature and a check but all of the DMs had to okay the arrangement verbally as it was a sizable commitment.

Kyle was suddenly having none of it.

For no apparent reason (at the time, but you and I know better—there is always a reason) he balked about everything from "ad guys", not trusting sales reps (a wide-reference that apparently included me), low performing ads they'd tried (from my competition) in the past, and his personal distaste for media being overpriced. I should have perceived this problem much sooner (I knew better).

I should have listened to my intuition, and asked Kyle about his former experiences. Using open-ended discovery questions would have accomplished this for me.

You can guess that in that moment I was wishing I had spent more time on figuring out how Kyle felt about media and advertising teams.

SALES SECRET #36:
Crucial Questions

A few of the most important questions to ask in a complex B2B sales situation are, "What were your experiences with your current or past solutions or providers?" and "How did they or how have they been working for you?" also "What areas of improvement would you like to see in a new business collaboration?"

Had I brought that up with myself during preparation between the second and third sales situations, or between the third and fourth sales situations, I wouldn't have been in the closing bind with Kyle that I was in—and now my sale was in the weeds as a result of my error.

I already knew the CEO was unwilling to override Kyle, and I actually wouldn't have wanted him to. There's nothing worse than having an account with an unwilling partner. You ice skate up hill through the whole contract as they roll grenades through every door you open while trying to fulfill. It's better to get everyone on board at the get-go. A bit more discussion only revealed just how deep Kyle had dug in.

A quick glance in Mitch's direction revealed his gesture toward the purchase agreement on the conference room table as he said, "Well. Looks like this little stack of paper is like yesterday's newspaper." I wasn't just in the weeds, I'd plowed through all the way to the swamp.

Mitch shrugged, stood to leave, and thanked me for my time. Kyle stood to leave as well but before he did, I asked him for some advice. He looked at me suspiciously and mentioned that he wasn't changing his mind. He "was out." I let him know my questions weren't about the purchase agreement—because they weren't. My Quad Close had just blown up and he was out in the wilderness of the Emotional Sale and I had to join him there.

SALES SECRET #37:
Power of Questions

Emotions are the prime movers of people and questions are one of the more powerful of the prime movers of emotions.

He let me know he had no more than a few minutes, so I didn't have much time to find out where he was in the wilderness. I decided to just get started anyway. Expeditiously.

TRACEY: "I was listening intently when you said you were sick of the low quality ads and the ad people who really didn't take suggestions or listen to you in the past. Would you share with me what you wanted to tell them?"
KYLE: "Who?"
TRACEY: "The ad people you became frustrated with. I'd like to hear what you would have said to them—what you wanted to tell them."
KYLE: "Why? I'm not buying, so why do you care after the fact?"
TRACEY: "With strong opinions like yours, the story has to be good or the opinions wouldn't be well formed and thought out like yours are. I'm curious to know what happened."
KYLE: "Well..." He paused to think, "I'm still not going to buy. I want to know why you want to know what I think."

SALES SECRET #38:
Don't "Ask" to Ask

Saying, "Let me ask you a question," followed by a question or, "If you don't mind me asking," followed by a question, makes you sound insecure, sales reppy, smarmy, and unsure. Just ask. State clearly and speak at an appropriate level in a consultative, friendly tone.

TRACEY: "There's one group of people that have the most valuable information. Usually the ones with the strongest opinions have formed

them over time. That often means they've analyzed a situation thoroughly. I want to listen. Would you share your experience with the last marketing group and creative ad team you worked with? Tell me what you wanted to tell them?"

Kyle went on to share his experience and shared several stories and past experiences with arrogant ad people and steam-rolling-marketing-teams that took a bunch of money but didn't deliver much—all while padding-the-invoices and not listening to Kyle. He felt lied to, bullied, and betrayed. When sales didn't improve even after the former marketers encouraged massive increases in the ad budget, ("You gotta spend money to make money!") Kyle wanted to explore other options for sales, marketing, advertising, and promotion. But the other decision makers wanted to stay the course and believed the marketers when they said "it takes time." I agreed, that it does take time, but I also mentioned that you should be able to see trending metrics. Indicators.

SALES SECRET #39:
Metrics Are Your Friends

If you're doing a great job with fulfillment, if any kind of metrics are available, they offer encouragement to you and will help steer your future decisions.

I listened intently. I nodded. He went on to share his frustration with the promotion of their company. As I listened, I responded minimally to his stories ensuring he knew I was listening, but what responses I did offer were brief and empathic. "I actually hear that a lot," and "That must have been frustrating," and "That would sure make anyone in your position feel that way," and then I would return to listening. And listening some more.

When Kyle was finished talking I had been listening far longer than I had initially talked and it turns out Kyle's objections were founded on logical reasons, past emotional experiences with advertising and marketing people, and a feeling of being somewhat powerless in the group dynamics of the decision. He wanted to avoid repeating that situation.

Once the right questions had been asked, he softened his resistance. Kyle let me know he had no more reservations about the sale. The P.A. was signed about a week later. Kyle's motives, once discovered through questions, were easy to see and understand because I had engaged in genuine **empathic active listening.**

Corporate positions such as RevOps, SalesOps, DevOps, etc., will be augmenting the CXO positions to counteract the siloed effects of some divisions. You can be assured this will be an adjustment for all, but also an advantage for you personally.

You are in a revenue generating position and anyone competent within RevOps will know (or realize) that the most important component of any company is sales. Especially the personal income of each seller. If that's not dialed in, the company can stack the metaphoric blocks any way they like—and even simulate capital gains, but true growth comes directly from you. The SDRs and BDRs are valuable sales support (engage them with respect), because without their help you may not achieve your numbers. This illuminates an important cannon of business; everyone, including the Ops and CXOs, are in sales support roles.

Everyone supports *you*—or they should.

"Just 'listening intently' is a tool few sales professionals ever fully master."

—ImmersiveSelling.com

Chapter 18

Empathic Active Listening

Strangers will often share secrets with you that they wouldn't normally disclose to those they know well. In a way it's a personal catharsis but it's also because the risk of exposure is low. Have you noticed that once they've over-shared, they often comment on how nice you are and may even mention that they like you or appreciate the connection? You hardly spoke. In fact, just about all you did was listen. People like you when you listen. "Earning trust" and "being likable" are two key components in selling and you can work on earning trust by listening and probably achieve likability status simultaneously.

> **"Listening is almost never a mistake. Talking sometimes is.**

Some DMs and KDMs are introverted and so you may have to draw information out of them over time. They will be apt to share little and seldom, and guard critical information that you perhaps might even need to properly assess their situation. Later they may just mumble, "Well, I didn't know you needed to know all of that other stuff."

At the other end of the spectrum are the extroverted personalities. They will be more apt to share their opinions. That does not necessarily mean the sale is advancing on its own, you still have to do the persuasive work. Also, spontaneous and impulsive personality types make a sales situation feel as if it's progressing quickly. That may reflect more on the DMs' personalities than on the actual progress of the sale.

SALES SECRET #40:
Being Likable?

Just how do you go about consciously being likable? One good way to do that is by listening. Empathic active listening, means hearing, nodding, being present and caring. Especially in video and virtual.

The quieter KDM may actually be more willing to speak than you realize but because of the cultural conditioning to avoid awkward silences at almost any cost, when a void in the conversation occurs, the sales professional often feels a compulsion to fill the void and speak. That quiet personality type of the decision maker often gets railroaded so they've learned to just take information in and make decisions later. You can accurately assume what may be happening to our likability when that occurs in our sales situations. If you're over-communicating, then you're likely missing out on cues and clues from others. You're certainly missing out on what they want to say.

The only picture you're ever going to get of your true sale which is in their mind, is going to come from listening and observing others who are in control of the decisions. You can't plot way-points if you can't see the terrain. You need the input. When you ask questions and listen, you're selling you. Effectively.

SALES SECRET #41:
Empathic Visualization

After you've engaged a sales situation and learned about a prospect's challenges, take some quiet time later and walk through an imagined day from their experience. Visualize their professional life and put yourself in that position using all that you observed. This will literally open up opportunities for you to see them, and may help you see yourself from their perspective.

If the KDM is talking in your sales situation, you should listen. ***Listening is almost never a mistake. Talking sometimes is.*** Many sellers aren't actually listening. They are thinking of their next statement, future moves, or are preparing their next question.

SALES SECRET #42:
You Can't Plot Way-Points without Vision

Listening and observing are information inputs. They are your vision of what's in the mind of the KDM.

You may find that in retrospect, nearly every time you compare the value of what you were thinking of saying (as it relates to the sale in their mind) to the value of what they are then-currently saying (that you should be listening to), their words win. That is nearly invariably true. You can repeat back to them, key points made by them, when it's your turn to talk to indicate you've heard them clearly.

SALES SECRET #43:
A Case for Preparation

If you have already developed several (or more) **open-ended questions in preparation for a sales situation, then during the situation you won't be preparing your next question while they speak and you can actually listen.**

Often the DMs and KDM are telling us what we need to know to advance the sale. We just have to listen. If you don't listen you'll also likely receive more **objections.**

A Question Creation Strategy

Many in sales find it frustrating to develop questions prior to a sales situation. When you try to think of a question, that endeavor can be similar to trying to think of what to say in reaction to a special holiday present. Until you know what the gift is, you won't know how to respond. A way to use this to your advantage is to develop new questions from what DMs and KDMs offer in conversation and convert statements and information to an interrogative format for *future* sales situations with other KDMs (and then put these on your Wall of Wisdom [*see also Strati-Tactical #3*]).

Tactical Example

KDM (in a current meeting): "You wouldn't think that the price of building materials would be affecting our sector of business as much as it has. In just one year the price per thousand board feet of lumber went from $360 to over $1250. That 255% increase can add over $40K to the cost of new home construction. We aren't even in the home construction industry but we use the same materials so the inflation has a definitive effect."

SALES PROFESSIONAL (in future meeting with a different KDM but in the same industry): "I've learned that the cost of building materials has risen 255% in just one year. Is there a downstream effect on your business attributable to inflation? If so, in what ways are you affected?" [they answer]. You continue, "So how have you been compensating for that? Are there other areas being affected?"

You can get them onto various topics in question form, based on answers and information from previous meetings. It literally pays to pay attention and listen.

SECTION 6

OBJECTIONS

Some Assembly Required

"We handled your price objections by making the rims and tires optional but hey, you got the price you wanted."

Chapter 19

Hidden Objections

Think of a goal you felt compelled to achieve and then did. Walk it all the way back in your mind to where that accomplishment began. The entirety of a long range goal began with an emotion, didn't it? You ***wanted*** to achieve something, get something done, acquire something or achieve something in your life.

> **Believing that hidden motives exist will help you see what they are.**

The same emotional basis you will find present in goals you will also find evident in resistance. Why? Because what we call "objections" or "resistance" is only relative to what we want. The decision maker is resisting an altered course often for reasons we can't see.

SALES SECRET #44:
Respond to the Emotional Motive

Sales professionals often respond to objections by addressing the literal words being spoken by the decision maker. A more effective response is to ask questions and dig for the emotions influencing the "why?" Once known, you can influence their motive and intent.

For every objection and instance of resistance, there's always a "why?" driving the DMs' decisions. They may not even fully understand the why themselves but most of the time they are well aware of what is driving their apprehension.

You've likely encountered a logical objection like, "It's not in this year's budget." If that resistance morphs into another logical reason, which again changes once that reason is resolved, you are probably encountering a hidden emotional objection being concealed by several logical ones. When you encounter hidden emotional objections, you should use discovery questions and engage tactical way-point thinking [*see chapter 4*].

"Sell the Dent"
Finding the Hidden Objection

While out prospecting for new business just after the '08 crash I could almost hear the hand-wringing and nervous pacing in the offices far above the streets. The decision makers had a better view of the burning economy from their offices above so I resisted joining them there until I could bring solutions to the meetings.

I'd been working on a sale for a few months in order to gain access to the decision makers of a factory-direct warehouse-type appliance center. They had a standing policy that the KDM never took a sales call. Ever. Everything was vetted at the lower levels. They had an agency-of-record and were in contract with a retainer, and so they had no motive to talk to me or hear about my advertising and marketing team. After receiving a lot of resistance from the executive assistants (GKs) of upper management (and hearing again and again how they already had an ad agency), **I went in on the ground floor. The retail floor. That's my least favorite approach but sometimes it's the only way in.**

Once I had figured out a solution set for them, I worked my way up through several meetings with the floor managers, middle managers, the VP of sales, and finally set a meeting with the KDM. My clarity of purpose in every step was solely to set a meeting with the next level of management (always try to go for the top KDM when possible. That wasn't possible in that company).

They advertised incessantly and doing some estimates from my outside perspective on their internal ad budget, the account would

have been in my top five income generators if I could close the sale. I wanted that account (for my business at the time it was ideal) and I knew I could help them.

The hard work paid off and I arrived to the meeting with the CEO "Calvin" after having prepared diligently. I'd shopped their retail stores, researched their ad history, read their entire website, their marketing collateral, disclaimers, and researched the history of the company online. I also ensured I had detailed knowledge of their agency-of-record.

Calvin's appliance center had overstocked units that were all brand new or had some small defect such as chipped paint, a dented door, or a scuff on the finish. They had every home appliance and wide selection of models and brands. The understated decor, big bold discount price tags, and sales banners in the windows, was the look of "factory-direct" they were going for. The visuals were reflecting Calvin's intense fixation on selling price.

After some brief small talk, Calvin advanced the Go Objection [*see chapter 20*]. "Okay. So Denise (VP of sales) set this up for me. She said what you've got is interesting. I've got a lot going on and can only give you a few minutes. So whatta ya got?" I answered with my sales story, the Three Minute Center Punch [*see also chapter 9*], interspersed with some details and facts relative to his business that I'd gained from research. While I spoke, Calvin began leaning forward a bit. Musing, he asked me some questions to gauge my understanding of retail price theory, product, total market area, serviceable market area, ad placement, current market area, foot traffic, advertising promotion, product sales, placement of ads, and promotion to generate foot traffic. I answered all of his straight forward questions and then shared a different take on my personal theory of price elasticity. I asked more than a few discovery questions to learn about his thinking which then led to a conversation between Calvin and I that was pivotal to the sale.

CALVIN: "So what you're saying is don't sell price? Like at all? You're kidding right? That'd be impossible in this business. I mean

that's the whole point of coming here. They get brand name appliances for less."
TRACEY: "I'm not thinking you *shouldn't* sell price. You could sell price *differently*."
CALVIN: "How? My current ad agency, your direct competitor by the way, has the ad campaign produced (what he was really saying there is he'd already paid for the ad production and was nervous about losing what he'd already put into the expense) **and they've been in business about 15 years longer than you** (he'd just asked about the history of my business)**. They've made it easy so we just rotate out the sales price in the ads and feature this month's sale** (what was revealed was his adherence to doing things the way they'd always done them and that he had an aversion to change)**. Don't you think if there was another way to sell price, as you suggest, they'd have thought of that by now?"**
TRACEY: "How long have they been your agency-of-record?"
CALVIN: "Like eightee—no, more like, I dunno, like 20 years."
TRACEY: *nodding* "They've done a good job for you. My team stands on its strengths and that is creativity. Unique advertising concepts that work because they're different, relevant, and engaging. Engagement is king in advertising because it translates impressions to foot traffic. Those are physical conversions."
CALVIN: "Yeah, I get that. I mean, they aren't the most creative agency. The ads aren't engaging. I've sort of been hoping people view a low ad budget as savings I pass on to the customer."
TRACEY: "That requires engagement. They aren't using critical thinking about the advertising quality until they engage. Which some do. But you want to improve. If those you wish to attract aren't engaging the ads, they aren't thinking about your ad budget."
CALVIN: "Well there is some engagement. Maybe not enough. I mean, it could be a lot better. But they get the job done and the ads generate some foot traffic. It sort of works."
TRACEY: "I agree. That agency will always be consistent for you. I'm also confident you've played with price elasticity every way to Sunday and are an absolute expert on moving dimes around on price tags and you understand the corresponding effects on the foot traffic at the door."
CALVIN: "That's exactly what I'm saying. Price down, foot traffic up. Price up, foot traffic goes down (a part of the definition of price elasticity)**. If it's not dialed in, the feet go to the mall to get a fridge."**
TRACEY: "What if you could add dimes to the price without affecting the door or even better, have foot traffic increase by selling a price

differently? Price up *and* foot traffic up. You could accomplish that with a new ad campaign that attaches price to something different."
CALVIN: "Attached? What do you mean?" (I'd been intentionally vague to create just a touch of anticipation).
TRACEY: "Just that. What are the prices attached to?"
CALVIN: "The product."
TRACEY: "Have you tried to attaching them to something else?"
CALVIN: "I'm confused."
TRACEY: "Exactly. So are your TV ad viewers."
CALVIN: "How so?"
TRACEY: "Price elasticity tells you much more than the tolerated brackets on the low and high end of tolerated price. It can reveal what customers see as value. What I saw when I was test-shopping all of your stores was some pretty impressive product knowledge from your team and managers. Are all sales associates in your locations that knowledgeable?"
CALVIN: "Absolutely. They're all trained and experienced."
TRACEY: "So if it were only price driving sales, why not just have price tags hanging off of product?"
CALVIN: "It wouldn't sell."
TRACEY: "What I'm hearing and seeing are trained professionals who can effectively sell, know the products, can make recommendations on size, volume, fit, finish and all manner of function and how that fits within a family's needs."
CALVIN: "Exactly."
TRACEY: "So you're not selling price, you're advertising it to get people in the doors. Then you deliver value and a buying experience that's consultative. You're selling consultative value. Does that sound accurate?"
CALVIN: "Absolutely."
TRACEY: "Then what you're actually trying to accomplish with your ad campaign is to get people in the door. Once here, you have to somewhat undo the customers' perception that only price matters and switch to delivering value worth the trip down here, right? Because it's not actually only price that matters."
CALVIN: "Yeah. Okay. I'll bite. What's your theory?"
TRACEY: "Price is actually not attached to the product in your ads, it's attached to a reason to come here."
CALVIN: "Splitting hairs, but okay."
TRACEY: "That means you can attach the price to something else and then you won't have to reframe their perception and undo work you've done in the market by driving price and then having to switch

to value and worth on the sales floor talking about product (because the price won't be attached to product). **So what I'm thinking is flip the script and instead of attaching the price to the product and running fire sale after one-week-only sales...where customers sort of know there'll always be another sale next week...I'm thinking you can instead, attach the price to the dent."**
CALVIN: "What? Dent? Huh?"
TRACEY: "Attach the price to the dent. Sell the dent. Each week instead of blasting the TV screens with the latest 'X% off of retail, stop on down, we'll take care of your needs. From this to that and everything in-between...' and then some cute reference to 'Having everything *BUT* the kitchen sink', you could sell the dent. Tell them how much that week's dent (or blemish or overstock or...etc.) **is worth on something. You'd get people coming in here trying to find the dents. When they find it, they get X% off for having found it."**
CALVIN: "Everyone would come in looking for flaws?"
TRACEY: "Yes, well, you're an overstock, dented, blemish good-as new-but-with-a-small-flaw factory outlet appliance center. You aren't hiding the flaws, overstocking, or factory-directness of it all.... are you?"
CALVIN: "We're not hiding it. It's part of our feature."
TRACEY: "You're already trying to feature the blem/dent/overstock feature and suggesting a lower price is the result. You could instead attach the low price up front as an experiential draw (to the dent) **and have their discovery, your quality, and consultative buying experience as the result. As it is, they're coming in here looking for *your* losses. You encourage them to. Their gain is merely implied. You could switch that and have them coming in here looking for their own gain with your losses being the implication."**
CALVIN: "I'd never thought of it like that."
TRACEY: "Almost like a dent-n-blem scavenger hunt. Retail style. That would encourage engagement. Involvement. This would deliver customer experiential enjoyment in your stores instead of vulture-thinking looking for your losses being their gains. You're swapping out the gain. Vulture-thinking is a negative emotional relationship on the floor that has to be undone every single time. That's placed squarely on the shoulders of every sales professional trying to sell value consultatively."

We started discussing how to feature dents, blems, scratches and overstocks with cool ad concepts, spokespeople and even a dent mascot/character (it would, of course, have to be "dented"). Our meeting had morphed into a mini-creative-work-session and Calvin appeared to be all in. He could see it in his mind working (because it absolutely would have). We talked for awhile longer before I started motioning toward scheduling a proper work session (because the whole concept needed a lot of work—you're reading about a rough concept because this is a sales subject and not marketing) and suggested including his partners, regional managers, and several store managers from various outlets to get input on market specifics. I wanted all of the decision makers in the same room.

Once a commitment was being discussed, Calvin looked down at his desk and then offered up the "Now is not the right time for changes like this" objection. I worked through that and he changed his objection to "not being not sure if one of his partners would go for such a vast change." After that was reframed, he changed the objection again. It was a sure sign of logical objections concealing a hidden emotional objection. It was clear he trusted me so I asked him open-ended questions to discover what his reservation *really* was. After another brief discussion he finally revealed his true emotional motive.

CALVIN: "Look. I think your team would do wonders with my ads and business but your competitor, 'Jim Gorgenson' (fictitious name) is our agency of record. He and I go way back. He was my college roommate and has been my best friend for 30 years."

He paused for a few moments. Intent on listening empathically, I remained silent and waited.

CALVIN: "I'm not going to use the dent ad campaign concept because that's yours (Calvin had already signed my NDA anyway). As much as I wish it were mine, retaining your team is not possible. I can't do that to my best friend. I just can't. He'd suffer irreparable damage in this economy. I just can't live with that."
TRACEY: "And bringing us on as consultants would probably offend the friendship."
CALVIN: "Yes. I'm sorry. I just can't do what I want to do here."

In this example there was nowhere to go from there. The emotional driver was friendship/affinity (a stronger emotion than "wanting-to-buy"). This is what drove Calvin's motive for change aversion. ***Believing that hidden motives exist will help you see what they are.***

SALES SECRET #45
Logical Objections That Migrate and Change

After you respond to an objection (and solve it), **if the decision maker changes their objection one or more times, you've probably encountered a logical objection concealing a hidden emotional objection. Open-ended discovery questions will help you reveal what it is.**

You may be wondering why I didn't launch into the whole, "Why let a friendship hold back your business?" and/or "If he is a true friend he'd understand you are growing with a new direction" angles. True friendship is something I respect. I actually agreed with him. It would have been helpful to know about the hidden objection back at the beginning, but he probably wouldn't have told someone he didn't yet trust *why* he had retained his agency. This was evident when Calvin had advanced the **Go Objection.**

"When a decision maker puts you on the spot and says, 'I'm busy, what have you got?' they are asking you to show them the value worth their time."

—ImmersiveSelling.com

Chapter 20

The Go Objection

There is a sales objection that has managed to remain nameless. It's seldom talked about (and it's time) so I call the nameless objection the "Go Objection" (G.O.). This objection is usually some variant of a firm request for you to just "get to it" with "it" being whatever value you promised would be forthcoming in the meeting. They're saying "Go" as in "get to the point" or "get on with it." An excellent response to the G.O. will be your Three Minute Center Punch (3MCP) [*see also chapter 9*].

> **When you're being pushed with some variant of the G.O. you should have a response ready.**

This objection can be subtle or direct, implied or expressly stated. You may get the feeling the DM doesn't want to be there, or they may state outright that they are pushed for time and they want you to "get right to it." That's the G.O. They want to know what's in it for them and they want to know now. You may have received the G.O. and just didn't realize it was an objection. That's because it can be disorienting and comes with some implied pressure that can be uncomfortable for sales professionals. Sometimes it's even accompanied by an air of apathy (they don't care to "go through it all" and just want you to get to the point). Other G.O.s will feel more like the traditional objections delivered with some emphasis.

Here are a few examples of the G.O.:

- A consensus buying committee grants multiple competing B2B vendors a rapid-fire chance to each pitch the committee, with each vendor granted some short allotment of time (20 or 30 minutes). The sellers that the committee members are interested in will receive a call back.
- The DMs or KDM are reluctant to meet, are busy or are just seemingly disengaged when you arrive. Your arrival could be to log onto video, engage virtually, or meet in person. You're asked to just get to the core value offering.
- The DM was actually about to head into another meeting and says, "I've been called into a meeting. I'll give you just a few minutes—what do you have for me?"
- The day got away from them, they can't meet but since you're there, they'll give you a few minutes.
- They, unfortunately, will have to cancel the meeting and reschedule far in advance—but can give you just a few minutes now.
- After agreeing to the meeting (some weeks ago) they've since reassessed their challenge and may not need to meet with you after all—but grant you a few minutes "just in case."
- They did a quick search online and found another solution—but let you have a few minutes to explain why yours is better.
- The DMs or KDM are having a bad day. They seem disengaged. You sense they are meeting with you reluctantly. The G.O. here is implied but that does not render it any less potent.
- The meeting isn't progressing well and the seller is asked to just send some information in email. If it's of interest, they'll schedule another meeting. Maybe (or not).
- The DMs and KDM are "pitched out" and don't want to hear another sales pitch. They may even say this and either request you move the value up front or skip the pitch/presentation.

You may be wondering why the G.O. even exists. The approaches that many in sales have been taking for years has culminated into a sort of saturation point with decision makers who are pitch fatigued. Many don't want to see another presentation about the sales rep, because, well, it's about the rep.

Few decision makers have time or patience anymore for spongy sales situations (not to be confused with valuable, brief, up front "small talk" to relax a situation. I recommend you still do that). Some DMs are tired of talking about golf, their trophy fish on the wall, executive toys on their desk and they just don't have time to play with sales reps anymore. They have a company to run and the G.O. can help facilitate that end for the DMs.

Imagine applying one of the go-to sales openings from the pre-2020 era to today's video and virtual sales situations.

Imagine for a moment getting a coveted meeting today with a DM or KDM of one of the prime prospective corporations you'd like to sell to. It's a video sales situation. Except instead of following the new rules of interaction, you engage the decision maker similar to how many in sales would open a sales situation pre-2020 (while trying too hard to establish rapport).

YOU: "Right, so, before we get started," you say with a tone of curiosity, "could you pick up your tablet or web cam and sort of just pan the room around you so I can get a sense of the space?"
DM: To which the shocked DM replies with, "Excuse me? Did you just ask me to pan the room with my web cam?"
YOU: "Yeah, I want to see what books you're reading, if there are any executive toys on your desk, or if there are any framed golfing photos to comment on, or a mounted trophy fish I can use as a springboard to tell a fishing story."

The conversation, if it even continued (unlikely) **would become weirder and more awkward by the second.**

If you've ever been in a sales situation and have seen a G.O. in the wild, you'll know that it can throw the seller a bit off balance.

SALES SECRET #46:
Perception Drives the Go Objection

If the decision makers perceive sales professionals as merely sales reps due to negative experiences buying within your industry, they are motivated to engage in vetting. The G.O. offers them an option for expediency to accomplish this. Be prepared with a 3MCP.

The objection is disorienting. ***When you're being pushed with some variant of the G.O. you should have a response ready.*** If prepared, you'll drop back to what you know which is why you need a tool like the Three Minute Center Punch (3MCP) [*see also chapter 9*].

SALES SECRET #47:
Humor at the Onset of Your Sales Situations? Maybe. Maybe not.

When possible, your default introduction should be to try and visit briefly with the DMs or KDMs so they feel comfortable. If you're funny, use light humor (only if that's a skill set for you). **If you're gregarious, then chatting is ideal. If you're a good listener, then ask an open-ended question and listen.**

What the decision makers want to know is if they can logically rationalize a time investment before paying you (with their time). You're already asking them for full price when paid for with time. You can use that as a base level of monetary confidence for yourself when **selling full price.**

Misleading information about price or options
will cause a reaction similar to the situation you see when lava from an
active volcano slowly absorbs an asphalt road in its path.
There's just no more road and no way to traverse
to the other side of the lava to proceed. Always be honest.
If discovered by the DMs and KDM, a sales professional cannot close
the financial sale using a method that erodes the Trust Sale.

"You either have to sell your sales manager on the idea of granting a discount, or, you have to persuade the decision maker to buy full price. Either way you have to sell a price to someone."—ImmersiveSelling.com

Chapter 21

Selling Full Price

Anything sold is a product. That means that when the decision makers are seeking terms for a discount, they are selling something back to you. The decision makers are "selling to *you*" the idea of granting a 10% discount to *them*. Their product becomes your-product-delivered-at-90%-of-the-price and they often seek it simply because they perceive it's possible.

Do you engage a sales situation more enthusiastically when you sense or perceive that a sale is more likely? Probably. You may even upsell additional options or ask for the sale with more confidence. You are more relaxed. You even have more fun in the sales situation, don't you? The reverse is also true.

> **KDMs use their personal power to make you feel like a discount is the only way to pull the sale over the line.**

When the DMs sense your product is of high value, will work for them, and is a viable solution to solve real problems or enhance their production, efficiency or experience, they may want to buy. If it's fairly obvious you're going to be willing to grant a discount, they "ask for their sale" with more enthusiasm.

SALES SECRET #48:
Commit to Selling Full Price

Once you commit to selling full price, there is often a change in how decision makers perceive you. They are also more likely to have some apprehension about asking for a discount. This is similar to how you may have felt in the past about asking for the sale—for similar reasons. They were exuding the same personal confidence and power within the buying role that you now possess within the role of selling.

When you deliver your full product for less, or you include extra value for the same or an even lower price, the DMs and KDM get a kudo from superiors, the board of directors, fellow senior staff, or colleagues. Many of them thrive on building a reputation within the company as a master negotiator or shrewd business professional. They may strive for that moniker-type-status of "You don't want to be on the other side of the table of [KDM's name]."

SALES SECRET #49:
Full Price Positioning

Industry and product knowledge and technical expertise are respected by DMs and KDMs. It's much more difficult to seek discounting from experts in a field. You should strive to attain a level of industry expertise. DMs will request fewer discounts and be more interested in buying from an expert offering consultative value.

You've probably heard a DM or KDM say, "It's nothing personal. It's just business." For you to accept that within your own mind, you have to see the discount request in simple monetary terms. Reducing cost and increasing efficiency, results in the same kudos that would have rewarded them for successfully securing a discount from you. This is true because discounting, revenue generation, and cost savings all affect the same bottom line. You can respond to discounting with their downstream costs [*see facing page*].

How often do you hear frequently given advice insist you "Sell value, not price!" What is the conclusion we arrived at within section 4? That when you sell value, not price, you're actually selling both and just merely leading with value. The quote at the top of chapter one also applies, "Product value without an emotional appeal is like an extension cord that wraps around in a loop and plugs into itself. The cord has value but doesn't have power."

Think about a KDM who is seeking a discount. What are they *actually* doing? They're trying to buy at a lower price, right?

SALES SECRET #50
Trying to Buy at a Discount, Is Still "Trying to Buy"

Try, at least once, to hold to your full price and see what happens. Often they buy anyway. "Trying to buy at a discount" is still "trying to buy." The confidence you'll gain from holding your ground (even if you lose that one experimental sale) **will boost your confidence and yield a return on that investment in your future.**

If they are trying to buy, that is a clear indicator that the Emotional Sale has probably closed. You may be thinking, "Yeah, well, what they're actually saying is, 'if you can sharpen your pencil a bit more we might be interested in buying' and that means the Emotional Sale is contingent upon my discount." That's what they're telling you they are thinking—but may not reflect what they are actually seeking. They could be looking for a way to rationalize the decision they want to make and they've assumed that a granted discount should be the validation. That discount is but one logical reason to buy. Just one. ***You can sell your price using their price*** (cost of not buying) by introducing other reasons that are just as compelling such as:

- **The price of the problem.**
- **The price of low quality from a low price competitor (should they opt for that).**
- **The past cost—which is the [ongoing] (cumulative) price paid thus far.**
- **The price of not having a solution when one becomes needed.**
- **The future price of compounding challenges that the product would have solved.**

- **The price paid when *their* competitors acquire the solution and gain an advantage.**
- **The price of lost efficiency.**
- **The price of inefficiency that your product would solve** (such as your product lowering utilities, or increasing safety).
- **The cost of not having you as the solution. You know what you provide, right? They *actually get less* when they pay less somewhere else because they lose your expertise.**
- **The price of the lost opportunity cost** (if they don't buy from you and have to invest more time contending with the problem which takes their focus off of more productive opportunities in their line of business).

That list is not comprehensive and could go on for pages but you get the gist. There's enough there to appeal to ***your*** mind to motivate you to appeal to theirs.

SALES SECRET #51:
Intrinsic Motivation

The best motivation is intrinsic which is based in the emotions of want and belief. You have to believe your full price is worth it. Then you have to want to sell that.

You should understand what you are actually seeing in the sales situation when the buyers are looking at the price on the table before them and trying to get that lowered. There's an inversion cost to lowering your price that can increase theirs somewhere else—especially if and/or when they end up not buying from you or not buying at all. You don't want to state that in a way that could sound manipulative (be careful), but you can point out the costs as beneficial savings they gain by buying from you.

KDMs use their personal power to make you feel like a discount is the only way to pull the sale over the line. Use your personal power to communicate, if even just via unspoken exuded confidence. Are you ever intimidated by some KDMs? Most everyone in sales has been. But why? There's nothing they possess, besides a title, that warrants more personal power than you have access to. If you think that title is the reason...you've met others with the same title that get metaphorically walked all over. It's not the title. It's personal power.

SALES SECRET #52:
Personal Power

You can exude the level of personal power required to ask for full price.

Would anyone actually buy a solution or result that will only provide 90% of the solution? Why would they buy a product that falls 10% short of delivering all that it promises to deliver? They wouldn't. So. That means they want to buy. They want the full solution. They want 100% of the performance—they have just figured they can get it for 90% of the cost. Are you communicating (maybe non-verbally) that a discount is at least a possibility?

SALES SECRET #53:
Corporate Poker

Discount requests are often a form of corporate poker when price is being negotiated. Try calling their bluff and see what happens. You might be surprised to learn they will often buy at full price instead of taking your competitor's lower price.

Once a discount has been requested or demanded, **you have a new set of rights.** You are now a key decision maker within a new sale they just introduced (their product becomes your-product-delivered-at-90%-of-the-price). For a time, until you make *your* decision as to whether or not you'll grant the discount (buy their product), what that situation evolved into is a "sale within a sale" and you're now a key decision maker.

So do you *trust* them? You already see where this is going, right? Do you *trust* they will be a long term account and provide a great working relationship? Do you *trust* them when they insist it's a one-time discount? Do you believe they won't be expecting another discount next time, at the reorder, next delivery, etc.? Do you *want* to give them a discount? Can you *logically rationalize* the discount to your sales manager? Can you explain the lower commission check to your spouse? Can you validate it to yourself? You can already hear your own voice as it trails off...***well it's better to have a discounted sale which closed than have no sale and besides the competition probably would have closed it any***

You might also be thinking, "*But—you don't understand, you're not there in the room. You don't feel what I'm feeling—the pressure. The intimidation. There are all those eyes looking back across big conference room tables, luxurious suits, lawyers in the room...important people with not a lot of time for games. They're brass-tackin'-me and I don't think they're messing around. I think they're serious when they say they want a discount and they'll go to my competitors if I don't give them one.*"

Okay, so they were scary at the table. The scary suits, big table, and brass tacks constitute *their* sales showroom where they sell to you (their product is your-product-delivered-at-90%-of-the-price). You're going to also have prospecting situations that have a similar level of intimidation. A lot can be said right here about confidence, quality of your consultative value, your own product and solution valuation, etc.

If you were offered an acting role in a low budget film (about sales) playing the part of a seller in a high tension sales close, you'd take the part (it pays well). Even if the simulation was intense, you could do it.

Our entire career exists because the companies we sell for need a professional—a specialist—that can go out there and play that part by earning the trust of decision makers. Except you aren't acting, you really care. The specialist (that's you) must help them want the result being offered, and rationalize the price difference between what the DMs want to pay, and what price the company you work for is requiring. When you take issue with your own price back at the office, you're saying to them, "You know that specialist you need that can help justify and explain full price? The difference in price between our competitors' and ours? Explain why we're better? Well, I'm not sure I can do that." Seeing it this way may also help you reframe your perception of your position within the company. In order to get yourself into the role of sales professional, you need to find the other actors (DMs and KDMs). That requires outbound **prospecting.**

SECTION 7

PROSPECTING

Prospecting Aversion Sales Syndrome

When you avoid making the decision to prospect (regardless of the reasons) the resulting sales inactivity is what I call, "Prospecting Aversion Sales Syndrome" (P.A.S.S.). At its core this is actually revenue aversion. When you succumb to this syndrome you will be intentionally averting new revenue.

Averted revenue is the same as lost cash. Everyone would retrace their steps backward to find a lost wallet...but not invest the prospecting effort required to avoid a lost future opportunity? Your strategy should be to connect within your mind any underperformance in prospecting to the resultant financial loss that may be happening.

There's no difference from the perspective of your bank account balance when you lose opportunities or lose Rock Hard Coin. Whether you go withdraw funds of $10K and lose it, or avert revenue over time that would have provided you with $10K in commissions, the net result is the same. One scenario you can prove. The other you cannot. That is why they remain unconnected. Just because you can rationalize the lost commissions, doesn't mean you should.

You wouldn't likely sit on a bus stop bench to take a break from in-person prospecting if the bench were some kind of coin operated privilege. What if it was $2 per minute to sit? Would you pay it? Would you thumb-in eight quarters every 60 seconds? Would you pay $120 per hour to sit on a prefab molded concrete bench? Taking a break is fine, but just make sure it's an earned break. When you develop an aversion to prospecting, it often becomes syndromic and will require you to seek out ways for reframing your perception.

"If you can perceive the need for a key, you can key a new perception."

—ImmersiveSelling.com

Chapter 22

Reframing Your Perception

While prospecting, top performers are seeking incremental commitments by influencing a series of mental decisions. The primary challenge in prospecting for new business is within the seller's mind and there's a similar process of incremental commitments.

> **"When you are prospecting, you are merely filing key blanks and trying to find the angles.**

What happens in your mind is the only long term variable that matters in sales prospecting. That's because while the sale resides in the minds of the DMs, the prospecting resides within yours. For this reason you need to reframe your perception.

Filing Key Blanks
Reframing Your Perception of Rejection

Imagine you were selected to participate in a game with a prize of Rock Hard Coin equivalent to three of your best months of sales commissions. The coin is kept in a room behind a well-built steel door. You have to gain physical access to the room without destroying or otherwise compromising the door. You must unlock the door without damaging it or using an existing key. You'll have to make your own key by filing down key blanks. You'll have access to the actual key that unlocks the door but it will be inside of a locked transparent polycarbonate case that is slightly bigger than the key. You'll have to copy the angles with small metal files just by looking at the correct key in the locked case.

You're assured there is nothing unusual about the lock and it's a knob similar to one you'd find on a steel commercial door like on a maintenance closet. Before the game begins you're shown that the existing key in fact unlocks the knob on the door. The door is then relocked, the key placed back into the locking transparent case and then handed over to you.

The rules for the offer are printed out in clear bullet points and as you look them over you see that you can't pick the lock, damage the door, compromise the knob or mechanism, or jimmy the thing in any way. You can't pry the door open or otherwise defeat the hinges or hinge bolts. You must open the door with a key to claim the three months' salary. That's the only acceptable way to win.

Your next questions are obvious, "Where do you get the key blanks and how many tries do you get?" You're then shown industrial-sized carts full of proper key blanks all identical to the correct key in the case, except they have no angles (which is why it's a blank). You're given a set of metal files and assured there are no restrictions on the number of tries. If you run out of key blanks, you can have another cart full. You can fill the room with piles of misfiled key blanks as you try to make a key with the correct angles and valleys that will slide into the lock, unlock, and then allow the knob to turn.

That's the game. There are no restrictions on either time or material, attempts, or key blanks. Your attention is directed to a series of cameras trained on various parts of the room around the door and your workspace, and a security screen visible to you that rolls through the images produced by the cameras. One of the images is of the opposite side of the door and the pile of Rock Hard Coin.

It's just you and that knob. Unlock the door within three months and you get your earnings replaced. Access the room in less time and you profit. If you can make the key in a few long days you can either take it easy for a few months or go back to selling and double your income (or some hybrid balance of vacation/double earnings).

Could you hand-file a working key by trial-and-error in under 520 hours with the solution key in a locked transparent case to look at? What would you do? Would you accept the offer and play the game or go back to selling never knowing? You may be thinking, "What if I don't get the key made and I invest longer than three months into this project? I'll go broke!"

But it's likely you'd get it filed far faster than you may think, using your hand-eye coordination and ingenuity. One thing isn't going to be happening though. No matter how challenging filing key blanks down into key shapes may become, and no matter how many you have to file, or how long it takes, you're never going to accuse the knob of rejecting you. You aren't going to experience any type of a fear of rejection. You may however experience anxiety, angst, frustration, anger, exhaustion, elation, hope, interest, intrigue, etc., but you won't fear rejection by that knob, the door, or the key blanks. That's because absolutely no one and nothing is rejecting you.

The gatekeeper is analogous with the door knob (this is not, in any way, objectifying human beings or suggesting gatekeepers are "doorknobs"—it's an analogous illustration to demonstrate gaining access to a door/gate through a trial-and-error process, not evaluating human life). The angles of the key blanks you've just filed and presented to the lock are analogous with the angles you present to a gatekeeper when calling, emailing, approaching in person, social selling, or networking. Each pin in the lock represents another step to getting the door opened for an in-person meeting, virtual meeting or video sales session with the KDM. You won't claim the knob has it out for you, because it doesn't; just as you won't claim the gatekeepers have it out for you personally. They have a motive to protect the time of the decision makers. So their rejection is real, but not personal.

When you are prospecting, you are merely filing key blanks and trying to find the angles. Nothing more. Nothing less. It's challenging but not impossible. It's involved, but not personal.

SALES SECRET #54:
Reframing Your Perception of Rejection

By reframing your perception, you change the reality of your sales efforts. This is NOT theory. It's actionable and concrete. You're in a career dominated by mental achievements and progress made within the mind. It only matters how hard you work if it translates to the minds involved.

In sales there are an unlimited number of doors, unlimited key blanks (prospective decision makers), and unlimited knobs. There is an unlimited potential pile of Rock Hard Coin available in the corporate world. Reframing my perception of prospecting is how I came to love seeking new business. Every call, text, email, screenshot, social query, search result and connection request is another angle on another key blank of many that I'm filing for many different knobs. Once you break free from prospecting aversion sales syndrome you will probably become excited about filing your own key angles on key blanks for knobs you've selected. The doors are just gates and the gatekeepers are just performing a locking function. The angles to file are your approaches to appealing to the gatekeepers.

Cold calling is highly engaging once you get into it because within each clue, piece, minor success, mini-movement of an account is another angle filed on that key blank and it's incredibly rewarding because when an angle works, it's a victory and an accomplishment.

SALES SECRET #55:
Mind Sight

Questions are your sight. Where's the sale? In their mind. What do questions provide? Insight. Asking questions and listening provides key blank angles. Yes, you can prospect with questions.

When prospecting, work a limited number of accounts (door knobs and key blanks) at a time. You'll get less accomplished working a thousand door knobs. Work from prospecting lists [*see also chapter 23*].

SALES SECRET #56:
Corporate Organization Charts

It's important to research a corporation's organizational structure/ chart so you know who the actual DMs are.

In many industries you'll probably want to avoid calling prospects every day. No one likes being harassed. But consistent, weekly attempts will eventually pay off. If you're getting through to voice mail? Use it and leave an effective message. Never become exasperated or make the decision maker feel as though they owe you a call back. Be helpful, cheerful, (but not over-the-top) and professional.

By adopting a different mindset and view point, you can achieve far better results. I've been asked many times why I think cold calling on the phone, social, and prospecting for new business is fun. This chapter is why. Once you get into it, prospecting is fun (really).

Prospecting, once reframed within your mind (filing key blanks) will likely prove to become one of the more fun activities in sales. In heist films, do you enjoy the run-up to the action? The planning? The technical stuff? The pieces that have to be put into place for a successful outcome (albeit an illegal one but we're not discussing ethics, just the process)? It's fun stuff because it involves risk and requires skill and experience. It's exactly the same part of the brain that is engaged when you really dig into prospecting except our endeavor is truthful, and you're being honest with yourself.

SALES SECRET #57:
Time Budget and Scheduling

You will need to reserve time in your schedule for a self-disciplined assurance that you prospect. Don't mess around with this. Treat it like the prime time it is. If you need time for something else, find it elsewhere.

Set your office up like a "central command." If cold calling and prospecting have historically been your least favorite activity, you may find that some prequalifying of prospects can help avoid some of the rejection. Just ensure that you don't invest more time pre-qualifying than it would take to just make some calls (and find out directly). Spending your time to save your time is still lost time you tried to save. A great way to find a balance that works is with **prospecting lists.**

Those who are mediocre in other areas of sales can stay in the game if they are stellar at sales prospecting. You cannot sustain a lack of leads. Most attribute poor sales performance to a lack of closing and while that is often true, more often it is a lack of prospecting that is the undoing of sales careers.

"Making and using lists, are probably base components of almost every worthwhile human accomplishment. You cannot even efficiently shop for groceries without one. Sales prospecting is more involved than a loaf of bread, a quart of milk, and a stick of butter."—ImmersiveSelling.com

Chapter 23

Prospecting Lists

You should make lists of prospects and then work those lists. They will depend on your product, industry, market, economy (very important in a recession/depression), goals, clarity of purpose, standards-of-qualification-mean, and outreach methodology. Your length of sales cycle for various products may be a factor as well. You will usually have several prospecting lists you can populate from your efforts in LinkedIn Navigator, Sales Force, listing services, purchased lists, trade journals, databases, web searches, etc.

> **"Using lists for prospecting can make cold calling more enjoyable.**

You should organize your lists into various categorical approaches and create a database, or utilize a CRM. Each prospecting list you develop should be sub-categorized by industry type, size of company, geographical location (if that is a factor), or any other information that will stratify your prospecting efforts. This is important because working within a specific industry can provide momentum and help you learn that industry's jargon. It will also help if you have existing clients in that industry as you can use your successes in that industry to contribute to the Trust Sale by citing testimonials when earning trust.

SALES SECRET #58:
Work Your Lists by Industry

Working your lists by industry will also allow you to use focused sales messaging for live calls and messages you leave on DMs' voicemails [*see Strati-Tacticals #9, #10*].

Using lists for prospecting can make cold calling a success. What follows are some ideas for the various lists:

---

1. Idyllic Accounts Prospecting List: These are the dream accounts that you will work on periodically. When one of these sales close, it is a career-changing event. You might keep the number of prospects on this list to around 10 or 20 and only drop one off of this list after you've explored every profitable way in. You may have a "back burner" subsection of this account list for those prospects in a holding pattern (such as when you must wait for a contract to expire).

2. The Short List: These are the corporations that would be premium high quality accounts. The number of companies you include on the list is going to range depending on your industry. A limit of around 50 to 150 prospective companies are a good start. You can move that total up or down depending on how it affects/rewards your prospecting time investment. Working a smaller list and doing a bit more research and custom messaging may yield more initial commitments.

3. The Practical List: This is where the majority of your qualified prospects will reside. Working with just a couple hundred or less will help keep you focused on qualified prospects while keeping the remaining companies in a bulk holding database. You can draw from the data set as you need more prospects to populate lists. Use subsets and subcategories for organizational efficiency. You might approach this list in a rotational manner. Elect a number of prospects you can realistically work and move them to the top of the list.

4. The Eclectic List: A varied-sourced list that has outlier components or reasons not to be included in one of the other lists. Lists can provide more clarity, and illuminate a deeper strategy with a tactical approach that will reduce **practice aversion.**

"When a seller fails to commit to practice, that preparation deficit will cause an inversely proportionate inflation of fear, self doubt, and apprehension within the mind of the sales professional. Practice and prepare so you will be confident."—ImmersiveSelling.com

CHAPTER 24

Practice Aversion

Even those sellers with extensive phone experience can feel apprehension toward the phone while prospecting. The less experience a sales professional has, the more intense the apprehension.

> "To become proficient you must practice.

Most everyone thinking about this (and most already have) come to the conclusion that experience encourages confidence and a lack of it creates apprehension. So what is experience? That sounds obvious and it will seem like the answer should be "something a sales professional has done or accomplished before—so repeating the situation is less of a stressor." That is all true, but maybe just a bit incomplete.

Experience is also practice. That's what it is. Unfortunately, the practice time invested by many sales professionals is limited to their real-time experience within sales situations. You may be asking, "So what's wrong with that?" Nothing, it's just not enough. What if professional baseball teams skipped spring training and practiced during their regular season series games? What if football teams only improved during in-game competition? Race car drivers don't wait for race day to hone skills but what if they did? You can imagine how surgery would go if doctors only practiced during actual procedures. Do you think they should limit their practice time to the operating table? Sales is one of the very few high caliber, highly skilled professions that limits practice to real time performance.

Why don't sellers practice? Do you?

Sculptors don't make their first attempts on pristine Carrara marble imported from the same quarry that masters have been harvesting stone from for centuries. Painters don't render an oil painting without some sketches. Pilots practice flying. Secret service agents practice technique and shooting skills. Law enforcement practice defense and breaching buildings. It may feel like, "Yeah but those professions have lives on the line." Your whole life depends on commissioned sales success. You don't get paid unless you close sales.

SALES SECRET #59:
Practice Isn't a Chore, It's a Tool

Practice provides you with relief from future anxiety, angst, fear and apprehension. All of these are emotions which impede your sales advancement. Just as DMs and KDMs buy emotionally, you also sell emotionally. When you're not at your top performance, those making decisions can sense that. Practice provides confidence.

Anyone on 100% commission, with no savings and has had to sell-or-starve, has the necessary experience to form a full and thorough opinion on sales practice. You should modify your opinion, ignore others who don't practice and understand it takes practice to become proficient at anything, especially selling.

Sales is a rewarding career and probably the most fun once you become proficient. ***To become proficient you must practice.*** Sales professionals will often log into LinkedIn, do a search to qualify ideal prospective DMs and KDMs and then proceed to send off mass mail type verbiage after plugging the prospect into their automation queue. Some of these automated touchpoints and mass-mailing form letters and templating may as well be called "lead burners." LinkedIn can provide stellar leads (so avoid burning them). To whatever degree you've worried about being replaced by AI, technology, big data, and robots, there may be an inversely proportional subconscious admission within your mind that you haven't practiced enough. If you're worried about being replaced, you see the automation and you've received a glimpse of what could be. Guess what AI sales replacement systems are doing right now? Practicing. Learning. Researching. It's even called "machine learning."

Getting sales professionals to practice extensively before interacting with actual gatekeepers, decision makers, and key decision makers and to work out strategy-and-tactics is a challenge. Many sellers are like that obstinate relative who just won't go seek medical treatment until it's an emergency. Don't be that person.

Invent and Perform

Most sellers practice in real time and use their sales situations as their primary (often the only) **method of practicing. The way that looks is similar to grabbing a musical instrument from the orchestra pit on your way up on stage in a performance arena of some kind..and trying to play whatever instrument it is you could get your hands on, for the first time.**

Sales is more complex than that. It's closer to walking past the orchestra pit and checking out what the instruments look like (checking out what other sellers do) **and walking up on stage** (arriving at sales situations) **to a box of bent wood, strings, tightening knob things and maybe a bow** (assembling components of a sale from a box of possibilities, words, phrases, questions and frequently given advice) **and trying to invent a stringed instrument while everyone watches** (create persuasive appeals). **And then—play it—well enough** (sell) **to receive some "applause" at the end** (gain the next commitment).

Articles often insist that leaving a voicemail is akin to putting a message in a bottle and tossing it into the Pacific Ocean. These are myths and usually precede selling you a social selling system or are manifested from an unknowledgeable status in the sales industry. The myths of traditional mediums "being dead" divert attention from the underlying issues such as the message being ineffective. Blaming the medium instead of the content is as old as advertising. That well worn path has lead many companies and corporations to underachieve their potential.

When you apply the very same mythical labeling to situations using absurdity, it helps to more clearly see the myths being fed to you by misfocused advice. Here are a few absurd logical assertions (If A, then B) that expose some of the fallacious reasoning driving myths:

- 100% of all loan applications written in blue ink are rejected from XYZ bank. **Blue pens don't work! Handwriting is dead!** *Could it be the applicants' income, credit ratings or savings? Maybe the bank's lending guidelines? Maybe the bank does commercial lending only?*
- 100% of all patrons leaving a big box store on Monday morning do not have a single oversized, giant, soft, stuffed animal in their shopping carts. **The stuffed animals are hard as a rock! Unhuggable!** *Could it be that people aren't buying stuffed animals* ***that*** *morning?*
- Every US ambassador calling their counterpart in Fakeistan for the past 9 administrations have failed to secure peace talks. **The phone is dead...and has been for 36 years!**
  Could it be what was or wasn't said into the phone?
- Every email sent to millionaires asking for donations to support the expansion of Crayon Coloring Awareness Week hasn't received a single reply. Not one. **Email is dead!**
  Could it be the request? Problems with messaging?

Many in sales are defensive about underutilizing practice and will point to widely-accepted myths as a way to dissemble, e.g., Why put effort into old school technology? Is practice really going to help?

Those are myths too. The answer? Get really proficient at what you do. Approach sales the same way you would approach something that requires a license, training, and proficiency. Bring your stepped-up game.

SALES SECRET #60:
Prospecting and Closing

Prospecting is the single most important skill, and activity in sales. Closing is the most important result.

Do you think DMs and KDMs can tell when you're winging it? Can they detect when you haven't practiced? When you're trying to ad lib? Practice improves confidence. A powerful tool and approach to prospecting is LinkedIn. This should be a central component of your **social selling**.

Tactical Advantages
for Remote Selling Within Video & Virtual Sales Situations

1. **Do the Obvious:** Use the proper camera angle, tilt, background, lighting, personal appearance/attire, etc. Eliminate background noise and use a background app if you don't have a suitable space.
2. **Question Prompts:** Go through the ideation steps in the Strati-Tacticals in section 8 (for analogies and an Emotive Gatekey). Use the ideation discovery process to develop your clarity of purpose and what you want to know before you go live. Have a list of primary and secondary questions ready to go (you can post them off-camera).
3. **List of Subject and Story Prompts: Use the tactical way-point thinking** [*see chapter 4*] **to plan way-points for your session so you have a clarity of purpose. Base your way-points on experience, guessing, agenda, ideation, known challenges, tech, and what you think the DMs and KDM may want. Use discovery questions to find out more from them.**
4. **Industry Expertise:** Have industry technology, articles, information and research at the ready (.pdf for email) in case you need proof or reference material.
5. **Research:** Ensure you do research on who you're meeting with prior to getting online with them. It can help to be well-read.
6. **Practice Commensurate with the Cam Tech:** You need to keep up with the technology so you should become proficient in virtual selling. A 360° video experience is here now and it's a powerful tool as well.
7. **Self-Record:** Using video or audio equipment, record practice sessions that you conduct either alone or with a colleague and then play them back. What you think you sound like on the phone or video and what you actually sound like are going to be different. Often you can't hear your stumbles and faux pas while focused on performing.
8. **Clarity of Purpose and Goal:** [*see chapter 15*].

Three LinkedIn Account Settings to Decide On.

- **Stealth Mode:** People know when you've looked at their profile. This is the default visibility setting within your profile viewing options, but you can change it to anonymous mode. This comes with a disadvantage. You can no longer see who's viewed *your* profile as long as your visits are hidden from them. Seeing who your visitors are is valuable while prospecting. In "profile viewing options" you can change your visibility.
- **Disable Notifications:** In your account settings within the "privacy controls," turn off your activity broadcast so that not every change you make to your profile is announced to your entire network.
- **Paid Membership Levels:** Upgrade your account for some seriously powerful prospecting and search tools.

Your LinkedIn Profile as a Showroom

There's no way around using LinkedIn if you're in sales. If you skip it entirely you look like you're out of touch. If you do a poor job on your LinkedIn profile, it's assumed you'll give even less attention to a potential clients' needs and challenges requiring your solution. The only option is the best profile you can build and it would be an advantage to have it function like a personal sales showroom.

To accomplish this, do an informal "audit" on your own profile and compare it to those in your industry. Use key performance indicators (KPIs) in LinkedIn to see how you measure up. Using that tool will show you areas of improvement needed. Usually content, new posts/videos, and improved messaging will equate to an increase in engagement and provide sales support if you are remote selling.

"If you don't have a message, social selling and technology will only amplify that deficiency, not conceal it."—ImmersiveSelling.com

Chapter 25

Social Selling

In the 1990s sellers were tripping all over each other on the phones because they all started at "A" in the phone book. This was easily solved by simply starting in the middle or back of the phone book to make cold calls. Today, sellers are tripping all over each other contacting the same prospects as their competitors are because they are using the same 1st tier keyword searches within LinkedIn (today's "A" section of the phone book).

> **Personalization will yield better results.**

The same search results among competitors means the same decision makers are being approached.

SALES SECRET #61:
Arriving Late in the Buying Cycle

When you hear sellers say, "There was another seller already positioned in the buying cycle and we came late to the sale," that's probably due to the lead generation method (competing for first tier keyword search results) **more than the sales approach.**

Have you ever wondered why you hear, often, about sellers coming into a buying situation where another seller has advanced the sale and the most common question is, "How do I compete with sellers already established in the buying process when I come late to the sale?" Sometimes the answer is to use different keywords [*see Strati-Tactical #7*].

You may also be wondering why the phones have such a high rate of rejection within many industries. Often it's the "1990 phone book dilemma" at play in LinkedIn with first tier keywords. Back in '90, "Andy's Whatever Automotive" got called all day long by sellers and Andy became annoyed and irritable. He was trying to conduct his own business. That's hard to do when you're listed in the "A's."

Strati-Tactical #7 walks you through the keyword tiers and has actionable examples that explain how the tiers and Boolean searches work in LinkedIn.

Back in the '80s and '90s whenever I would call any business anywhere in "A" through about "F," I just heard, "I'm not interested," and the *click* of a hang up was heard repeatedly. They wouldn't even listen to four words past the point they'd figured out I was in sales. The same was true of walking into businesses on the busy main streets. The most visible and obvious are also going to be the most pitch-fatigued and least receptive to sellers. Turn the book to about "L" through "Z" and the business owners would listen, ask a few questions, and many more would agree to meet. They were far more receptive.

SALES SECRET #62:
Mastering Key Word Searches Is Imperative

In the next decade you'll benefit from utilizing creative thinking to discover second and third tier qualified leads others haven't thought of searching for. LinkedIn is a perfect tool for accomplishing this. The keyword contest is one you can and should win. Boolean advanced search is the secret to winning that.

Today in LinkedIn a similar mindset dominates. You feel like you "should cover all the bases" or "ensure you don't skip over the low hanging fruit." Using 1st tier obvious keywords is picking at the same cherries as everyone else and with that many hands clicking, dialing, messaging and requesting, you've set yourself up for competition and a much higher rate of rejection.

SALES SECRET #63:
Start Small. Then Scale.

Start small, if even for a few shifts, then scale. Get your location, geographical, verticals or horizontals (if your products cover a wide range of customers) **all set in Navigator and then start with search and advanced search to familiarize yourself with what query results look like.**

Navigator:

If you're trying to find stellar leads that are receptive, less pitch-fatigued and more apt to jump on a video call, LinkedIn Navigator is an excellent way to accomplish that.

SALES SECRET #64:
Join LinkedIn Groups

Joining the same LinkedIn groups as decision makers can put you in the same orbit. This provides common ground and an excellent way to initiate a conversation. You can often message them directly if you're both in the same group and they have an open profile.

Advanced search will probably provide results and lead you to people interested in new ideas (because they haven't been as inundated with sales calls). Using Navigator is going to give you an edge especially if you are remote selling. Even amid other sellers using the same tool in the same industry. The advantage is in how you think (of keywords).

SALES SECRET #65:
Human Keyword Ideation

Humans are thinking of terms to describe themselves on LinkedIn and other humans (you and I) **are thinking of what to search for. If they thought of the words, so can we.**

By using advanced search effectively, you can dial down into specific group searches in your subject (like lean manufacturing), and specific positions in companies.

SALES SECRET #66:
Ditch the Pitch with Your New LinkedIn Connections

It's annoying to almost all people who agree to connect with you on LinkedIn to then receive a "pitch message" from you right away. Engage but don't be spammy. At least wait until you've communicated a bit before "trying to sell them."

Regional or territorial constriction for specificity, is also possible. The more specific searches can benefit greatly from Boolean search in Navigator [*see also Strati-Tactical #7*].

SALES SECRET #67:
Inmail (LinkedIn)

Inmail is almost always received and read because you are limited in the number of inmails allowed in each month's billing cycle on LinkedIn. Decision makers know this and so they know you aren't sending one unless you have something to say (so don't waste the opportunity).

Your Network:
LinkedIn limits the number of 1st tier connections you can have to 30,000 and your monthly connection requests limit have been lowered (to perhaps as low as 400, down from 3,000).

The connection requests that you send can be responded to with three actions:
1. **"Accept"** it, which makes that person one of your first tier connections.
2. **"Ignore"** the request at which point your request simply moves to their archived mail (they can retrieve it later) with no penalty to you.
3. **"IDK"** or "I Don't Know [this person]" and if you get just a few (maybe like five) of these gems LinkedIn responds (research this online).

Beware of the IDK:
"I Don't Know" [this person] **is called an IDK. You are allowed a very low number of IDKs when sending connection requests so be careful with invitations so they don't "IDK you." Avoid agressive connection efforts and don't be spammy.**

The strength of your social selling is going to largely revolve around your networking efforts and skills in advanced search. Actively networking is sending requests and inmails wherein you reach out to connect. LinkedIn success will involve producing content in long form posts and commenting on others' posts and articles.

SALES SECRET #68:
Follow Notifications

When you follow someone on LinkedIn (such as a DM you'd like to meet with) **a notification is sent to them that you are following them. That sometimes puts you on their peripheral radar. You'll also keep up on their content and activity.**

Your network is a cached resource that you can search and query often to find professionals that make decisions. The larger your personal database, the more effective your searches will be. Often someone you are connected with may know a KDM you are trying to connect with and can provide you with a warm introduction on LinkedIn. You'll want to avoid hard selling your 1st tier connections, but reaching out when you have a specific reason or request is what LinkedIn is for. The whole point of advanced search is to find profiles. The whole point of networking is to connect with them so you can contact them.

Commenting:
You'll definitely get noticed if you can comment intelligently and with relevant knowledge on others' posts. Actually read the content you are commenting on and don't ever fake it with a general comment. Those are benign anyway and won't impress the decision makers you are attempting to attract, who will all see your public comments.

Commenting on content posted by DMs you'd like to approach

at some point is an indirect but effective way to generate interest and gain visibility. It's using a circular approach to prospecting instead of a direct approach, but it can be very effective. Comment intelligently with knowledge, and you can actually get on the decision makers' radar. Many decision makers are pitched-out and tired of the barrage of endless automated outreach.

Personalization:

Sellers often buy into the misfocused advice that automation can simulate personalization but inserting a DM's name at the front of a message and using a clever script—no matter how ingenious, still reeks of automation. The DMs are highly intelligent. They can tell when you're doing the work of personalization and when a machine is doing the work. Your comments on their content, when intelligent, show you are insightful, have actually read what they produced, and are genuinely interested. You aren't pitching to them, you're bringing something to a conversation. One they are more inclined to have with you after you've invested some effort.

If you can learn something new about the subject of a decision maker's post that isn't mentioned, you can work that into your comments so make sure you either know what you're talking about or research it before commenting. You're sharing through a back channel and impressing the decision maker. Is that labor intensive? Absolutely. It also counters the advice to automate everything. However, ***personalization will yield better results***. This is hyper personalization and it will probably get you noticed, gain respect and earn trust. That's the whole point. It can be an effective way to gain new leads, because that decision maker will be more receptive when you begin a conversation or send a connection request. The downside to all of this, is it will require patience as it takes time to see an ROI. While remote selling you will need to have self discipline and commit time to this every day.

LinkedIn is not Twitter. When you are followed by someone in LinkedIn, you may not want to reciprocate each time. When you follow someone, their activity gets pushed to your feed.

The number of followers you have is unlimited. In Twitter, "following" IS the method of connecting whereas in LinkedIn it's more of a notification service for new content and activity.

Groups:
There are thousands of groups to choose from and joining those within your industry will pay dividends on your time investment. By joining the same group (as a prospect you'd like to connect with) you can send a message to other members even if you're not 1st tier connections, provided they have an open profile.

Your Showroom Content:
The LinkedIn profile you build isn't ***just*** a minimum requirement or a task like entering data into the CRM or leveraging your sales stack/tech stack.

SALES SECRET #69:
Showroom Features

You should focus your LinkedIn message on offering something of value. Show how you solve problems and show how you provide results. Use a story, case study, example or even a hypothetical scenario.

The LinkedIn profile is built by you and more importantly, everyone knows it. If you're going to lead thought, offer consultative advisement within sales situations and build relationships, the content you publish on LinkedIn matters. It should be as effective as a print ad.

SALES SECRET #70:
KPIs and SSI

Your Key Performance Indicators will help you track your influence and success. Your SSI is your Social Selling Index and measures success according to four metrics: brand, people, insights, and relationships.

If your current LinkedIn showroom features only your resume with your past employment history, you need more. Content is incredibly important and you need to have engaging thought leadership or infuse your profile with curated content.

SALES SECRET #71:
Showcase Pages & Video

LinkedIn has "Showcase Pages" and a video platform wherein you can feature your content and the result you are providing in your sales. The pages are affiliate pages to your profile/company's page.

Long Form Posts:
LinkedIn offers you the unique opportunity to write blog posts right in your profile. You can also recreate your blog posts from work you've done outside of the platform, such as on your blog.

SALES SECRET #72:
Membership Cancellation [LinkedIn]

Should you ever cancel your paid membership portion of LinkedIn membership, you may lose your saved data, searches, lists, etc., in some of the paid services areas of your membership.

Once your content starts gaining some traction the stunning power of this publication platform allows you to write an article about anything you want—so here's your chance to get known in your industry as a source of thought, information and answers.

The phrase "social selling" sounds snappy (which explains the name) **but if the name were to more closely describe what it is that social actually does in sales, it would probably be called, "social prospecting."**

Try and create something new and post it on LinkedIn frequently. Making this commitment will serve you well when you integrate video and begin **social selling with video.**

"Cast yourself as a guide within your sales video so the decision makers will see themselves vicariously as the main characters. Lead them to imagine the result you're offering."—ImmersiveSelling.com

Chapter 26

Social Selling with Video

Using video with social selling adds an entire dimension to others' perceptions of you. If you're looking for an edge over your competition, use video in your social selling. When you introduce video tooling to your social media presence, the right video can become what are commonly referred to as "evergreen social media posts." These are a perfect utilization for social selling because evergreen content has staying power, and remains prominent and effective over time. The content says on top, has broad application, and ages well. Keep this in mind when producing video vignettes.

> **"Your video may be the first real impression you make.**

Uploading a video of yourself, your product, the result you offer, or industry knowledge within your area of expertise and then promoting it within one of many social media platforms will add dimension to their perception of you. Video brings you, your image, voice, intonation, personality and thinking directly into the mind of those who engage your social accounts. You can convert your LinkedIn profile into a showroom experience that features your result or your thought leadership. You can also upload your prerecorded videos to other social accounts and gain multiple returns on the investment you made in production.

These can even feature your sales stories, analogies, Emotive Gatekeys, appeals for your component sales, etc. All can support your video efforts with content. Brevity is key and it's within this approach that you can refine and hone your verbiage in writing first so that you aren't speaking from the top of your mind in real time (unless that's a strength of yours).

SALES SECRET #73:
Speaking Prompts

Memorize some speaking prompts such as the first sentence in each subject or component you'll introduce and talk about in your video uploaded to social sites. This way you won't have to sound like you're reading from a script.

If you're using stories, an Emotive Gatekey, analogies, or introductory bio-type information for your video, most of that should be fairly easy to recall with some practice. A major deterrent to using video is a fear of performance, technical skill requirements, and editing. Performance anxiety is mitigated with practice and there's no one forcing you to upload a video to LinkedIn or promote it on any number of video streaming sites, until you're ready. There are simple video editing software services and online apps that remove most of the technical skill requirements.

You can utilize many different types of sales videos. Introductory videos are effective for putting your face to a name or communicating with new social contacts that arrive on one of your platforms. Sales videos are also an excellent way to convert your LinkedIn presence from just a profile to more of a showroom motif. You could also include a sales video in your LinkedIn feed to guide understanding of a complex subject in your industry. This can lend enhanced credibility to your message and place you in a thought leadership role. You can also send video links in email and social, and in many places actually embed content right in the pages or features.

When developing a sales video, your content and message matter more than production tech—though don't go short on that effort. The lighting, setting, delivery and your appearance are going to matter as much as the messaging. ***Your video may be the first real impression you make*** so attend to the variables that will affect the result. You'll need to determine the type and application of your video so that your clarity of purpose is focused for the intended application.

During video production and message development you can utilize some of the information you will be synthesizing in Strati-Tacticals #4, #5, and #6. This will assist you as you produce the components of a successful sales video. The considerations may include some of the following.

1. **Who are you speaking to? Receiver/viewer.**
2. **What challenge are you going to identify for them? Will it pique their curiosity and resonate with the viewer?**
3. **To keep it simple will you just focus on the one challenge** (but elude to others)?
4. **What format will you use** (e.g., aspect ratio of 16x9, or square 1x1 for social)?
5. **Utilize similar types of persuasive appeals required for the component sales that you will, or have developed, for such tooling as your sales story, 15 Second Segue, etc.**
6. **Utilize social support by referencing your social accounts or information, articles or long form blogging you've done that support what you are referencing in your video.**
7. **Underscore the benefits, results, or your solution that they can expect for agreeing to make the next commitment you are asking for on the phone or in voicemail.**
8. **Keep your video as short as possible. A short introductory video may be just about as long as a voicemail message or up to a minute or two if your product or industry is complex. A full story approach on video where the product's result is an exposition-by-video may be several minutes long. To keep your length manageable, you should write out the verbiage and familiarize yourself with it [*see also "word count to time conversion" at the very end of Strati-Tactical #10*]. Memorization is also recommended so it feels natural and extemporaneously delivered.**
9. **Be prepared. Ensure you put in the effort to make the environment as pleasing as possible.**

10. **Use proper lighting** (it's very affordable now). **When possible, buy lighting support that is balanced: for example a light capable of 6500K color temperature. This closely mimics what you might see on an overcast day outdoors. Try different lighting placement locations relative to you and pick the most enhancing option. If you want to get deeper into lighting theory** (helpful) **you can research the concepts of key lighting, back lighting, and fill lighting.**
11. **Don't publish until several trusted colleagues or true friends** (willing to critique you honestly) **have viewed what you've produced. You'll be surprised what they see that you may have missed. Take notes and revise.**
12. **Watch many videos in a similar application you propose to produce so that you may see what others have done. Don't copy them but do meet and exceed their production bar** (now if possible, or down the road when you can).

What you want to remain focused on throughout video production is your core message, which should be about the viewer. You should know who it is you intend to talk to.

SALES SECRET #74:
Add Captioning to Your Videos

Many videos will be viewed in professional situations or social settings and public places. Headphones won't always be an option for sound and the viewer may have to mute their audio. You can caption your videos and increase the likelihood of repeat engagement.

All too often we approach social selling from a number's perspective and view potential decision makers as metrics. This tendency becomes exacerbated once a prospect's information has been entered into a CRM (customer relationship management software). This can obscure your observation of potential opportunities preventing you from finding **the pearls in the pipe.**

"Movie stars are larger-than-life while acting on big screens. Sales professionals are smaller-than-life while selling on little screens. If you don't prepare and become a consultative resource, you may be viewed as just another app on their small screen."—ImmersiveSelling.com

Chapter 27

The Pearls in the Pipe

The customer relationship management (CRM) systems are amazing assets and tools. The leads and opportunities that represent the prospective decision makers are inserted into your CRM system and become useful data. An unintended result that can develop over time is a tendency to form an attitude toward the data. The data is tracked, reorganized, uploaded to the cloud, downloaded for meetings, and will be used to populate reports for sellers' accountability. The data takes on a numerical life-of-importance within the pipeline.

> **"There are few tools with more advantages in the day-to-day career management of sales than a CRM.**

In many organizations, sales runs on data. CRMs thrive on it, technology moves it around, your tech stack and/or sales stack allows you to access it. The CRM is an essential and powerful tool you would be foolish to underutilize. What you can do with the technology is empowering and there's a tendency to grow to respect the technology. It's also important to avoid feeling impersonal toward the data because over time it can become all about the data in the pipeline. In some organizations it's all about that pipe.

Decision makers can develop an attitude that encourages commoditization of us and our products. We know how that feels. If we aren't mindful, we too can slip into a similar rut by seeing decision makers as data, opportunities, and deals moving along in the pipe.

SALES SECRET #75:
What's on Their Desk?

The missed opportunities we don't see when we're hyper-focused on the data are real people that have real decisions to make and real work surfaces in front of them with real stressors. What's on their desk? What do they care about?

Management watches the pipe. The CEO is directing the sales manager to fill that pipe and the manager is in turn pushing you to, you know, fill the pipe. Fill the pipe now. It can become all about that pipe.

There are few tools with more advantages in the day-to-day career management of sales than a CRM. The advantages are obvious and its utilization is a near-requirement to keep up. What isn't obvious is "how" it's used. Just as you should sell the result instead of your product, with the CRM you should buy into the result instead of the features and options.

SALES SECRET #76:
Trust Can Help Prevent Commoditization

It's more difficult for decision makers to commoditize someone or something they trust.

Use and deploy only those modules and components that facilitate results within your career. Are the touchpoints in your cadence and sequence automated where they could be actually personalized and more effective? The DMs are intelligent and intuitive. This allows them to see a seller's motive and intent.

SALES SECRET #77:
Personalized Touch Point Sequence

You can (and should) **personalize parts of your touchpoint sequence with specific details. By incorporating information from their LinkedIn profiles and company websites, you can manually-compose personalized outreach.**

They can literally feel the difference between a sales professional truly striving to find and solve a problem for them and a sales rep trying to move them down a pipe.

The Pearls in the Pipe

Would you ever store a high value pearl in a foot long piece of galvanized water pipe? You could pop that pearl into a pipe and cap off both ends for safe keeping and carry the thing around with you. It would never get crushed and would be secure but the pearl would become deeply scratched. It would lose its translucency. The pipe protects it from the external world threats like being crushed, but the interior surface treatment ruins it.

How we treat data in the pipe is a reflection on our attitude toward our sales. Those data sets are worth far more than pearls and they're about as hard to find. If a pearl were to be put into a pipe, you would line the interior of the pipe and wrap the pearl in velvet. You'd personalize the care, storage and handling of the pearl, just like we should personalize our touch points and customize our approach in prospecting. Our attitude about the pipe should assume that within that galvanized CRM are pearls.

You will need to facilitate engagement from the accounts you are working. What can accelerate this is utilizing the next section's **Strati-Tacticals.**

T-shaped professionals
are those who have a wide general understanding
across an industry (represented graphically by the top of a capital "T").
They also have an area of deeper focused expertise, education, or certification in a subject area within the industry
(represented by the base of the "T" plunging down
deep beneath the top surface
line of a capital T).

You should strive
to become T-shaped (or even "M" shaped)
in your industry.

SECTION 8

STRATI-TACTICALS

Strategy • Tactics • Tools • How-to's • Concreteness

STRATEGY (for Strati-Tactical #1): **Go In with a Plan**

There will probably be four strategic outcomes for you from Strati-Tacticals #1 and #2:

1. **You will be better able to develop an interrogative strategy for yourself by figuring out what you need to know from the future companies you approach by observing the sales situations you're currently in** (viewed from the illustrations' viewpoints).
2. **You'll likely be able to visualize the 2D diagram and 3D model** [*see Strati-Tactical #2*] **in your mind while selling, and transpose them over the events you see unfolding.**
3. **You can use this diagram prior to your sales situations to help you plan your clarity of purpose.**
4. **You can use this diagram as a post-mortem analysis on those sales that end up in the weeds** (so you can improve).

TACTICS (for Strati-Tactical #1): **Search Zones Approach**

The "zones" in diagram Fig 1.1 (in Strati-Tactical #1) **won't necessarily be followed in numerical order. This is similar to deep sea exploration for sunken ships. Their search grid consists of columns and rows laid out on the ocean floor and they follow a process. If, however, the explorers see a barnacle-laden 1600's era cannon shape protruding from the sand outside of their current zone, they will move outside of their planned search. They will then establish and work on a new zone around the opportunity while still simultaneously progressing on the former zone. Their search area zones may increase to a third and even a fourth. Their numbered progressive search plan by zone can be modified by the situation similar to new opportunities that arise in your sales situations. You can work multiple zones in Fig 1.1 and not necessarily in numerical order.**

STRATI-TACTICAL

ONE

The Quad Close in Two Dimensions

Fig 1.1 shows an overhead view of a 2D diagram of the Quad Close. Within your sales there may be more or less emphasis on each component. The size of each zone is not indicative of a heirarchial importance.

Fig 1.1:
2D Diagram of the Quad Close

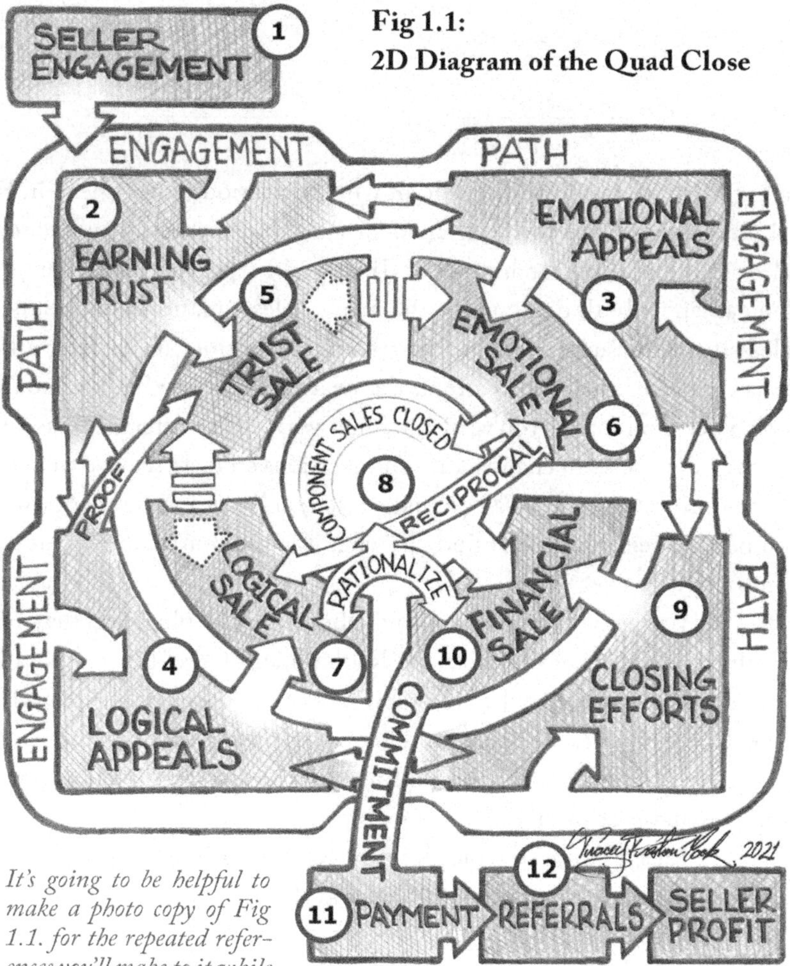

It's going to be helpful to make a photo copy of Fig 1.1. for the repeated references you'll make to it while in this Strati-Tactical. You have my permission to make copies for yourself.

Fig 1.2: Graphical Legend (references and explains Fig 1.1)

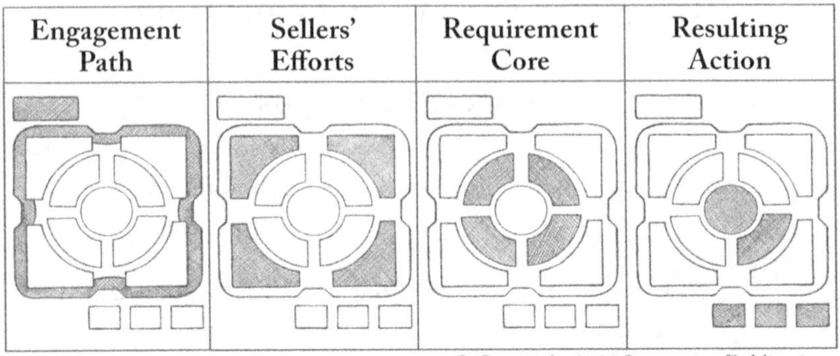

In Fig 1.2 you are shown a legend of what the various zones mean in Fig 1.1. The first panel is the "Engagement Path" (or how you would enter a sales situation or overarching sale). This would represent your approach. You can apply both diagrams to the macro sales situations, or the micro sales situations such as "asking for the next meeting" or "getting a key decision maker to agree to attend the next meeting you have scheduled with a decision maker you've already met with." Also referred to as your "clarity of purpose" in chapter 15. Your questions strategy may be launched at the onset of your first sales situation so you'll need to figure out what you need to seek out or just find out what it is you don't know about that company.

As you gain information you'll be mentally plugging that into the third panel above which is the "Requirement Core" (we temporarily skipped the second panel). This represents those supporting materials, appeals, documents, discussions, demonstrations, emotions, trust, logic, information, etc., that a buyer will need to receive from you and your company in order to make a decision.

A "pack of gum" buying decision requires a brand name, craving for gum, logical reason to buy it then, and the few coins or card swipe it takes to purchase it.

A geological survey determining whether or not investors in a corporation with mineral rights speculating on extraction at various strata of the earth, will require volumes of information. That decision could take a year or five. The pack of gum takes about 10 seconds. Both require the same components but in different volumes and with different weights ascribed to credentialed consultative talent within the decision making process.

The second panel in Fig 1.2 is what efforts you invest and put forth in any given area of the component sales. Ideally your efforts would be hierarchical. You may lead with discovery questions or a 3MCP depending on the situation. This would be followed by intuitive speculation on your part to proceed in directions revealed within the sales situation (a key skill set).

The fourth panel is the resulting action or "what happens." You can almost follow it backward through a sales cycle to see how that result came to be. What you would find is a result of the fulfillment of the requirement core, seller's efforts invested, and the seller's initial approach (and reception by the decision makers). Those "zones" greatly simplify the diagrammatic presentation of the Quad Close in Fig 1.1. In this way, by using Fig 1.2 to isolate functions, you can see the differences between functions.

What you have been doing within sales situations is likely asking open-ended questions that, while effective, are guessing-questions (that's actually a good way to start so this isn't critique). For example, let's assume a sales professional is selling a time management software system, or a module within an ERP (enterprise resource planning) software system of some kind. You and I are observing the situation. Let's also assume that through the course of the initial conversation with the decision maker some production challenges have emerged. It's revealed that there is pressure to get production caught up with incoming orders but there is some internal debate as to why the production schedule delivery rate is lagging. It's not as easy as, "We're waiting on part #2356 and we can't assemble without it." The seller might ask an open-ended question like, **"Would you share with me some of your thoughts on how this past quarter's production goals seemed harder to fulfill than in the past?"** Once answered, it's discovered that the challenges are actually intensifying so the next question might be, **"What has changed to increase the challenge?"** The DM answers and the seller continues, **"So what occurred just prior to that change that may have contributed to the challenges?"**

Those are excellent questions that have revealed a lot of valuable information. Most sellers with even moderate experience would likely figure out that interrogative course; e.g., you don't need the Quad Close to figure that out. But then what? Where is your sales situation headed? Why are you going in that direction? Who is leading? Where do you need to make a change in direction? For what purpose? Should you stay-the-course? What are you trying to learn? What do you need to tell the DMs or KDM? What more should you ask? Why? Should you be listening or talking?

SALES SECRET #78:
Preparation and Practice Are Tactical Advantages

Implement a strategy and deploy tactical questions for an effectual application of persuasive appeals. Doing this with preparation and practice will probably result in a distinct advantage over competitors.

So let's assume those initial open-ended questions are answered by the DMs and the seller learns that a good portion of their production problems are due to a deficient time tracking system (or total lack of one). As the next questions engage with specificity, the answers stop coming and some angst can even be detected within the vocal responses of the decision maker.

Much of the time, in fact, almost all sellers will feel a pretty strong compulsion at that point to seek out a way to position the product as the solution. It's all on the table, right? They have a production problem. It looks like data is missing or incomplete. The sellers system tracks and captures production data, parses it for useful analysis and can spit it out into any form of metric-magic. Most sellers are going to proceed with scheduling a product demo for the next sales situation augmented by perhaps a slide deck of capabilities of the software, a live demo of various modules, functions, options, capacities, versatility, customization aspects and user interfaces.

Many sellers will bite and you can understand why because it's tempting, isn't it? Even if your motive is to help people and companies, that's an encouraging invitation. What happens at that very moment in your mind and those of most sellers is the insertion point of this Strati-Tactical's purpose. We know some of what the seller has discovered. We should now analyze some of the outstanding questions that may be lingering. Let's take a look at what the seller *doesn't* know:

1. **Does the DM trust the seller yet?**
2. **Does the DM know that it's a lack of "time tracking" that is causing the production problems? Even if advanced as a theory, would it be believed?**
3. **Does the seller know it's time tracking related?**
4. **Is it known who the other DMs are? There's little chance that a production challenge company-wide that will require an ERP system replacement is going to have just one decision maker involved** (more like impossible).
5. **How are decisions made in that company? Who is the KDM?**
6. **Is there a budget** (and who controls it)?
7. **Are there any GDMs** (genie decision makers)? [*see also Strati-Tactical #8*]. **Could they kill your sale?**
8. **Is there a timeline and will that exacerbate any interdepartmental conflicts or ongoing tensions?**
9. **Does the DM want to see the minutiae of the seller's software solutions when the macro questions haven't yet been answered?**
10. **Are they willing to fund solutions to solve production or have they resolved to just endure and suffer through until next year's budget so they don't have to do battle with the board for funding?**
11. **Who would actually sign a requisition? Would it be the real KDM or would the KDM make the decision but the CFO would have to release the capital? Are there two KDMs then? Would a committee be empaneled for a consensus buying decision?**
12. **Do they have a current vendor or are they currently using time tracking software in any way?**
13. **Does the seller know the ins-and-outs of the KDM's current system** (e.g., sharing the sparkle and glitter of an ERP system that can do what is already being done with theirs would be benign)?

14. **What does that system cost per year?**
15. **What are their production problems actually costing per quarter?**
16. **Is it a macro problem or a micro?**
17. **If the seller asked right at that moment, for another meeting, would one be granted based on what was advanced in terms of value worth the DM's time** (not likely)**?**
18. **Should a mini demo take place first? A discussed overview of capabilities instead of a demo? How long should an in-depth demo be withheld then, if at all? One more sales situation? Two? Should it take place at the next meeting? Will it be online or in person? What will be included and more importantly, "Why?"**
19. **What will engage the DM to realize the seller is a solution source for efficiency problems?**
20. **Are they using Six Sigma processes or lean manufacturing for their production?**
21. **What kind of thinker is the DM? Big picture? Detail-oriented?**
22. **Are they introverted or extroverted?**
23. **Does the DM seem to be a visual person or an auditory learner?**
24. **What does the seller need to accomplish to get the next sales situation requested, scheduled and secured? What will be the agenda of that sales situation? Why? For what desired result?**
25. **What are the seller's and buyer's defined purposes for clarity?**

Those twenty-five questions seem to be somewhat comprehensive but you could easily identify many more within complex B2B sales situations. Would a consensus buying committee be making a recommendation to a KDM who makes the final decision or is it committee-approved by vote? Who will be held accountable should the product underperform? Will there be a potential board of directors over-ride on complex decisions? Is there private equity in the corporation? Are investors involved in major decisions that may "pop in" and disrupt a sale acting as genie decision makers (GDMs)? The point being that there are more moving pieces within your sales situations than you perhaps realize and in order to prepare your strategy and tactical approach, you need thinking tools—which is what we're talking about.

So what do you do with all of those questions and identified needs for your sales situations? Yours will be different, obviously, but the relationship between what you need to know, what appeals you advance, what decisions you make, etc., are all going to correlate to what the decision makers need for their mental requirement core so you can close the component sales before asking for the Financial Sale.

Strati-Tacticals #2 and #3 are going to help you synthesize this into tooling you can actually use (you get to build a Wall of Wisdom in Strati-Tactical #3) based, in part, on the thinking tools in this Strati-Tactical and that of #2. This will help you strategize how to approach your overarching sales approaches so that tactically you can sell the result (because you'll be better equipped to see it yourself). In this way you won't be as tempted to strive toward your product demo, which is often pulled out a bit too early. There are challenges to identify using open-ended questions. There is trust to earn and a relationship to establish. There are emotional appeals to be made and logic to advance that can act as sales support.

The way that will look using Fig 1.1 is to see the arrival at a product demo as more of a process of tactical way-point thinking where you can match your sales efforts to their requirement core [*See Strati-Tactical#2*].

SALES SECRET #79:
Work Session or Product Demo?

In some industries with some products, you can use a work session as a segue to demonstrate the result a product can produce. Sometimes you can even refer to a product demonstration as a work session but only if that's actually true. You then need collaboration.

Those emotional appeals would have to be carefully constructed to work in tandem with logical appeals to offer proof that a potential solution could work and be beneficial [*zone #4 on Fig 1.1*] because the DM would need to have proof [*zone #7 on Fig 1.1*] and believe whatever it was that was being advanced by the seller [*zone #2 on Fig 1.1*]. The seller reviewing and understanding this would have reviewed Fig 1.1 and saw that trust may be required before believing the emotional appeals or proof [*zone #5 on Fig 1.1*]. The diagram works on paper but what does it look like when someone jumps to the logical proof?

Blurted Proof Mid-Trial

Imagine one of the assistants at a prosecuting attorney's table within a criminal trial blurted out, "The defendant was at 1105997 Chestnut Street at 7:05 PM on the third. I have proof!" That means nothing to the jury (it would be a procedural violation so the judge would likely interject, but that's beside the point). **No one cares until the logical construct and facts have a frame of reference and relevance. Sellers offering proof devoid of relevance may be making a similar case.**

To gain that frame of reference and earn trust prior to advancing technical demonstrations, Fig 1.1 might reveal a need for a sales story. Extending the use of the ERP example a bit more, a story that described another client's/company's production problems that were solved with the software would be an effective tool to use [*zone #2 on Fig 1.1*]. Reciprocity would need to occur between the effects of the emotional and logical appeals [*reciprocal arrow between zones #6 and #7 on Fig 1.1*] so that at some point rationalization could occur [*rationalize arrow between zones #7 and #10 on Fig 1.1*].

Many sales demonstrations occur before emotional want or trust have formed enough for the DMs or KDM to engage mentally. Many Financial Sales closing attempts take place before the component sales have closed. At various points throughout your sale you will need to gauge the amount of trust, emotion, and logic that is required and has been earned. This will always be a guess on your part but if you think of it in three dimensions, it will be easier to visualize. To illustrate why, we'll take a look at 2D blueprints and a 3D model.

2D Blueprints and a 3D Model?

In Strati-Tactical #1 the 2D diagram (Fig 1.1) illuminates the zones and relationships of the component sales but is not able to illustrate a volumetric representation. For example, if additional trust were earned, would that then reduce the amount of logical proof a KDM would need to support a decision in your sales situations? Would a high level of emotional want for a solution (to a challenge that may be causing a company intense pain) mean that more logical proof would be needed in your sale (to avoid repeating a situation another vendor placed them in)? While no book can suggest what these ratios should be, or even could be, what you and I can do is extrude the 2D diagram in Fig 1.1 into three dimensions and then pull the 3D model apart so you can see the volumetrics. Why progress from 2D to 3D?

Two dimensional blueprints for a new home construction give an important overview of the structure and show human traffic flow and the position of one component in the home, in relation to another. The addition of a 3D model or virtual walk-through of the structure would reveal the volume of each room, and sight-lines through various spaces, such as in an open-floor concept. Using solely 2D, you would miss out on the volume the spaces or how kitchen cabinet doors, when opened, might interact with traffic patterns or other appliances.

Using solely 3D you would not have an overview "bird's eye view" that blueprints provide and you could wind up with a garage on one side of the structure with the kitchen on the opposite side of the home—something not obvious when solely using a 3D model but it would be very conspicuous as you one day carried groceries from the car parked in the garage, down the hall, through the living room to the kitchen. A 2D blueprint would illuminate that immediately. Three dimensions provides a sense of internal space which is why we will next take a look at **The Quad Close in Three Dimensions.**

STRATEGY (for Strati-Tactical #2):
Volume, Effort, and Timing

Adding the third dimension illuminates (at least some of) the volumetric aspects of the Quad Close. Knowing that your efforts can be better matched with requirements is empowering. Matching the volume of your efforts, the type, and utilizing more specific timing is better determined from a position of insight. Three dimensional modeling provides that for you. Insight, literally "sight" into the Quad Close provides a strategic construct to build your future sales efforts upon.

TACTICS (for Strati-Tactical #2):
Emotive Gatekey Way-Point Tooling

In chapter 4 we discussed tactical way-point thinking wherein way-points were plotted after joining the KDM where they were in their thinking. The symbolic radio tower on the horizon is the clarity of purpose with major way-points being contributors to the component sales of the Quad Close. Fig 2.1 introduces the volumetric aspect to this concept by illustrating the terrain of a third dimension in your sales situations.

Volumetrics, timing and effort allow you to strategize and then tactically adjust your approach within sales situations (often in real time) because you will be able to overlay the diagrammatic modeling within your mind. You can and probably will, adjust your focus on your directional sales situations' subjects, and in what ratios of effort-to-requirement. You may even blend persuasive appeals for compound advantages. Without the 3D models, it's more difficult to see sales in this way. Once you see the Quad Close three dimensionally, you can then go back and plot more effective way-points using two and three dimensions together similar to blueprints of a house construction project coupled with a 3D walk-through.

STRATI-TACTICAL
TWO
The Quad Close in Three Dimensions

Fig 2.1:
3D Quad Close Model

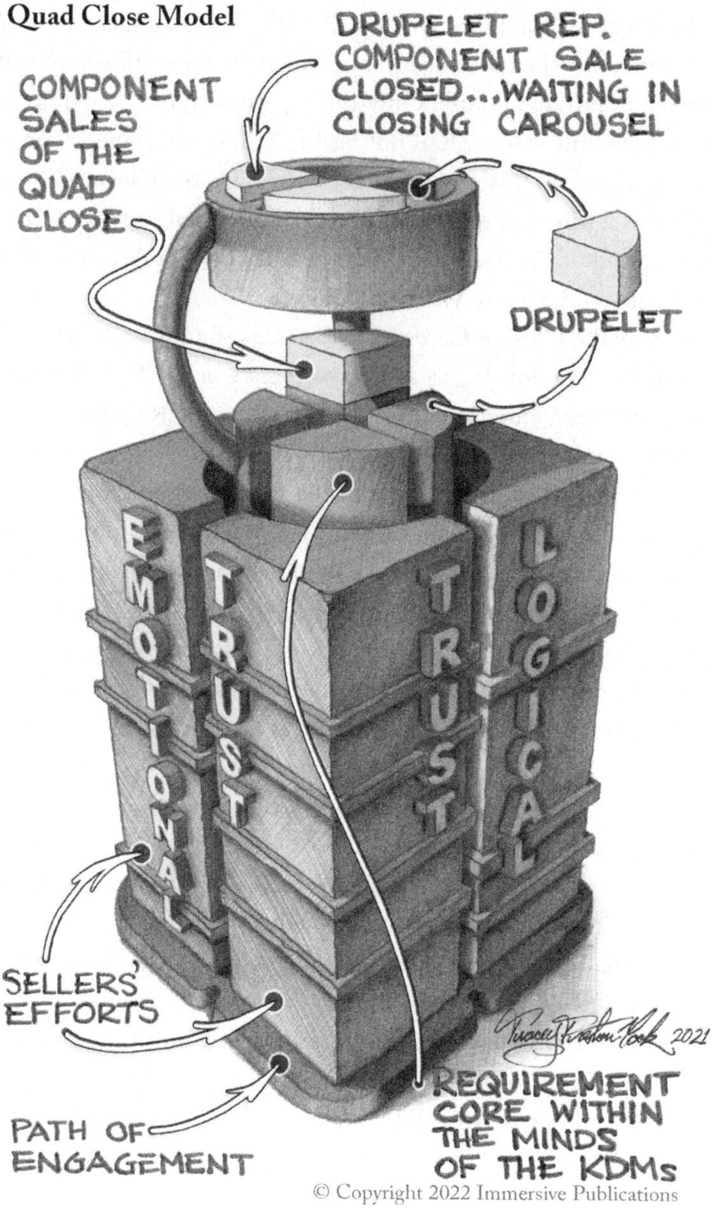

The 3D model in Fig 2.1 is a direct upward extrusion of the 2D diagram in Fig 1.1 in Strati-Tactical #1. Fig 2.1 has been rotated 180° so that emotion, trust, and logic are facing forward (instead of financial). This is because those three subjects are discussed before the Financial Close can take place.

What's occurring in the 3D model of Fig 2.1 is an identification of the visible pieces—the outer quadrants, which are your efforts that affect the internal requirement core. Only the top portion of the requirement core is visible—but it has detail not visible in the two dimensional diagram of Fig 1.1. I call this area at the top of Fig 2.1, the Closing Carousel. This provides a physical representation of the mental process occurring within the mind of the decision makers as component sales close. Which is something you'll need to visualize while selling.

The way the Closing Carousel works is, as you invest effort into the Sellers' Efforts quadrants [*zones #2, #3, #4, and #9 in Fig 1.1*], those efforts are having an effect, either positive or negative on the Requirement Core in the DMs' minds [*zones #5, #6, #7, and #10 in Fig 1.1*]. That relationship between the Sellers' Efforts zones and the Requirement Core zones is a process that is further explored in Fig 2.3. For now, we know the result as simply fulfilling the requirements the DMs need in the areas of the component sales. To visualize the filling of the Requirement Core, we will call the requirements "units" (so we can illustrate volume). The units (when accepted by the DM) are then awarded, meaning our efforts are having a positive effect and each situation or accomplishment represents some number of units.

Once a component sale closes, the Requirement Core "awards" the accumulation of the total required number of units by granting what could be called a "drupelet" (as in quadruplet—or like a section of fruit, like an orange, wherein each section is actually called a drupelet). The drupelet in the Quad Close is granted and is then moved from the top of the Requirement Core up to the Closing Carousel where it will wait for the other component sales to close. This process repeats until the component sales are all closed.

When your persuasive efforts produce the remaining drupelets that

Fig 2.2:
3D Pull-Out Revealing the Structural Interior of the Quad Close

represent the closing of the remaining component sales, three of the four drupelets are in place in the Closing Carousel and the seller can then ask for the Financial Sale. Any of the component sales in Fig 2.1 can close in any order and while the effects of the component sales are interdependent they can also accumulate (or be lost) independently.

In Fig 2.2, the Closing Carousel has been removed as the focus is "zooming in." This model represents the internal structure of the Quad Close and has been rotated back 180º close to the original position you see in two dimensions in Fig 1.1 (in Strati-Tactical #1). Fig 2.2 is a sort of in-between frame of action between Fig 2.1 and Fig 2.3. Its purpose is simply to let you see there is an interior space we will be talking about (up next).

To discover the amount/volume of what you need to advance (Sellers' Efforts) and the types of appeals to use, you need relevant information derived from discovery questions that are based on your clarity of purpose, your intuition, and your experience which should be available and recorded in some form on your Wall of Wisdom (W.O.W.) [*see Strati-Tactical #3*]. That relevant information is going to give you a mental picture of the internal structure in Fig 2.1 that can then be "zoomed into" similar to Fig 2.3. There you will see a relationship between the outer quadrant of the Sellers' Efforts. In two dimensions this would be zone #4 in Fig 1.1. In three dimensions this would be Fig 2.3 (showing that relationship between zones #4 and #7 on Fig 1.1). For reference, that "arrow" in Fig 1.1 in zone #4 pointing into zone #7, the Logical Sale, on Fig 1.1, is the exact location being illustrated in Fig 2.3.

The right column in Fig 2.3 is what they, the DMs or KDM, will need to receive for persuasion to occur in each of the component sales. The left column in Fig 2.3 are the Sellers' Efforts. Each letter represents a different area of logical proof.

For example, letter C in Fig 2.3 might represent a requirement that your company be of a minimum size corporation. Decision makers from a Fortune 100 company are less likely to hire a start-up company with five employees to provide a pivotal service for their company. Once the decision makers see that the seller is representing a legitimate operation with the resources to provide support, parts, warranty, etc., they would then be satisfied.

The illustrative suggestion being made by Fig 2.3, is a scenario you've likely witnessed wherein a seller shows up to a sales situation or joins a video sales situation wielding a slide deck. The first slide is the company logo. Slide two is a photo of the facility exterior. Slide three is the interior or some proposed expansion of the facility. Slide four is the grainy photo of the group of employees wherein most are squinting into the sun. Slide five is a bulleted list of achievements and awards with slide six featuring some kind of award or certificate. What is apparent to the DMs but often not known to slide-deck-wielding sales reps is that it's far more logical proof than is needed.

This is graphically visible in Fig 2.3 as what is required in the right column requirement core is of a much smaller volume than the amount

Fig 2.3:
Close Up (Zoomed In) **View**

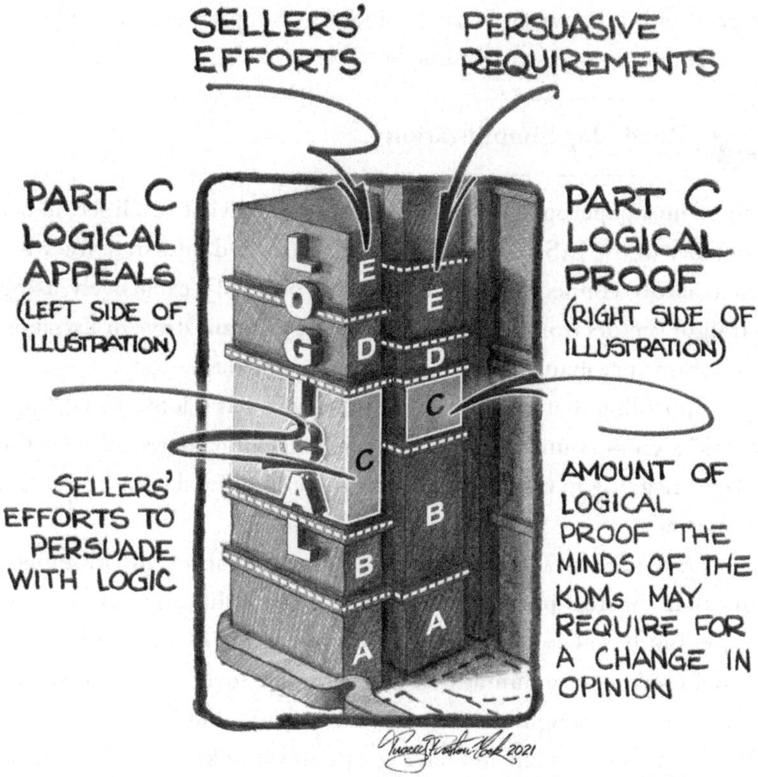

or number of appeals being advanced. Because you're likely employing critical thinking it should be obvious that the illustration is no authority and the suggested volumes could be inaccurate. However, the volumetric relationships are unknowable and will always be a guess. The way you can know is if you see lots of nodding but not necessarily in "agreement," but more like the "let's move along" nods, yet the slide deck just keeps over-presenting proof after slide after bullet point. This is hypothetical, so don't cut something short without analyzing it thoroughly. We could just as easily demonstrate the opposite—that the seller is sailing through key points but the DMs are really wanting to drill down into some more details before moving on.

Some may be thinking, "All this modeling stuff is just complicating the sales process. I like to keep things simple. You know...rapport, discovery, positioning, demo, etc.?" That's similar to simplifying a road map with a marker and a ruled straight line between two points.

Road Map Simplification

Open up a paper road map of any country and what you'll see, in the instance of the U.S.A., are meandering lines and interstate freeways that hardly connect all point A's to all point B's exclusively using straight vectors from point-to-point; e.g., you can't drive in a straight line from very many places to other cities or destinations.

Spreading that map out, it could be said that it looks like it "confuses" a cross country trip. Taking meandering routes all over the place are going to complicate what can be simplified with a ruler and a marker.

Drawing a straight line from one city to another, and illuminating that shortest possible route certainly simplifies travel plans on paper but has absolutely no effect on the reality of geography. Your pen doesn't move mountains or create bridges-over-rivers for you. So draw that line straight through and then try to follow it. It won't work. But studying the map and having a plan would keep you heading in the right overall direction just as planning for your sales situations will provide a general direction to follow your plotted way-points. Both "planning approaches" accommodate actual terrain you'll be encountering.

You can apply the concept of tactical way-point thinking from chapter 4 and use it both two dimensionally to plot points [Fig 1.1 in Strati-Tactical #1] and three dimensionally using Fig 2.3 for all three component sales. Even though just the Logical Sale was featured, the Trust and Emotional Sales both have their own sections "A, B, C," (or your sale may have additional sections like "D, E, F," etc.). Keep in mind that each letter in each section would represent a different area of proof required; e.g., section A might = warranty proof, section B might = cost savings, section C = size of corporation, etc.

The tactical way-point thinking, combined with the 2D application of the zones and hopping from one to the other and around that diagram as you navigate your sales situations, also has the vertical aspect you can move up and down within in Fig 2.3 to visualize volume, effort, and timing separately for each component sale. They all work together for a cohesive mental hologram of your sales.

SALES SECRET #80:
Volumetric Parity

Match your efforts in persuasion with the requirements of the DMs' and KDMs' minds. The absolute ratio of your efforts to their requirements is unknowable but you can get it close with experience. Questions about what they wish to accomplish will help dial that ratio in tighter. Asking about their decision criteria and what their former experiences have been will provide further information for you.

What will simplify your sales situations' preparations are your understanding of what's going on in the minds of the DMs and KDM. The more you understand their buying process, the simpler things become while designing your sales process. Understanding provides clarity which can result from knowledge and experience. Those can be applied to tooling as you discover **how to build a wall of wisdom.**

STRATEGY (for Strati-Tactical #3):
Build the Wall

A Wall of Wisdom (W.O.W.) offers what strategy? Imagine you have a challenging quota set and some new market disadvantages or disruptive technology rolls out at about the same time that the economy decides to go off its meds. Where will the sales team likely go to strategize? Right, a conference room or meet virtually online. But if you have a W.O.W. built? You already know that's where the sales team will head (and that could also be in a conference room or virtually online).

When you have visitors to your home, everyone ends up in the kitchen, don't they? That's where the food (and hosts) are. Your W.O.W. is sales support food. Once everyone begins marinating in the information, a solution or the tool you're working on will often emerge. If it doesn't, you keep adding data and ideating until a solution does.

A W.O.W. is a low cost tool with a high yield. It's an effective sales support tool that can lead to the development of tooling, techniques and tactics worth millions or even billions in new sales. Your strategy should be to build the wall. The best part is you DO NOT need to invest massive up-front time. You can start and build it one card at a time gradually.

TACTICS (for Strati-Tactical #3):
Low Cost, High ROI Sales Support Tool

You have a tactical advantage when you encounter challenges while selling. Your W.O.W. offers you ways to respond to objections based on your past experiences that will have produced the then-current index cards on the wall. You'll have the objection on one card and some effective responses ready to go on others. You'll have question-based tooling ready for discovery. These accompany you in your memory.

STRATI-TACTICAL
THREE

How to Build a Wall of Wisdom

Fig 3.1
Index Cards Representing the KDMs' Requirement Column

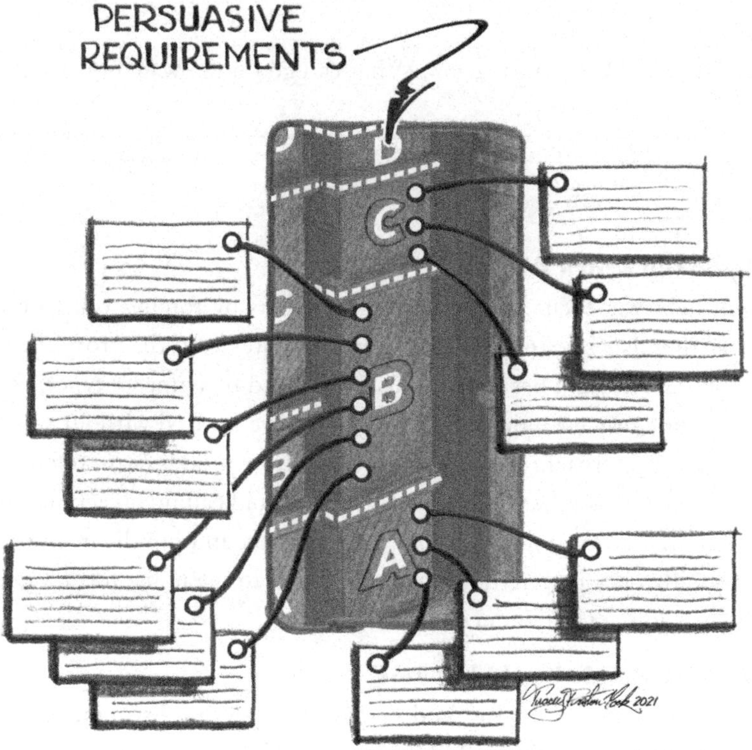

A Wall of Wisdom (W.O.W.), is your place to go for wisdom, strategy, knowledge, and the construction of tactical tooling. You'll either be converting a wall's purpose or building a binder with protective sheets containing pages to pin, tape or affix information to. Or you may elect to build a W.O.W. electronically that can be portable on your smart devices. It's a place where you can write, draw, denote, and capture your observations of sales situations, research, and prospects. We will go through the components involved in developing a W.O.W. in three parts:

Part One	Why you want a W.O.W., what you do with a wall, and what form it should take.
Part Two	Your efforts while selling and appealing to the minds of decision makers and the corresponding requirement core contents and amounts required by the minds of the decision makers for persuasion to occur. Fig 3.1 illustrates some of this.
Part Three	Wall information. What can go on the wall, how to get it, and why.

Part One

Why do you want a W.O.W.?

It will help you focus your prospecting efforts by forcing you to build prospecting lists [*see also chapter 23*]. If you write down the prospects you are seeking within a list (if even just organized by name or type), you'll see a picture of your industry you may not have noticed without this organizational approach. This is because the information is cross-referenced and grouped with other information (such as cold calling objections) that can illuminate strengths, responses, weaknesses, and pitfalls in your call strategy. This is a picture that is more difficult to see in list form. On the wall you can see it all at once.

The Puzzle Box Lid Picture

Think of developing and sorting prospecting lists like fiddling around with a large 2,000 piece puzzle. Without the box lid picture, the puzzle is far more difficult to work out. Even if you organize the pieces by color (organize by lists), **you aren't sure if those blue puzzle pieces are sky or water, or the blue car parked on the street. Using your W.O.W. to organize your strategy is like having a puzzle box lid.**

You'll also be using the W.O.W. to assist you with the creation of your Emotive Gatekey, analogies, sales stories, Segue Story, Center Punch, and cold calling messaging approaches. I've been using a W.O.W. for almost three decades and I would estimate most of my revenue has come either indirectly or directly from its use.

Remember that really challenging objection you received awhile back from a decision maker? You probably remember what it referenced but do you remember why it occurred? What happened just prior to its advancement? What, specifically they said, and what you said to respond to it? Was it that objection which put your sale in the weeds? Did you have to go get a metaphoric 4x4 truck to get your sale back up onto the road? Using that 4x4 response again someday might be of great value—all of that would. But you probably can't remember all of those details. A W.O.W. would bring that experience right up to any present need you had or might illuminate a sales support angle you had not previously considered. You build some of your persuasive tooling based on what you project you'll likely need and some based on reactions to the illumination of recurring situations.

What do you do with a W.O.W.?

You create it to build other tools, provide answers to difficult challenges and use it as a source of ideation. Whatever you think about what you're currently doing in sales, positive or negative or somewhere in-between, you need new approaches. You'll gain additional success with new tools and skills. This is especially true when new challenges or variables arise in your industry.

SALES SECRET #81:
Observation

As you observe sales situations (both yours and those of colleagues) **you can make mental notes of the DMs' and KDMs' motives, reactions, facial expressions, questions, requests, and pain points revealed by open-ended discovery questions. Objections, resistance and acceptance are also revealing. You can then put all that you learn up on your W.O.W.**

The reason that matters is when you start hyper-focusing on your sales situations (to feed the wall data) something happens that would never have happened. You begin noticing that the resistance you thought was responsible for your sales ending up in the weeds, may not have been fully responsible for the entire causation. You'll notice other contributing factors, and things people say in an almost after-thought-voice. You'll notice challenges you hadn't noticed before. Resistance you thought was minor turns out to be more substantial than you thought.

When I was faced with the industry-wide-objection [*see also chapter 10*], there came a point at which I decided to solve the problem. I literally ceased trying to sell and started using my time with decision makers to learn about their operations. I asked a lot of questions about what they were doing so I could feed my W.O.W. new data about their pain points. I learned a few things I wouldn't have, if I wasn't driven to feed my wall data. They trusted me sooner and more intensely than if I had talked "at" them about insurance. They shared (very often over-shared) their challenges, fears, pain points, struggles in business and what they were really up against. They were very open to discussions. Sure, I'd give them the overview of what I was offering, but as soon as I could, I switched the topics to them and their operations. This fed my wall more data, faster, than any other possible option. That's what I did with my wall. It was great data too. Accurate, relevant, meaningful and insightful. And yes, by putting down my sales agenda, using open-ended discovery questions, I ended up selling more than if I had talked and pitched insurance.

What format can you build your W.O.W. within?

The wall approach: The reason for "the wall" approach is you can see it all at once and if in a private area, you can leave it up. Should you ever decide to collaborate or have a separate one for that purpose, colleagues can interact with a wall if they are there in person (if not, see the electronic version).

With your wall, you can contribute to it over time and easily move information around to form various associations, lists, groupings and experiments. Seeing the information all-at-once offers the ability to make mental associations that are more challenging in other formats.

If you don't have a large bulletin board and don't want to put a zillion holes in a sheetrock wall but you need a temporary W.O.W. (or it will have to move), **you can use temporary tape. The blue painters' tape has varying adhesive levels or you can use drafting tape** (available online).

The binder/page approach:

If you want to keep your W.O.W. private or portable then build it using a binder with protective sheet pages. The protective sheets allow you to draw on them as well with some types of markers. Test this out before investing in colored sets. The binder approach also gives you the opportunity to use sections, dividers, include pictures, diagrams and marketing collateral as well as maps, sales support resources, quick reference info, etc. The binder has some advantages over the wall as you can take it home.

Electronic/digital W.O.W.:

You may also want to make your W.O.W. electronic and there are many graphics programs that would facilitate this should you want to "scroll left and right" to see your wall. You can also use notebooking and note taking software or simply snap photos of the wall with your phone. Also effective is the use of a multimedia interface screen/board on the wall. This has the advantage of ease of distribution.

Modular W.O.W. approach:

Another way to modulate, control and track information for your W.O.W. which will work exceptionally well for large corporations, complex tech companies, or those with involved information sets is to build a modular W.O.W.

The way it could work for you is to use the binder method above for each subject, type, subtype or data set and then use the wall method above to have reference index cards. So for example a W.O.W. in a conference room could have diagrammed and index carded components that reference various binders, some of which everyone would have a copy of. This way large numbers of participants can track complexity with simplistic visuals that act as modules. Migrating all of that information onto a server, the cloud, into software that can be accessed from multiple devices brings your efforts up to a broadcast spectrum everyone can use.

Part Two

Your sales efforts and the decision maker's requirement core featured in Fig 3.1 show a hyper close-up view of what Fig 2.2 showed as a bi-section of the Quad Close. So Fig 3.1 continues to zoom in past what Fig 2.1-Fig 2.3 illustrated. In Fig 2.3 we saw two columns side-by-side within the 3D model with the left column being the Sellers' Efforts and the right column being the Requirement Core of the decision maker. Fig 3.1 shows a close up so you can first see you need index cards or an electronic version of what the decision makers in your industry require to see, hear, understand, know and believe before persuasion can occur.

It's assumed that you'll be able to extrapolate from that close-up, what the other column would look like and see that it will be a mirror image (as close as you can make it) so that you will have a set of similar index cards (not shown) representing your efforts. Those cards of your efforts will have recorded what has worked well in various sales situations. At some point you'll have a repository of your own tips, tricks, phrases, situations, and ideas.

Part Three

Once you've curated enough content for a wall, you can organize it by genre; e.g., "objections all go over here" and "responses to objections are to the right of that" and "opening questions are to the left of objections" and "discovery questions are over in this area." You can then also have areas for raw information, related but not directly organizable data, and historical information or industry-specific research.

You may doubt the need for a W.O.W. and think, "Well I know all that (no one "knows it all"). **Why would I put what I already know on a wall?" Even if true, can it be held up in the mind for review all at once? Even Einstein had notes.**

Pay very close attention to what your stressors are. Trace those stressors back to their sources. Depending on your industry or approach you may want to have some of the following:

- **Your clarity of purpose:** [*see chapter 15*].
- **DM/KDM dossier and/or company profiles of ideal client types:** The mindsets, opinions, approaches-to-buying, apprehensions, fears, problems, challenges, etc., are outlined. The companies you approach will need to be identified by type, size, challenge, application of your result, ROI they seek, challenges they face, what they have invested to fund the temporary solutions, what they will be funding in lieu of a solution, why they would want your result, why they wouldn't, and who the typical DMs are.
- **Your product results:** What it can do, strengths, weaknesses, reasons people have purchased in the past, why they will/won't again.
- **Your competitors:** What are they doing? What is effective? Unique? Weaknesses?
- **Your strengths:** What areas do you excel within? What are your product strengths? How is the result you offer exceptional? Are there bold print bullet points you can draw from? What about the metaphorical fine print?
- **Reasons for not buying:** Different than "objections" these are the actual conclusive and reasoned causation for past decisions by DMs and KDMs to not buy or not buy from you. These reasons are not necessarily delivered in the "objection voice" of resistance but are more similar to explanations.
- **Objections & Responses:** Those you've received, anticipate, others have heard, and what worked well in response to them.
- **Questions:** Your discovery strategy and tactics for persuasion.

You will appreciate your former efforts invested in a W.O.W. and you will see a need for a wall as we discuss **how to create an Emotive Gatekey.**

STRATEGY (for Strati-Tactical #4):
It's about Them. When It Becomes about You, You're Probably Off-Road.

The first strategic step is to accept that Emotive Gatekey development is involved. It's difficult to develop. It's worth it, but it requires an investment of time and effort. The more simple and basic the result, the more involved the development will probably be (yes, you read that right). Simple is harder. Effective is more involved.

There are a few places to look that are the most likely to contain gatekey material. 1. Their pain. 2. Some kind of enticement. 3. Some form of saving something: time, money, the environment, a relationship, investment, effort, etc. 4. Some gain or accomplishment they could have. 5. Protecting something of value/preventing something from happening.

You'll notice that all are emotional and you'll also probably notice it's all about them and their result you offer. An Emotive Gatekey is all about them. When it starts becoming about you and what you can do, you're probably going off-road. When you need to talk about yourself or point at your product or company, do so in a way that immediately translates to their result.

TACTICS (for Strati-Tactical #4):
Gatekey Single & Multiple Way-Point Tooling

While an Emotive Gatekey is often used for initial engagement, it can also be a tactical advantage as a mid-stream persuasive vehicle to advance to each way-point. If your sales are complex, you can treat each tactical way-point as a sale within a sale and develop a different Emotive Gatekey for every way-point or just those that are technical or complex.

STRATI-TACTICAL FOUR

How to Create an Emotive Gatekey

What follows are ten phases of "how-to" creative development that will also prepare you for what you can expect to pass through as you create or discover your Emotive Gatekey. You may elect to skip some of them. The point is not the process but the result.

If you think of your Emotive Gatekey within four minutes (not likely), you've succeeded. Congratulate yourself and go sell with it. If it takes you four hours, or four weeks, or even if you work on it for months, that's okay too—it's not like you're going to need fewer successful engagements or leads a month from now, right? You'll still be trying to generate new business so whenever you succeed, an Emotive Gatekey will probably begin helping you with engagement almost immediately.

Phase 1. The Challenging Phase:
This tool, an Emotive Gatekey, is a challenge to build. It will require an investment of time. Your desired result will probably be one that is simple and effective. To create anything that embodies simplicity is more difficult to build.

That is the very first component you really need to accept. It will make it far less frustrating if you know up front you're going to be at this awhile. People manage the patience to climb mountains or trek long distances because they have managed expectations. You would probably get frustrated waiting at a toll booth for an hour for no apparent reason, only to later arrive at your destination where you don't mind waiting six hours in a line to get into a venue of high interest. You expect to blow right through the toll booth and you expect the venue line to be eight hours long. When it's only six hours, you are elated. Choice is a primary difference there but it's also reason, causation, expectation and purpose that drive the difference in emotional reactions.

This is the most important first step because having developed an Emotive Gatekey successfully many times, I can assure you it's very involved but absolutely worth it. You should also know that while I did it in one all-nighter in chapter two, that is not typical. It was also under extreme conditions (I didn't fully expand on how bad my financial situation was, but it was dire). I had a lot of extrinsic pressure and had to perform or lose.

Manage your expectations by initially understanding that you can theoretically hit on the answer after thirty minutes but it's more likely to take many hours across many days and you may even need to let it sit for a while and come back to it with a fresh perspective.

Phase 2. Finding Phase:

Do you already have an Emotive Gatekey buried somewhere? Take a look at whether or not you already have a gatekey but just don't know it. Pump the brakes here and focus for a minute because you can save yourself an immense amount of time if you can recognize a gatekey from within that which you already have.

Look in your own sales approach or that of others. Read your marketing collateral. Go visit the marketing department and ask them what they think and what research they've done. You have no doubt heard about the person cleaning out an old storage building out back of a historic estate that once belonged to a great grandparent only to discover an heirloom worth a million dollars on the antiquities market. Brashly blowing through the storage space would cause the person to have missed the value, or worse, discarded it. So as you go through your sales approach in search of potential Emotive Gatekeys, focus and be careful not to miss anything.

Phase 3. Framing Phase:

Your W.O.W. can reframe your thinking. The "two-hand-gesture of a rectangle shape" that you see movie directors use when scoping out a location or scene or making a decision on what or how to film next, serves a purpose. That "finger frame" is a rough preview of what the viewer would see on screen and serves to emphasize what's visible within the frame while blocking extraneous distracting scenery that won't enhance the scene. It's "framing." Even other forms of framing highlight what to look at. A painting on the wall that's framed is saying, "Look at this. It's important or enjoyable to look at."

You'll benefit during the gatekey framing phase if you zoom into what's in it for the DMs and KDM. What their experience was, is, will be, could be or should be. What they care about. What's affecting them. Discover what they don't know but should.

Phase 4. Ideation Phase:

You are developing a tool to make decision makers care about something affecting them. Keep in mind, it's already affecting them and you're merely tooling up to feature that persuasively. Questions will greatly assist you in both discovering what it is they care about, and help them see what that is if they haven't already.

Here are (some) examples of affect/effect/emotional impact questions you can ask of yourself. You're searching for what is responsible for emotions surrounding the need for your product.

- **What do DMs miss out on if they don't have your product?**
- **What happens in each of those two "states of having"** (have or have not [*your solution*]) **when you follow events downstream?**
- **How does the result differ from competitors?**
- **How can they access the benefits?**
- **How does it save time, improve performance, etc.?**
- **Why does the experience of having your result matter?**
- **Why does the time savings specifically matter** (e.g., saving time on mowing a corporate lawn is not the same as saving communication time amongst senior staff)?
- **What problem does it solve, specifically?**
- **Why would it matter if they didn't have your product's result?**
- **Who does/doesn't benefit in the absence of the solution?**
- **Is there something almost no one knows about your product?**
- **Why don't they know?**
- **What does everyone know about your product? Why is that?**

- Do you have to explain technology before revealing the value of your product that is worth their time?
- Who is affected by having, not having, solution, etc.?
- Where did you find that information?
- Read online negative reviews of your product—what are people upset about? Read reviews of your competitors.
- Is that a misunderstanding of the product or do they have a point?
- Can you take the negatives and feature them in a solutions-based feature?
- On negative reviews, how are the word choices articulated?
- Eliminate every noun, verb, and fact. Can you interpret or list all of the emotion or frustrations without the nouns and verbs distracting you?
- Are positive reviews mentioning anything specific?
- How does that feel?
- What is affected?
- What does that alleviate?
- What does that improve?
- Why do they care?
- Why are they frustrated?
- Why are people pleased?
- Who is affected?
- Who isn't?
- Who else has your solution?
- How do people use it?
- Who truly benefits?
- Clues on where to look?
- Have you missed anything?

The search for the mental switch isn't "too hard" for you. It just requires some patience, diligence, learning and adjustment of the focal length of your search for data. Questions let you "see." This will lead to an adjustment of your approach to questions.

Questions asked of yourself to determine why DMs and KDMs that DO meet with you are agreeing to meetings:

- What am I hearing from KDMs that is common to more than one or most?
- What are the commonalities within their expressed frustration?

- **What is the primary reason KDMs are meeting with me in the first place?**

A great way to adrenalize the ideation phase is to go interview your current clients and listen as you ask why they bought, did so from you, and their entire thinking process as they considered the purchase. Was there a point at which they almost didn't buy but then decided to? What enabled that? What you are looking for is a mental switch in the minds of the decision makers so you can flip it on with your Emotive Gatekey. A switch that is common to all or most of those you'll be approaching. You'll need to seek out and write down answers for what is affecting them, will affect them, and the resulting emotions.

Questions asked of yourself to determine why DMs and KDMs that DON'T meet with you are disengaging from committing to meetings:

- **Are they often irritated with the seller and I'm stepping into that role and feel the transference of emotion?**
- **Am I representing a seller they don't care for? If so, why?**
- **Are they tired of the products in my industry breaking? Are they annoyed by the maintenance required?**
- **Is there confusion that's common to most?**
- **What are the areas that everyone seems to stumble on?**
- **Are they transferring this annoyance to other areas like price?**
- **Is there a common point in most sales situations, where interest seems to drop for most KDMs? What's occurring at that point?**
- **If I moved that to meeting #2 would the drop-point also move? Is there a way to test this?**

Questions asked of yourself to determine why DMs and KDMs that *don't* buy but *do* meet with you:

- **Are they learning what they need from me and then going online or to a competitor and getting the solution for less? If so, why is my information valuable but my result less so?**

- Being honest with myself, do I actually know where I may have made a misstep but don't want to admit it?
- More importantly, is there a consequence common to most for approaching their purchase in that way? Do those KDMs ever regret their decision to proceed with my information but not with my consult—and is there a downstream cost for that decision?
- What part of the sales situations do I find the most challenging? Is that where I need a gatekey? Or would practice solve that?
- If I could magically apply an Emotive Gatekey to any specific point in the sales situations or prospecting process, where would I apply it? At what specific point? Disregarding "what the gatekey needs to be," at what point would I advance an Emotive Gatekey (that can tell you what problem you may actually be trying to solve)?

Questions you can ask of your existing customers (if possible and only if you have earned trust and it won't affect your relationship):

- When you were considering the result I was offering to deliver with our product, what were some of your frustrations with the industry as a whole?
- Were there any points in our discussions that were confusing?
- Were there things that many or most of the sales professionals that you've visited with all shared in common that you found especially helpful?
- If you could change some things about the process of buying, what would they be?
- How important was ________________ to you when considering a purchase?
- How difficult did you find it to accept that some change would have to be adopted to go in the new direction (or replacement/installation/tech change/process change/etc.)?
- What challenges arose during discussions with multiple people weighing in on the decision?
- What did you agree on? What did you disagree on?

- **What did you find was the most challenging aspect of the consideration process?**
- **If a trusted colleague who was in an another industry or a non-competitive position to you, asked you for advice on how to buy, what would you suggest they do or consider?**

Consider the questions you're going to ask because you aren't going to be able to ask an unlimited number. Use these questions you find here as a starting point but keep in mind your own ideas and knowledge may produce a question approach that better reflects your industry and experience. You should not ask every question suggested here (you'll annoy people) and the intention is for you to pull some ideas from the lists.

SALES SECRET #82:
During Ideation, Flip all Assertions from KDMs 180°

Write down every assertion, (positive statements or negative objections) **in one column on your W.O.W. Then next to that create a second column and convert every statement to its opposite. Why? The left column will show you all of the objections, stressors, interests and positive statements. The 180° column will show you the mirror image of their vocalized thinking. In the 180° column the positive statements** (opposites of their actual negative objections) **can reveal what may motivate them. The negative statements in the 180° column** (opposite of the positive things they've said) **can reveal fears or things they'd likely like to avoid. Using this as an ideation tool gives you a different working snapshot. It jogs your thinking with a new perspective and offers new inspiration and lines-of-thought.**

Seek out information online and physical sources like marketing collateral, and top sellers:

- **What are your competitors currently doing and saying?**
- **What do their websites say? Their social accounts?**
- **What is your industry saying? Are there national ads running?**
- **What are top sellers in your industry saying to open up sales situations or using for engagement?**

- **If you type into a search engine the very same questions the decision makers you are appealing to are asking, what comes up as results? What are the questions? Could the answer to one of those questions be reframed as, itself, a question or statement and serve as a gatekey?**
- **What do the marketers in your marketing department have for resources and research** (have you made friends with them yet)?

Phase 5. Dig through the Data:

Putting it together and pulling it apart. Now that you have some data to mess around with, what do you see? Step 1 of the next Strati-Tactical has a series of questions that will help you. Here are a few additional ones to consider as you dig through the data. You're looking for:

- **The decision makers' pain or that of their company.**
- **Some kind of enticement.**
- **Revealing a liability.**
- **Some accomplishment.**
- **A way to improve their image.**
- **New opportunities.**
- **Untapped potential they haven't yet seen.**
- **a system, technoloy, or approach you have experience in.**
- **A topic they care about.**
- **A way to save/accrue time.**
- **Missed opportunities.**
- **Illuminate what they're missing.**
- **Protecting something of value.**
- **A way to save/earn Rock Hard Coin.**

In the digging phase you are seeking out the topical subjects or overarching facts or data that illuminates the subjective or objective.

SALES SECRET #83:
An Emotive Gatekey Needs to Be "Good," Not "Epic"

Your Emotive Gatekey does not need to be epic. You only need to get their attention and make them curious enough to care about what you're engaging them with.

Phase 6. Rough Conceptual Drafting:

Work out a rough draft and remember this is short and to-the-point. It's a statement or a question. Work out different ways to ask the question, say the statement, or advance the observation you wish to use as an Emotive Gatekey.

Phase 7. Standby Phase:

During development it's a good idea to shelve your gatekey rough draft for a week. Giving your mind time to think it over will either develop improvements, affirm what you have, or encourage you to question it. If you are stuck, this may help. You can always come back to it. If you are seriously stuck, just know that your mind will continue to work on it in the background, like an app that churns away as you check email or whatever.

Phase 8. Testing Phase:

Try out your new idea(s). When possible, try out what you've come up with on those whom you trust first. Do not try ideas out on those whom you feel self conscious around.

Phase 9. Revision Phase:

Revise. Take the feedback you receive and revise where possible and rework what needs replacement.

Phase 10. Implementation Phase:

Go try it out. If you feel it's not dialed in and you feel stuck, there's another ideation and creativity process up next which cross-relates (and this one can help with that next one as well). Keep this in mind as you work through, **how to develop analogies.**

STRATEGY (for Strati-Tactical #5):
Define Your Clarity of Purpose

Think of analogical strategy like a fire extinguisher. Don't use it everywhere or all of the time, but when you do need an extinguisher, it strategically prevents a larger blaze from spreading. For example, you don't need to put out the charcoal fire in your grill on Sunday with a fire extinguisher. The grill fire would be analogous with a simple question in a sales situation. You don't need a major tool to answer it. Your strategy should include becoming proficient at developing this tool so that you can apply the solution to larger problems that are complex.

TACTICS (for Strati-Tactical #5):
Associative Situations and Comparative Parallels

Once you know what you're trying to accomplish (your clarity of purpose), development begins. The parallel comparison is the next leg of the stool—the choice you've made in subject and how you've authored the comparison. Both tactical stances require proficiency so practice will be the third leg of that stool. Your delivery, charisma and personality matter to the analogical success. You're going to make tactical mistakes and that's far better than non-use of analogies because once you get this tool dialed in, it's like calling in the crane to erect a building. Intuitive judgment is the fourth tactical leg of the stool. Intuition supports knowing when to use an analogy and at what point, for what reason, to accomplish what purpose, and told in what way to whom. Much of that can be learned with experience.

STRATI-TACTICAL

FIVE

How to Develop Analogies

What follows are the eight steps I personally use to develop most of my analogies. By fulfilling these steps, you will likely arrive with an analogy you can improve, work on, or use.

Step 1. Clarity of Purpose:
Define the challenge.
What is ***your*** challenge (not that of the DMs and KDM that you're solving with the analogy). It must be definable. No one buys what they can't or don't comprehend. Analogies sell ideas, communicate, change opinions, simplify complexity, make the abstract more concrete, and educate. You should be able to clearly define what it is the analogy must do because it is solving ***your problem*** in communicating ***their problem***. When you write down your challenge that the analogy will solve, it should be similar to this example:

> **The decision maker is not understanding why his company must buy a foundation package for the system. It must be installed prior to the technicians' arrival on installation day. He feels I'm trying to get more money out of him now and while that's technically true, the motive is so the foundational package will have the kinks worked out prior to installation. Doing it on the same day/week means that any problems will be diagnosed with too many variables to troubleshoot. Isolation of variables will be far more difficult and my team will look incompetent, even though they aren't.**

It's probable that the only way that challenge is going to get solved is with a sales story or analogy. Get an analogy to solve that dilemma, and not only will it be likely the decision maker will allow for a change in opinion, but will probably admire how you went about changing the opinion. Keep in mind throughout these lists that you are defining ***your*** problem in communication and persuasion—not ***theirs***. You may be referencing the decision makers problems or challenges but only as it relates to your challenge in persuasion concerning that problem. This tool is about them, but it's *for* you.

What are you attempting to do with the analogy?

Are you educating?	Informing?
Changing an opinion?	Persuading?
Creating a new opinion?	Discussing efficiency?
Seeking a commitment?	Earning trust?
Solving a problem?	Aligning new ideas?
Expressing complex variables?	Instilling new values?
Encouraging persuasion?	Transferring ethics?
Proving a logical construct?	Sharing a new vantage point?
Demo how something works?	Revealing something?
Repositioning an idea?	Explaining mechanics?
Communicating complexity?	Adjusting an ideal?
Explaining why something is/isn't?	Responding to objections?

Are they based on emotional opinions?
Are they logical but based on misunderstood/confusing processes?
Based on entrenched opinions?

Is your challenge addressing:

Time?	Performance?	Expectations?
Process?	Quality?	Reliability?
Opinion?	Customer Service?	Warranty?

Will your analogy convey a process of physics?

Volume?	Longevity?	Performance?
Tensile strength?	Capacity?	Reach or range?
Quality?	Traction?	Reliability/corrosion?

Or is your challenge related to an if/then situation, or action/reaction such as: a causal relationship between two things. Is it immediate gratification versus patience? Or is it an experience-over-time or expense that accrues?

Will your analogy communicate efficiency?

Hidden value?	ROI?	Productivity?
Labor?	Materials?	Process?
Known costs?	Time savings?	Increased capacity?

Will your analogy be idea-focused?

Belief?	Rumor?	Group knowledge?
Superstition?	Bias?	Fallacies?
Misunderstanding?	Filters?	Misconception?

Will your analogy address monetary aspects?

Hidden costs?	Training?	Raised costs?
Learning curve?	ROI?	Market fluctuation?
Expectations?	Economy?	Unseen latent value?

Step 2. Define the DMs' & KDMs' Challenge:
Using the same question matrix found in step #1, define clearly, what the analogy will actually be communicating or solving ***for them***. You will need to write in sentence format answers to the questions (those that are applicable) in step #1 that reflect your perspective and what you need as the seller. Do the same and answer them again fulfilling the ***decision makers' perspectives and needs***. There may be overlap.

Step 3. Your Goal/Desired Result:
Remember that analogies, especially short ones, are tactical. They get into the mind quickly and efficiently so that you can get back out (while the positive effects of the analogy remain) and you are then able to move on. Analogies change opinion, so what do you need the analogy to do?

Step 4. Analytical Approach to Finding a Topic:

The three most important ideation questions for analogy creation are:
1. What are you trying to accomplish?
2. What does that sound like? Not phonetically. By subject.
3. What situations, scenarios, or comparisons of things represent a parallel to what you are trying to accomplish?

Example Challenge:
Let's assume that there is a recurring challenge you face with many DMs and KDMs. It may be a situation involving a cumulative risk they face that builds over time. If the effects of the erosion of quality or performance aren't visible in their current situation, facility, or product, they may not take it seriously. Because you are experienced, you've seen this fix-and-repair scenario so you know what happens over time (erosion, degradation, increased repairs, etc.). **Without an analogy, it will be difficult to persuade them.**

The next example of ideation illuminates the thinking process (I'm "showing my work" like you did in the margins of a long division math test back in the day).

Ideation of Sample Analogy (my development notes):
Arriving at analogical concept of termites/carpenter ants—predecessor of "Sunburn at the Beach" analogy). What follows are my stream-of-consciousness as I came up with ideas to solve the "cumulative effects of neglect" problem to be solved by an analogy.
Ideas for Analogies:
Idea #1: Neglecting rust on a car? (yes, but that's visible). The cumulative neglect/corrosive/damage needs to be invisible or not visible as it's occurring.
Idea #2: Neglecting friendships—potentially weakened by the various emotional external variables. Concept is weak.

Idea #3: Dust building up inside of a computer— clogs the cooling fans, the CPU overheats, the hard drive puffs and you lose immense value? (good, but we'd have to explain the CPU fan's function). It's also not something most people are even aware of as they replace computer equipment every two years so the "fans get cleaned" via whole-replacement of the unit. Many are unaware of the liability.

Idea #4: Not shoveling intermittently during a snowstorm. You end up with four feet of snow to shovel all at once at the end of the storm? (most people do it that way so while the relevance is there, the urgency isn't accessible). Also the percentage of the population living in the snowbelt isn't inclusive of all who would receive the messaging.

Idea #5: Termites or carpenter ants eating the wood in a home? (that has promise).

Step 5. Let it Simmer and Come Back to it Later:

There's something not quite right about the ants and termites idea. It's invasive alright and the cumulative effects are devastating but it's something external intruding inward instead of "happening" due to a decision to neglect. Yes spraying for termites is preventative but do you want to be seen as a pest control service (a respectable business to be sure but maybe not a relevant association for all industries)? Very often it requires dozens of ideas to be considered. Sometimes it will feel like nothing is working (but it is working at the subconscious level in your mind). Give it time and let it simmer. Come back to it later and often fresh ideas emerge because you've been mentally working on it in the background.

Step 6. Improvement Phase:

This next analogy took that base premise of the termites and ants and built on it. I may not have come up with this next analogy had it not been for the ants/termites concept showing a "cumulative" effect of neglect. I let this simmer and the result was the next example, "Sunburn at the Beach."

Sunburn at the Beach

Sunburns are cumulative. Sun exposure from yesterday still counts toward a potential sunburn today. It doesn't seem to warrant sunblock when you have an hour here, and 45 minutes there of exposure. You're not likely going to feel the accumulated exposure to the risk of sunburn.

Once burned, that result prompts the surprised question, "How did this happen?" often followed by, "I was outside for like an hour today!" People don't often realize just how much exposure to risk they are absorbing because it's intermingled with other activities that are distracting...just like production in a facility as busy as yours. You lose track of the exposure to risk until there's a problem.

It feels very sudden but often the exposure was all trackable. It just wasn't noticed. Once your skin is burned, you're shut down and it literally stops everything you were doing until you heal. That healing is a time-based process you have to wait out. In a production or business scenario, solution time can be more expensive than preventative measures.

Now you have an analogy that everyone can relate to and it conjures up actual pain (very effective) and transposes that pain to being felt by the corporation for the neglect/oversight. The cumulative effects become associated with that feeling of being out without sunblock and knowing you're pushing your luck. Your product's result starts to feel like SPF30 protection.

Step 7. "What Does That Sound Like?" Forecasting Experiential: You're in sales and presumably creating analogies, so now everything around you becomes an inspiration, data, models, situations, and scenarios that can feed into analogical development. Pay attention and observe your surroundings everywhere you go (if even only at a low level awareness on the lookout for something that looks unique).

Stuck in traffic? Waiting at a auto lube place for an oil change to be completed? What's around you? Waiting for road construction? What machinery is being used and what is it doing? Waiting for an elevator? What's around you? Heading into a corporate building? Again, what's around you? Potted plants? Mirrored ceilings in the elevator car? Is it echoic? Is the lobby carpeted? Tiled? Reflective brass around the buttons of the elevator? You don't have to be weird about walking around someone's lobby being all overly-observant, just pay attention to what you're doing and where you are. Everything you see, hear and experience is raw material now.

Pay attention to other situations and activities you do as well for inspiration and material to commit to memory. Washing dishes? Repairing a car? See someone riding a horse off of the road out in a field? You'll notice more things and situations once you realize it's all material for analogies. Instead of always having to ask of yourself in the moment of need for an analogical comparison, "What does that sound like?" Now you can notice things and ask, "Where does that apply?" or "What challenge does this resemble?" It's a 180° flip and similar to being given an answer on a written exam and being asked which question it answers. Practicing the formulation of analogies in your off time can sharpen your skills and memory. Let's take some of those situational observations and introduce them into ideation for analogical concept creation.

The next four pages have back-to-back analogical examples:

For example, I mentioned seeing a horse in a farmer's field. Horse hair on a horse tail swats flies out of the way. That's very "farmy," but horse hair put on the bow of a violin, affords the ability for a symphony orchestra to play Mozart. This could demonstrate repurposing something or a harvest that is benign or underutilized, that has the potential to produce something extraordinary from something very rustic, rural and farmy. It's an interesting analogy because it has that element of surprise and ends with some refined sophistication of the music of Mozart.

Referencing that oil change mentioned earlier, if the technician forgets to put the drain bolt back into the underside of the oil pan before filling the engine with new oil, it will all drain out and you'll be running the engine dry. The vehicle will run for about four miles (maybe five) until the engine seizes...never to run again. That's a relationship between a small oversight and a very large price to pay for the neglected process protocols.

How many other situations are you in every day that provide a lot of material that you can collect and apply analogically? Taking note, mentally, of things requires little mental resources and can be of high value later.

Self-winding watches wind up as you swing your arm and walk. You don't think about it and it's automatic. What mechanism drives that? The relationship could be something like explaining that one action happens while concentrating on another. Or activities meant for one purpose (walking), can achieve several (winding the watch) for a result (knowing the time).

Window screens keep out bugs but let in fresh air. Off street parking is deemed expensive until the car is vandalized or damaged—there's an unseen cost involved. Baseball and softball have the same bases but very different games and very different fans. One are primarily parents and friends. The other requires stadium seating.

Scissors require one blade to move against another blade to function. That could act as a visual representing two sharp performers in an office that are somewhat in conflict. By directing the rub and tension like you would steer scissors, you could illuminate a way to get a result not possible by letting each of them work solo, conflict-free. This could be two different departments as well.

The cap on a car tire stem (where you put the air in) seems like it's to keep the air in but it's actually to keep the dirt out. The nozzle in the stem is what keeps the air in. Someone might think some part of a sale is really important but it's serving a different, and very low-priority function in the sale. That perception is hindering concentration on what would be your valve stem core of the sale.

DVDs and CDRs are the same shape and size but hold very different amounts of data. A box style fan in your home has a speed control that goes from "0" to "3" then to "2" then to "1" instead of progressive. It's non-intuitive but highly accepted. It's one of the only appliances you walk over to and turn the speed control all the way up with one click position, but you must keep turning to step down the speed. If you need a DM to get accustomed to a counterintuitive interface that becomes accepted, that's a comparative example.

You can use crayons on paper and then a water-based paint over the top and it won't stick to the crayons...meaning you could use white crayon on white paper and at a later time see what is there. That has a "reveal" component as well as a hidden message, or a concealment aspect. Something you do now is revealed later when it becomes wet or painted.

Bamboo is a long pole-like structure with individual water-tight compartments and is exceptionally strong for its weight. That might work for a compartmentalized analogy wherein something needed to be equal in strength but separate in content. Like departmental guidelines. Or a structure that needs to have its own provisions within the strength of the structure.

Fireflies fire off a sequence of light and then change direction in the dark. Probably so they avert a threat or maybe to communicate with other fireflies? The signal-and-change-directions relationship could be used to compare to vehicular traffic. Vehicles signal their intentions and then change directions the same way fireflies do. But fireflies appear to be random directions with the only predictability is that "a change in direction" is coming.

You may be thinking, "I thought analogies were serious sales tools? We're in here talking about bamboo, fans, crayons and fireflies?" If the analogous topical comparison fits, gets a point across, and you construct it with resulting relevance...the topic of the analogy doesn't matter because the topic isn't the topic—*the comparison is*. Just make sure there's a point. Ensure it's solving a real communication or persuasion problem.

Using an analogy to explain why papers in a stack need to be stapled doesn't require an analogy. If you're selling commercial copy machines, however, and there's a stapler unit to upsell that affixes to the end of the copier accessory units and they aren't interested because of the cost, well then, you may want an analogy. Comparison of doing something manually that could be automated applies there.

A state's geographic borders lock a mental affinity and loyalty directly to a point on the earth wherein across a border feelings or loyalties change even though the distance traveled is short. That could be useful analogically if you were trying to demonstrate the physical movement of something having an unintended or unexpected emotional effect like interdepartmental corporate challenges.

Fixing a loose leg on a table and stripping out the screws that were sort of holding it together before (and now do not hold at all) could illustrate a reason to wait and leave something alone until a full replacement is available. If they are considering a half measure or temporary fix instead of buying from you, something like that situation could help make a point to wait for your full replacement option.

Most office buildings have elevators and most lobbies have a table, seating, plastic plants, the big logo somewhere, etc. What if you noticed maintenance temporarily slide one of the plastic plants over in front of the elevator buttons to mop where the plant was? What could be done with that observation? The plant is now obscuring "the way up" but "the way up" still exists if you know where to look for the button. Consider how many situations you witness in just one day. What if you parked your car in a parking ramp and upon exiting your vehicle you took a look around. On your way to the elevators at either end you considered the structure and how it may apply to a future sales analogy.

Parking Ramp Security

A parking ramp has those half walls on the outer perimeter with the top half of the wall on each level open to the outside, to let exhaust fumes out. So that structure is very robust and strong but ineffective at preventing temperature changes, keeping out bugs, or insulating against sound or temperature.

Assume that you sell a computer security system and the KDM doesn't want to invest in further protecting his system. There's never been a problem and there is advanced tech support on site. The KDM

has mentioned that their current system is "structurally strong" and "their existing security will hold up for another few years."

That is true. Like a concrete parking ramp with those open exterior walls, the structure is strong and it will hold up for years. But their computer hardware system shares some things in common with that concrete parking ramp. It's open to bugs from the outside (internet) and their system won't insulate against the exterior conditions. It will be a challenge to keep out the noise and exterior threats because of the open sidewalls of their system (spam, phishing, hackers, etc.). You could use this analogy and explain that you have a "whole net" approach to cover their entire system similar to putting a net over the parking ramp. They would see your product as valuable.

After using that analogy a prospective KDM would probably change their perception. You have a product that offers whole-building-netting (your product) that keeps bugs out of the parking ramp (their system).

SALES SECRET #84:
Differentiation by Analogy

It's easy for DMs to confuse one vendor for another. An effective analogy can help you differentiate yourself from competitors. DMs will remember you as "the one with the analogies."

Step 8. "What Does That Sound Like?" Hindsight Experiential: Seeing the examples in step 7 demonstrates how seeing a situation illuminates a potential for a future analogy. You'll need to walk back through your memory and search for parallels to the problem in front of you. The questions being, "Is it easier to see scenarios and try and find a future analogical parallel application?" or, "Is it easier to identify a challenge and then search your mind for a comparable situation?" You'll obviously do both. Step 8 is looking back in memories and step 7 is projecting forward. This same approach can also help you learn **how to develop a sales story.**

STRATEGY (for Strati-Tactical #6):
A Story Is the Shortest Distance between Two Challenging Persuasive Way-Points

Your strategy for using stories is to drop your likely associative meaning with the word "story" and look at the sales story tool for what it really is. It is the shortest distance between two challenging persuasive way-points. Imagine you eliminated just chapter 2 from this book and handed the rest of it to a colleague and then asked them to integrate an "Emotive Gatekey" into their selling. Would they? Probably not because it's the story in chapter 2 that does the work.

TACTICS (for Strati-Tactical #6):
Development and Application

The tactical advantage you gain from utilizing stories literally positions your result in the minds of the decision makers. To continue the strategic thinking above, after taking out chapter 2 of this book, put whatever you want back in its place (except a story). Would anything else work better?

The Tactical Advantage of a Story: It affords you the ability to literally install whatever scenes you want into the mind of the decision maker.

Tactical Development: Most sales stories begin with the setting and/or time to put the listener into the moment. During the Renaissance era of oil painting many of the masters would call this moment the "immediate present." Your story's immediate present should feature something intriguing.

Tactical Application of the Story as a Tool: Your story can let them take a peek at their moment of pain, need, or want that is associated with the result you offer. You can also tactically position your sales story within the sales situation for delivery to pique their curiosity at a potential peak time of need.

STRATI-TACTICAL SIX

How to Develop a Sales Story

Fig 6.1
Elements of the Sales Story Illustrated

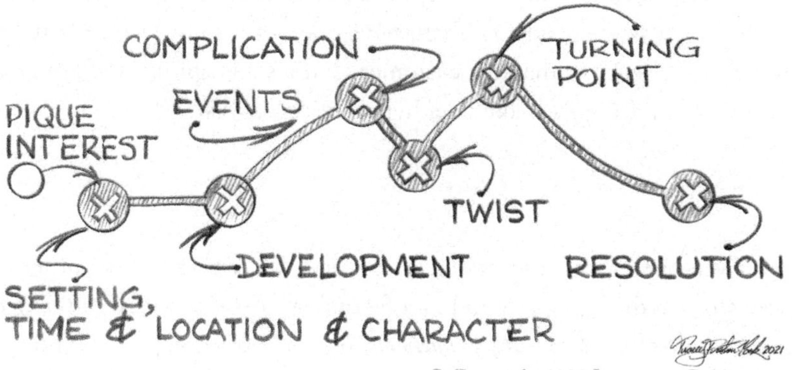

Write your story and take as many words as it takes to do it. Slug that story out in long form. It literally doesn't matter if it's thousands of words long. The first draft of the story about the Emotive Gatekey in chapter 2 was at least four times longer than it is now. You can eliminate 500 word blocks and whole paragraphs and even entire pages of text and replace them with single lines or short descriptions like, "Just as the sun was rising I found my Emotive Gatekey buried within the fine print of one of the policies." Instead of telling you about the all night work session and how brutal it all was, that one sentence implies it. The full description was in the first drafts and then was taken back out during revisions. You can't replace what isn't there, so as the author, put it in your rough draft and then take some back out later. Then you can use a sentence to *show* their mind instead of telling them.

Always remember that sales stories should usually be about them, relatable to them, or be about what's in it for them (even if the subject is you or your company, you're implying the relevance to them). If it helps explain why your company does what it does, then that's probably highly relevant. If it's just to convey the founder is a hard worker, then maybe that's not relevant or interesting.

What if you don't have a story?

You may be thinking back over your sales career history searching your mind "for a story" and whether it be a long career history or short, you see repeated situations where you try and grind out the sales close. You may (incorrectly) assume you just don't have a sales story. So what to do about the lack of a sales story? Or if you have one but it's not ideal? Or if you have an experience or that of a customer's but it's uninspiring and not great material? You can just make up a hypothetical sales story.

Really?

Yes. Everyone in sales can have a sales story. You can write a hypothetical sales story and it's just as good as a factual event-based story—***as long as you let the listener know it's hypothetical***—it's 100% acceptable (and will likely be just as effective for you). Whether writing a hypothetical story or a factual event-based story, the creation process is nearly the same with three primary differences:

1. The introduction on a hypothetical story.

2. You will be recalling facts on an event-based story, and making up the events in a hypothetical story.

3. The listener can be inserted directly into the cast as a main character when using a hypothetical story. This is a very big advantage.

You might use a hypothetical sales story when someone asks you why your product is better than a competitors—or when they just simply request a more in-depth explanation for the product's actual application or result. They may want to know what your competitive advantage is. Or they may ask how they can apply your solution in a tone that's really asking, "Why should I care about this? Why you?"

You can respond with a hypothetical sales story like this: "Let's say that you're in [the following predicament]. What you'll find you will need are [continue story here]. So your challenge in that situation is going to be...[continue on with the story]."

Or...

"Imagine a scenario where your company needs to accomplish [some want or need] and it must be shipped [this would be your product's result] the next day...[continue on with the story]."

Or...

"What you might do if your company found it needed to accomplish [some want or need], you would likely have to seek out options for...[continue on with the story]."

What offers the "disclaimer" for your hypothetical sales story being based not on fact or events but on a likely scenario that did not happen but *could* happen to them, are the words, "Let's say," or, "Imagine you are in a situation where..." or, "Suppose you're in a situation when..."

In a factual event-based sales story, you might hear an introduction that inserts the beginning of the story factually into some part of a historical scenario's timeline and either moves forward or back in time—but that date/time is included along with the introduction of the main character. This is the signal to the mind that what follows is a factual retelling of what happened.

Step 1 — Step 4.

You'll need to define your clarity of purpose, define the DMs' challenges, determine your goals and engage an analytical approach to finding your story topic. These are all found in the first four steps of Strati-Tactical #5. Strati-Tactical #4 also provided some helpful baseline information in the first phases of your work there that would apply here as well.

Step 5. The Concept or Scenario:

Similar to how a book must lay out the scene, setting, and characters in a situation that is interesting, during development you need to metaphorically sketch-in the situation that will fulfill your clarity of purpose. Will your scenario feature a corporate titan stressing about stock movements and market fluctuations? Is it a maintenance professional trying to remove gum from the carpet? That will depend on your product, result, clarity of purpose and mission. Your product solves or provides something. Create the overall scenario that will have a climax or turning point "immediate present" that can feature the apex of need or a highpoint in the value provided.

Step 6. The Elements of Your Sales Story:

Here's what will need to be included in your sales story. If you are just recalling a pleasant experience one of your other customers had, great, you don't need this because that's a testimonial. If you need a sales story (likely), then you need the following elements:

1. **Main character (MC)**
2. **Supporting character(s)**
3. **Beginning of dilemma that piques interest**
4. **Time**
5. **Setting & location**
6. **Challenges or dilemma**
7. **Events**
8. **Complications**
9. **Twist or surprise**
10. **Turning point**
11. **Resolution**

The progression of what these elements look like is illustrated in Fig 6.1.

Your story development will need to assemble the pieces into the elements of your sales story. Not the other way around. Try and avoid sitting down and writing a story from the top of a blank page (screen) down in a linear writing approach. Even then you may find the process outlined here will produce a more impactful story.

Step 7. Creating Modular Sentences from the Elements of Your Sales Story:

We will be developing modular sentences from the elements in step 6. By rephrasing them into question format you can "answer the questions" instead of "trying to write the story." Your answers don't have to be complete sentences (yet) but should be complete answers as they relate to content, occurrence, facts, etc. You need to have it all in there, you just don't need to worry about how it's written or how it sounds at this point.

Elements of Your Sales Story Rephrased as Questions:

- **Who is the main character** (MC)?
- **Who are the supporting character**(s) (only if necessary and as few as possible)?
- **How did this situation or dilemma start** (intro that piques interest)?
- **When did the story, or when would a hypothetical story, take place** (time)?
- **Where does the story take place** (setting/location)?
- **What are the challenges** (development of story/dilemma)?
- **What took place or hypothetically would occur** (events)?
- **If a complication occurred or would occur hypothetically, what happened or what would happen?**
- **Was there or would there be, a twist or surprise?**
- **What was the turning point where things improved? Why did they improve?**
- **What resolution will make a business, sales, or persuasive point?**

Answering these questions with relevant details that you know (or are hypothetically common) provides you with the basis of a story. To demonstrate the process, the sales story from chapter 10, "Stories Can Solve Industry-Wide Objections" is used in the next example.

Example Basis of a Story:

What is shown here are my development process notes.

Who is the main character (MC)?

"Alissa" is a business owner with a production company. Before she became my client, we had a long discussion about her production business challenges.

Who are the supporting characters (only if necessary and as few as possible)?

"Gary" was a key employee of Alissa's. She had other employees, some of which had been working for her for 10 to 15 years. Gary had 23 years in at her company.

How did this situation or dilemma start (intro that piques curiosity)?

A key employee of hers was in a car accident on a Sunday night and didn't report to work the following Monday morning.

When did the story, or when would a hypothetical story, take place (time)?

On the Monday morning following the Sunday car accident, Alissa became worried. It was the first time he'd ever failed to show up for work. To her recollection, Gary hadn't even called in sick at any point in 23 years of loyal employment.

Where does the story take place (setting/location)?

Within Alissa's company that relies on a production line with complex machinery that requires trained technicians to run.

What are the challenges (development of story/dilemma)?

Alissa had several challenges. She needed to replace what Gary was providing.

The second challenge was how to financially support Gary who could no longer work, but who's life was requiring full pay. Paid by Alissa. She felt obligated to continue paying him even though he wasn't able to work. After showing 23 years of loyalty to Alissa she felt she owed him.

The third struggle was how Alissa appeared to her other employees who were all watching to see how she treated a loyal employee of 23 years, who through no fault of his own, became injured. Many of them were planning on staying through to retirement. Alissa's response was potentially being scrutinized.

What took place or hypothetically would occur (events)?

Alissa was stuck in an emotionally-charged circular argument she couldn't win. She was challenged if she continued paying Gary's high salary, and looked cold and uncaring if she didn't. Many had to continue working overtime (including Alissa) to cover his shifts.

What stressors or emotions were developing for the characters?

Alissa felt obligated, guilty, stuck, frustrated, nervous, leery, self-conscious, and had regret for having touched the situation in any way. She could not see any way to not become involved. She felt stuck.

If a complication occurred (or would occur hypothetically) **what happened?**

Everyone in the company was watching how Alissa handled the Gary dilemma and transposed how she treated Gary over how they perceived she felt about them. It was a company-wide stressor. If she stopped paying Gary's bills, employees' morale would suffer. This could result in increased attrition, additional training costs for new hires and H.R. hassles. Simultaneously Alissa's product quality could suffer. If she did continue to help Gary, her other employees may respect her more but she's paying the salary of a key employee without getting any benefit of productive work. Because he was a key employee, others were also having to pick up Gary's shifts, perform unscheduled overtime and work harder to cover the labor shortage caused by the injury.

Was there, or would there be, a twist or surprise?

Learning that Alissa was actually paying all of Gary's bills, food, house payments and other expenses for family members, even though Gary was no longer reporting to work.

What was the turning point where things improved? Why?

One of my insurance products that I think of as, "paycheck insurance," would have paid Gary's expenses with cash benefits he could have used to solve his problems—that were being carried by Alissa. Every employee had experienced the effects of Gary's accident.

What resolution that makes a business, sales, or persuasive point?

My product would provide the business owners like Alissa with absolute deniability. Once the policy has been offered, the employers' responsibilities are fulfilled. Business owners would eliminate all emotional liability and protect their employee morale should anyone become injured.

Step 8. Connect the Elements into a Sequence:

Here's where you can experiment with chronology, revealing events or solutions, beginning with the problem and ending with the solution. The start of the story could even be at the apex of the challenge. Because the answers are modular, you can copy and paste them to rearrange their order.

SALES SECRET #85:
Advancing the Story

The elements must advance the story. When this happens, the listeners are engaged and you get more of their time and attention. Each sentence advances the story and buys this time for you.

Once you get the sequence the way you like it, you can then start connecting the modular sentence elements you produced in step 7. Use connecting statements that form transitions to bridge the elements.

Step 9. Write the Introduction:

Why are we doing an introduction last? If you write that first, you'll get stuck on the hardest part to write. You won't move along until you get the intro tweaked and it's unlikely you'll get the result you want until the story is written. Why? Because even if you write your introduction and then move along, writing the rest of your story will reveal ideas and angles you hadn't previously considered. These new ideas will probably inspire your introduction.

If you get stuck here, go watch the intro or first one minute of a dozen TED Talks online. Those videos, especially the actual TED (and not necessarily the TEDx speakers), will have a very impressive layout for their story and start with an absurd question that sounds impossible to prove or be true (be very careful with that if you use that approach as it requires skill to pull that off). That unique or unusual question gets attention, piques interest, and encourages participation. What it does is buys another 60 seconds of the listeners' attention. That result is what you're going for but you can engage their mind with a story that begins with a question.

Your introduction should not telegraph or ask permission to tell a story. It should not feature its onset or even contain the word "story." For example don't say, "I'll tell you a story about a customer we had about a year ago that had that same challenge..." That reduces the impact. Why? What is problematic is the "I'll tell you a story" phrasing. That's telegraphing your intentions and cues their mind to react to the "telling of a story" instead of just engaging.

A better way to start is to simply mention, "Last year another customer of ours had a similar experience." You're telling a story but not announcing or asking permission. The story (hypothetical example) would likely continue, "One of their maintenance workers locked himself outside on an overnight shift. He'd left his keys inside and was standing on the shipping dock trying to figure out what to do. It's one of the reasons that company reached out to us the next day and had our keyless entry system installed." That story could obviously be expanded out to show the frustration or fear, or perhaps a tense situation such as he'd left the water running in a mop bucket in a maintenance closet and found himself trapped outside. Obviously, if you're not using a hypothetical approach, it would have to be true. It's easy enough to make that same scenario hypothetical however by saying, "Suppose one of your maintenance professionals stepped out for a moment but forgot the door keys inside..." You then have the added advantage of dramatizing the situation for more impact.

Where will your story begin? In the middle? At the apex of the dilemma or problem most of the way through the sequence? Right at the beginning? Does it entice the listener to ask some questions or stick around mentally to see how it's resolved or how the main character got into that situation? Encourage curiosity? Will the listener stay engaged to see how your result solved an intriguing challenge? Have you tried posing a question as an introduction? Perhaps not TED Talk absurd level but an interesting question?

Let's assume your product saves time or improves efficiency. You might be tempted to start your story with, "What if I told you our product could increase efficiency by 23% annually in the following areas?" But that's annoying. It's salesy. It telegraphs that "there is a pitch coming."

A simple intro is just fine, such as, "Last year one of our customers felt the same challenges you're experiencing and they had a unique way of looking at their challenge..." That induces curiosity and piques interest.

Step 10. Revisit Your Clarity of Purpose:
Your story should probably be about the KDM or be relevant to their result, or allow them to transpose their own self into a situation where they identify with the main character. So work-in a conclusive point to the story they can relate to. Recheck your clarity of purpose and make sure your story is fulfilling your objectives.

Step 11. Revise the Length—How Long Should Your Story Be?
Once you get the content worked out you can work on length by taking out everything that doesn't advance the story or contribute. If you need additional length, you can add in missing details.

The spoken word speed for advertising is about 96 words for a 30 second ad spot or 192 words a minute. You're sort of looking at 600 words or less as an ideal story length with probably no more than 900 as a maximum. To convert your word count to spoken delivery time, see the "utility tips" in the index section in the back of this book. There you will find, "word count to time conversion."

Step 12. Critical Review:
This is the time to "see if your story hangs together." Does it? Do the elements at least closely mirror what's illustrated in Fig 6.1? Did you forget anything? Do others understand it? What are their reactions? Does your story make a business point? Seek out critical reviewers that will give you honest feedback.

Step 13. Put It on Ice:
Put the story aside for a week if possible, and then read it fresh. How does it sound? Does it work? Fresh eyes and ears can detect what you will miss when immersed in ideation and creative writing zones.

Step 14. Rewrite:
Writing involves a lot of re-writing. That's a very tough reality to accept. Many put time and effort in, and once invested you tend to defend what you've done if only to yourself. As you work your story out you may become frustrated. That's normal and it's a challenge.

Step 15. Final Test/Implementation:
Fix any issues and take your story into a lower priority account to test it on actual decision makers first. Then if you feel ready, use your story more often (where applicable). Don't ask permission...just tell it. With confidence. It's three minutes of their time. Having that confidence will help you transition to **social selling, LinkedIn, and advanced search.**

Is your product something you, yourself,
would actually buy? Try assuming the role of decision maker
(like in another market for your same product)
and go through the consideration process
with a competitor.

Pay close attention to what you're thinking,
questions you have and reservations about
the process you see from the buyer's perspective.
The chances are good you may have a similar experience
to that of the decision makers you appeal to when you are selling.
This experience will offer you valuable production support
while ideating and writing any sales story.

STRATEGY (for Strati-Tactical #7):
LinkedIn: Prospecting with Advanced Search

For many in sales, LinkedIn is synonymous with social selling. I tend to largely agree (but I engage on other platforms as well). Your strategy may be to become recognized as an industry expert. LinkedIn is a perfect platform for accomplishing that. The showcase pages, ability to include media and posts from other platforms as well as descriptive features and video makes LinkedIn a synthesizer for promotion. You'll be searching the LinkedIn database for new leads and this is where the DMs and KDMs typically are.

TACTICS (for Strati-Tactical #7):
Search, Navigator, Content, Your Showroom

Your LinkedIn profile should become a showroom that showcases those elements of the result you offer. You can feature your industry expertise and continually update content which will provide you with a tactical advantage. Using the long form blogging platform, you can write articles that will get you noticed. You can also utilize the showcase pages to feature accomplishments, media stories on your company or product, and social links to external content. LinkedIn also offers you a media platform where you can promote and hold virtual events.

LinkedIn Navigator, a paid option within the platform, will greatly assist you with advanced search functions. A prime tactical approach is to master advanced search in Navigator so you're contacting DMs and KDMs that your competitors haven't thought of accessing. You've heard of "arriving late to the sale" wherein a competitor is already established as a viable option while you play catch up? Using advanced search as a tactical advantage can keep you ahead of that competition.

STRATI-TACTICAL
SEVEN
Social Selling, LinkedIn & Advanced Search

Using LinkedIn for advanced search functions empowers you to discover leads before your competitors do. Much of the time, advanced search will provide results your competition may never find. The advanced tools, called "Boolean search" allow you to query the LinkedIn database in ways others cannot without the knowledge. Even if and when they know about this search, they still have to think of the keywords you'll be using for search functions. It's within that creative ideation (for keywords) that you can leverage a substantial advantage for yourself. This also demonstrates a concrete example that explains why "prospecting is in the mind of the seller." Because your competitors cannot read your mind, you retain your advantage indefinitely (if you're actively prospecting for yourself).

Boolean search functions access search results from the cloud of information similar to how radar illuminates aircraft for air traffic control. You can think of Boolean search almost like "cloud penetrating radar" with "the cloud" being a double entendre describing both actual clouds and the vast database within LinkedIn.

Without Boolean (cloud penetrating radar), you're relegated to using the same keywords as everyone else and that is like looking up into the sky for planes you can see with your unaided eye. This is exactly why many sellers are "coming late to the sale" where other sellers are already established. Everyone is just going for the same planes they can see between the clouds. Boolean's cloud penetrating radar advantages are based, in part, on your understanding of the functions and how keyword tiers works.

Keyword Tiers:

Searches in LinkedIn for new leads using advanced search in Navigator operate on keywords and phrases that you think of to most closely match who it is you are looking to find and/or connect with. The keywords and phrases search for DMs by region, industry, job description, job title and their position in a company. The most commonly used (or thought of) keywords that everyone is using to find these DMs are what are called "first tier" keywords. The more detailed and specific keywords and phrases describing the same criteria would be second tier keywords. The difference between first and second tier keywords being the specificity (and likelihood of) being used to describe that person's position, job, industry, etc. The most specific keywords (and least likely to be used by your competitors) would be the third tier keywords. Together these three tiers of keywords can describe and find nearly anyone in LinkedIn.

Most people think of "keywords" as meaning "the main ones" in a list. But that's not what the term means. The term literally means what it says, "words-that-function-like-keys." Keywords open secret doors others can't access without the same keywords. The keywords you use produce lists, contacts and leads.

So a seller who provides a productivity improvement software package like an ERP system for supply chain management would need to reach out to those in production, I.T., business administration and several C-suite executive positions. These might be the CFO, COO, and CEO along with newly created positions in the 2020s and 2030s in RevOps, SalesOps, ProductionOps, etc.

Provided a seller conducting the searches has gained enough traction in social selling to pass through whatever gatekeeping and vetting a decision maker has set forth, the chances of gaining a commitment for a first meeting increase substantially using Boolean. This is because as you move from first tier to second tier and on to third tier keywords you aren't calling upon the same decision makers your competitors are [*see also the "1990 phone book dilemma" in chapter 25*].

Gaining control over your search proficiency can reduce rejection rates, improve engagement, and garner results not possible with the obvious search approaches you might take with the standard free and default search bar. Advanced search in Navigator will work supremely well and provide more impressive leads if you match it with advanced skills. Obviously if you aren't engaging the leads with effective email, inmail, phone and cold outreach methods, the quality of those leads will be masked by the ineffective approaches taken. So it's important not to burn your premium leads coming from advanced search with "me too" email and inmail.

A quick sidebar on that before moving on. Inmail should not be underestimated. It's perhaps one of the last communication channels left (almost) unspoiled by a spammy takeover by reppy reps in our industry. That's because you have a limited number of inmails available until you buy more/subscribe to higher membership levels. Conversely, the LinkedIn inmail is an almost magical tool as most of the time inmails get opened and read. Combined with stellar searching skills, which we're talking about next, you can give yourself a serious boost.

Examples of Keyword Tiers:

Let's assume you're selling a difficult and involved product with a longer sales cycle in complex B2B settings. The product will be a cloud-based ERP system and we would be interested in finding decision makers who are in lean manufacturing and/or Six Sigma (perhaps black belts in Six Sigma).

As you may know, with enterprise resource planning software (an ERP system) every single department in a corporation is affected by the purchase. It's unlikely that you're going to get that sale closed without the inclusion of departmental decision influencers (DIs) and probably more than a few deal-killers will get involved. That scenario is perfect for advanced search using Navigator in LinkedIn. You may need to find decision makers or influencers in multiple levels of a corporation. The more time you spend in first tier keyword searches, the more competition you'll encounter (others in sales approaching the same prospects). You should still conduct the first tier keyword searches, and you may get new ideas for more specific keywords. It's also obvious that if a good lead comes up in a first tier keyword search you should always process the lead. We're discussing a mindset and approach that may prefer second and third tier keywords.

First Tier Keyword Search Theory and Application:

Most sellers would be thinking of the obvious first tier keywords to search for leads while selling an ERP system such as:

- Supply chain manager
- Vice president of production
- VP of business administration
- Chief executive officer production company
- Production
- I.T. director
- ERP technician
- Enterprise resource planning coordinator
- Productivity manager

Also in that list above would likely be departmental manager titles, etc. Using those terms isn't necessarily the worst idea, but combining them with something more specific or using terms that have more specificity would mean the seller searching in LinkedIn might be using second tier keywords.

Second Tier Keywords:

- Vice president strategy and architecture
- Change control supervisor + [industry]
- CEO collaborative team efficiency synergy
- Six Sigma
- Lean manufacturing
- Efficiency team
- Lean Six Sigma
- Maximized productivity
- Profitability through efficiency
- ERP enterprise resource planning

These terms are mock queries of the LinkedIn database by a sales professional seeking leads from within the manufacturing industry. *Your* search terms would reflect *your* industry. The literal terms being discussed here are irrelevant to you. The process is being demonstrated so you can see how the keywords become more specific in each tier. "Manufacturing" is just the example industry.

Third Tier Keywords Might Include:

- **DMAIC** (the acronym that stands for **D**efine, **M**easure, **A**nalyze, **Im**prove, **C**ontrol)
- **DMADV** (the acronym that stands for **D**efine, **M**easure, **A**nalyze, **D**esign, **V**erify)
- **DOWNTIME** (the acronym that stands for **D**efects, **O**ver-production, **W**aiting, **N**ot utilizing talent, **T**ransportation, **I**nventory excess, **M**otion waste, **E**xcess processing)
- Outdated legacy system Six Sigma ERP
- Lean manufacturing eliminating eight kinds of waste
- ERP supply chain efficiency specialist
  enterprise resource program for [insert industry]
- Six Sigma black belt
- COO Six Sigma
- Lean manufacturing expert
- CFO lean manufacturing
- Supply chain [insert industry]

What those results will be showing you are different levels of professionals' profiles in LinkedIn with job positions, titles, experience in, or interest in that industry.

SALES SECRET #86:
Paid Membership on LinkedIn Is Worth It

Until you upgrade to a membership level in LinkedIn, the number of free searches you can conduct is limited. You also DO NOT have access to Navigator and the advanced search approaches being discussed here without a purchased upgrade (I recommend buying the upgrade).

Revisions Based on Your Wall of Wisdom:

You can take your dossier that you either reference or directly post on your W.O.W. describing the ideal candidates for your product and enter their interests into the advanced search in Navigator. Your W.O.W. is data. You're the processor and interpreter and Navigator is the cloud penetrating radar that lets you see the picture of the database that your then-current ideas are generating. So what that means is the advanced search function works for you and is available 24/7/365. By continually revising and refining your queries and interrogative skills interacting with a database will continually improve the quality of the results.

Boolean Search Functions:

Boolean search functions within LinkedIn (especially searches within Navigator) are advanced approaches to searching for leads that can empower you to access the LinkedIn database in a different way. Boolean works by using modifiers (a word or symbol that performs a function) to accompany your keyword searches. The 2nd and 3rd tier keyword searches are going to produce nice results and can be expanded further by using Boolean.

Boolean Search Exclusion Ability

What if you wanted to search a geographic area that happened to include a collegiate-dominated metro area with a tech school? If you search for "Six Sigma lean manufacturing" you might receive results that include college students studying for a manufacturing engineering degree who've included your keywords as a minor, area of interest, future career, etc. To exclude all students then and focus only on decision makers, you could use the Boolean function of "NOT" (all caps). **It would look like this:**
"Six Sigma lean manufacturing NOT student of."

There are five basic Boolean search modifiers of your search query. You would type these into the search bar in conjunction with your search terms (keywords) to modify the results you get. The five modifiers are:

Quotes: **" "** (*the literal use of quotation marks*)
NOT (*the actual word "NOT"*)
AND (*the actual word "AND"*)
OR (*the actual word "OR"*)
Parenthesis: **( )** (*the literal use of parenthetical symbols*)

The functions that correlate with the modifiers are:

" " This provides results of profiles that only include an exact phrase. For example **"ERP supply chain efficiency."** Instead of returning results for profiles that include "efficiency" as well as others that don't include "efficiency" but do include "ERP" using the quotes will prevent that and return only those profiles with an exact match to what's in quotations.

NOT Type this before any term or phrase you don't want to be considered for query results [*see example on facing page*].

AND Use this term for search results that include all of the terms you would normally include in a list. For example, **"Six Sigma AND lean manufacturing AND supervisor"** This provides you with the ability to search for profiles that ***must*** contain all three. This would allow you to see middle managers within lean manufacturing environments and would be potentially good decision influencers for you (middle-up strategy for prospecting).

OR Use this to include a list of terms like company names or cities or any other information that might normally be tabled or listed. For example, **"Six Sigma OR lean manufacturing OR change control supervisor."**

( ) Parenthesis allow you to conduct more complex searches. For example a search that excludes some portion of an industry. Essentially you need to perform two functions from the above Boolean search options at the same time. For example, DMAIC and DMADV and DOWNTIME are all within lean manufacturing but you want to find those profiles with just **DMADV.** Your search would be: **DMADV NOT (DMAIC OR DOWNTIME)** Both the "NOT" and the "OR" Boolean functions are being used simultaneously for a compound/complex search.

Once you've gained query results and have a prospecting list, it's time to then figure out how to connect with them. You can do that by sending a connection request, or reaching out to them via inmail. Because reaching out involves the risk of rejection, you may encounter one of the **twelve frequently heard objections.**

STRATEGY (for Strati-Tactical #8): **Objection Preparation**

Debate teams, political debate events and highly effective leaders all prepare for discourse and communication situations by practicing. They know that their endeavor will involve others with differing opinions and in order to communicate with those people, preparation is required. You must know what those differing opinions are. You must know their intensity (are they entrenched or just lightly held opinions?). **You should know who it is you will be talking with. Much of that is your whole purpose in sales—to "change opinion" that affects a "change-decision."**

Our strategy is to help decision makers change from what they have been doing, using, and buying, to what we offer as a new result (or purchase our result again). **Your strategy is to be a consultative guide and prevent and/or respond to objections with tools, skills, your mindset, knowledge, preparation and practice, etc.**

TACTICS (for Strati-Tactical #8): **Anticipate and Develop Effective Responses**

Your tactical strategy should be to anticipate those elements of the conversation possible to know beforehand and come up with an effective response. For that which cannot be known prior to a sales situation, you should develop a question strategy for discovery. If leaders in the communication and sales fields all have strategies that involve practice, research, preparation and anticipation, so should ours.

STRATI-TACTICAL EIGHT

Twelve Frequently Heard Objections

There are literally hundreds of sales objections that you may encounter. What follows are twelve of the objections you're most likely to receive organized into four categories which are:

1. "The Go Objection."
2. "Now is not the right time. Come back next week/quarter/summer."
3. "Send me some information or an email."

4. "I don't think this is anything we need right now."
5. "I don't understand or see the value."
6. "I can let the other decision makers know what it is we've talked about here."

7. "I need to talk to so-and-so first."
8. "It's not in this year's budget."
9. "Your competition has the exact same solution" (commoditization).

10. "Your price is too high."
11. "I need to think about it."
12. "I'm just not interested at this time."

You will find that many of these objections can and will be received at times that differ from what is denoted, but often if you do receive them, they will probably be in a category from the list above. We will explore each of the objections in the list (except for those which are covered extensively elsewhere in this book). What follows is a discussion that includes the objection, cause, and an effective response. Some objections will also have a few thoughts on typical mistakes or misfocused advice.

PROSPECTING OBJECTIONS:

1. "The Go Objection."
[*see chapter 20*]

---

2. "Now is not the right time. Come back next week/quarter/summer."

They may also say, "I'll take your [business] card/email/phone number and keep it here in case I have any questions," (they probably won't) or, "We're connected on LinkedIn and I have your email, I'll drop you a message when it's a better time."

Cause of objection:

The DMs and KDM don't care, or your result hasn't been revealed, or you aren't a priority. They may not be engaged mentally. Whatever curiosity you piqued initially has chilled. There's no sense of urgency. They likely don't see a need, believe the consequences or rewards for having the result, or feel there will be a net gain for them at that time.

Effective objection response:

If this objection is received during a sales situation, then reschedule when you can. At minimum, always ask for another meeting. If the DM throws cold water on that, then the objection may be a logical objection concealing an emotional one [*see also chapter 17*]. Switch to asking them a question about their decision making process (so that you "may return at their discretion, more prepared"). See if you can work in an open-ended discovery question to find out what emotional apprehensions may exist or what their true thinking is. Often just listening to them solves a lot. If you do uncover a reason for their decision to wait, either respect that, or if it's fixable, attend to the reason if you can.

You can also respond to their, "now is not the right time" objection with a softly-delivered, "What are you thinking may work better for you?" They may do the whole, "I dunno, we'll be in touch" or "We'll let you know" or "When I know, you'll know." They may also just tell you what they're thinking. Try and look at this objection systemically from a career-wide perspective and seek out the causation if you hear it often. You can also ask DMs and KDMs that trust you, why they elected to wait, or go a different direction, use another vendor or put off a buying decision all together (i.e., if you've received a definitive "no" and only if they actually trust you—and you feel it's appropriate to ask). You may get an answer that surprises you.

Ask for a referral, introduction, reference, or recommendation on where to find more companies, similar to theirs, to assist with the result you are selling.

---

3. "Send me some information or an email."

The decision maker is saying "no" in a neutral way.

Cause of objection:

Whomever is disengaged right in front of you, listening to you in the moment where you are fully available for any questions or thoughts...who then claims they will later become engaged and interested from an email, a stack of brochures, or some general information—is actually telling you "no."

Typical misfocused advice:

The oft-suggested work-around may come in the form of discovery questions such as: "I'd be more than happy to send you information in an email. May I have your email address?" The DM expects this and will willingly give that to you. The misfocused advice then suggests, "I have hundreds of pages of material. So that I can send you the most relevant information, could you tell me what it is you'd like to see in the email?" And so the conversation goes...and it goes swimmingly, leading the seller to feel like they've really done something productive when in fact the sales professional has accepted the most humane form of "no."

SALES SECRET #87:
It Is Retrogressing, Not Progressing

If a decision maker enthusiastically suggests you "shoot something over to them" in email as a way to proceed, that isn't progress. That's retrogressive. It's converting a real time discussion over to an email spam-filter-dodging-exercise.

Effective objection response:

This objection is very often received while prospecting or sometimes during a first meeting. They don't often know what it is they are saying "no" to. They aren't engaging and don't see your result as a priority, probably because they don't see your result.

Would an Emotive Gatekey initially increase their engagement level? Can you use a story to make an emotional impression? Can you work your 3MCP into the initial engagement (before you receive the "shoot me something in email" objection)?

The sharper your tooling and greater your experience, the more effective *future sales* situations will be.

OBJECTIONS RECEIVED DURING FIRST MEETING

4. "I don't think this is anything we need right now."

[*see chapters 13, 14, and 21*]

Their current situation may work for them but at what cost? What price will they pay? Remember, you can sell them their downstream costs and their return on investment. When a company is losing money, the more they sell, the more they lose. Even when a cost they are paying is less than the purchase price of your result, their current cost is a loss—your result is an investment. If capital is going to leave their building, should it leave in the form of a loss or leave in the form of an investment that will come back in the form of profit or cost savings? Their purchase price with you is an investment that has an associated ROI.

---

5. "I don't understand or see the value."

[*see chapters 13, 14, and 17*]

Chapter 17 has a good approach to asking your way out of the weeds. As a sidenote, this objection (and all of the objections in this Strati-Tactical) can be included on your Wall of Wisdom.

---

6. "I can let the other decision makers know what it is we've talked about here."

This is essentially, "I'll re-present your product to others and do your job as well as you can (some think, even better than you)." This is one of the least fun objections to have to respond to because it emanates from their ego. They are essentially insisting they are as good at discussing your product as you are.

SALES SECRET #88:
Present a Few Questions They Can Expect

A DM who insists on re-presenting what you've shared with them, with another DM who wasn't in attendance (doing your job in your absence) **may think again after you prepare them with a few answers to typical questions they will receive that they don't know the answers to. The subtext there is powerful.**

The decision maker proposing to re-present the result you are selling (do your job for you) may be highly intelligent and skilled, but they haven't invested the time and don't have the product knowledge you have.

Effective objection response:

Agreement works well along with "assisting them" with some quick preparatory material they can take along. Here's where you pull out some technical material requiring an explanation of some component like a regulation, compliance issue, physics aspect or compatibility component. Done in a very helpful way, you will probably hear the DM say, "You know, maybe it would be best for you to just explain it." I discourage "tech talk" with DMs until the right time, but this may just be the right time. If you didn't need to know it, you wouldn't know it. They don't know it. So they should if they're going to insist on doing your job.

OVERALL SALES OBJECTIONS

7. "I need to talk to so-and-so first."

This is what I call a GDM or a "genie decision maker." They pop up out of nowhere and all of a sudden are somehow pivotal to the decision, yet have attended no meetings and are nearly uninformed.

Cause of objection:

You can't always prevent or anticipate the GDM because KDMs aren't always forthright about who's really making the decisions. If you earn trust, they may tell you beforehand and give you some notice that "Their [spouse/partner/investor/lawyer/etc.] will need to take a look at the proposal" before they can sign.

Effective objection response:
Try and ask them some variant of "Besides yourself, who else may want to be involved in a decision like this?" Then ask if they can invite those other decision makers to the next sales situation. If not, gently ask if you can meet with the others briefly to bring them up to speed. They may likely say, "I can brief them on what we've talked about here," which is a new objection. See objection #6. As outlined in objection #6, technical information may be your friend here.

---

8. "It's not in this year's budget."
A way you can sell the idea of budget inclusion is similar to selling full price.
Cause of objection:
As with most objections, this is another form of "no." There are multiple modes this objection resides within. Is it not to be included in any budget? Is your result wanted and needed, and will be in next year's budget? Has the result even been suggested at the budgetary level discussions? Is it assumed it won't be approved? Who is assuming that? Does that mean you aren't actually talking to a KDM and are hearing this from a DM that doesn't want to expend the political negotiation chips required for inclusion? Could it be that the person saying this may not have authorization to approve investments of the size your result requires? When you determine which of those (or other reasons) are contributors, you'll be better able to respond.
Effective objection response:
There are costs associated with not buying and/or paying for the alternative to a solution and result...their answer of not buying could be a bandage strategy. Budgets are obstacles to progress sometimes, but if a company really does want to get something accomplished, budgets manifest like a GDM (genie decision maker). In the case of the budget, a "good" genie

can manifest.

If you are up against an implacable budget wall, then you may have to address the sale as if it were a longer-cycle sale and get into the budgeting process. Which will mean you are going to have more moving pieces, middle managers, inter-departmental dynamics, internal power struggles, and pressures on your sale that have nothing to do with your product, solution, or result. The likelihood of a GDM appearing is much higher. Internal champions, and decision influencers are going to be very helpful.

It's also highly recommended that you engage in relationship selling so that your mutual respect will transcend the budgeting cycle. Ensure you are genuine and truly try to help them form the construct needed for a requisition to include on the next budget. Remember, to get a budgeted item added, they will have to rationalize the investment and it will be the sales professional's job to provide that sales support. Work out the downstream numbers (costs, ROI, savings, etc.) of your result discussed in chapter 21.

---

9. "Your competition has the exact same solution" (commoditization).
Cause of objection:
The sales professional hasn't tied their own value and worth to the sales situation and buying experience. The implication is that the competitor not only has the same available solution, but for less. Often your competitors are told the exact same thing about you and the KDM may be fishing for a discount. So ask yourself if the KDM can't see the difference, or you haven't shown them the difference. This objection is a clear indicator that the component sale you're jammed up on is the Emotional Sale. Why? Because when they want your result, they find all of the logical reasons to rationalize that. When they don't, they find all of the logical reasons to object. That's what you're probably receiving.
Effective objection response:
Do your competitors have a sales story? Differentiation by professionalism? Do they work as hard as you? Are they truly as knowledgeable as you? Sales isn't just the product, it's the total value received and net worth realized. You're a big part of that value. The net worth of the sale is important and

will help you avoid being commoditized (often the attempt of this objection). Section 4 discusses the value worth their time, and active listening in chapter 18 sets you apart from most in sales that prefer to talk. When you listen you hear the differences they are seeking—you may also see what your competitors all missed. A missed challenge or potential result that they didn't see, but you do, differentiates. Asking, "What would you really like to see done differently in your future relationship with your next ______________ provider?" will provide you with a framework for what to build your approach around. Asking what they *did* like about their last solutions provider dials into what is important to them.

CLOSING OBJECTIONS:

10. "Your price is too high."
[*see chapter 21*]

11. "I need to think about it."
You may also hear, "Rome wasn't built in a day. I just need some time to go through all of this. It's a lot to take in all at once."

Cause of objection:
The human mind doesn't usually engage high value decisions with spontaneity. The impulsive personality types that do act in a spontaneous buying manner also have a long, memorable track record of buyers' remorse to remind them that "thinking about it" is wise. They also typically have surrounded themselves with others not prone to impulsivity.

The situation and timing where the objection is advanced matters and will determine what you should probably do or not do, more than most other variables being considered. One of the component sales could be either leaking or wasn't closed. This was the theme of chapter 17 which landed my sale in the weeds.

Effective objection response:
Often, "thinking about it" is absolutely part of the consideration process of buying. Trying to counter this can work but the best advice is to really nail your sales situations and have confidence that the persuasive work you did on the run up to the sales close was solid. "I need to think about it" does

not equate to "no." What you do before they think about it *is* often "what you do about it." Have you ever thought about work while at home? On the weekend? In down time? What do you think about? Challenges left unsolved, right? So are the decision makers. If you have solid tools, a great approach, have done the work, and what you did was impressive—thinking about buying is part of buying.

Mistakes sellers often make:

Avoid a "hard sell" to "get it closed before they think too long." You'll likely damage your sale with a hard sell or pressure.

---

12. "I'm just not interested at this time."

Cause of objection:

This is a temporal-based objection and so it's illuminating their priorities. That means a sense of urgency or need hasn't been revealed to them (or theirs, to you).

Effective objection response:

You need to find out if this is a hidden emotional objection posing as a temporal one, or if it's being deemed to be actually, "not the right time." Try asking open-ended questions ***with their objection inserted right directly back into your response question;*** e.g., "I'm just not interested at this time." You could ask, "What are some of the criteria for determining the timing of decisions like this one?" or "Does your division coordinate the timing for replacements like [insert your result] with other events? (If so) What events?" or "What time of the year do you typically consider these types of investments?"

Listen closely to the answers as they will likely start talking about process—that's what you're looking for (add the answers to your Wall of Wisdom). You can learn about priorities and then assemble and position your result alongside downstream costs they may incur by not buying. You may also align your result with savings, efficiency, productivity, etc., (laid out in chapter 21. Chapters 13 and 14 will also help). Working through these objections will assist you in creating **messaging for voicemail.**

STRATEGY (for Strati-Tactical #9):
Objection Preparation

The most common reasons to leave a voicemail (VM) in B2B sales is to receive a call back from a prospective decision maker. You may also leave a message so that when you do connect in the future, you already feel a bit familiar to the decision maker (or so they'll take a future call). A third strategy could be as a cross-marketing approach for brand awareness, name recognition, or to coordinate with a product or social account promotion. The strategy you will use most often, however, is to get a decision maker to call you back.

TACTICS (for Strati-Tactical #9):
Voicemail as a Radio Spot

Your tactical approach to get a call back should be to develop your sales messages for voicemail around the goal of piquing the curiosity of the decision maker. You can do this by inclusion of some element (but not your whole product benefits list) that conveys something mildly intriguing so they'll want to know more. If you leave some parts out, that may encourage curiosity to form.

If you don't have that, or cannot think of anything intriguing, the next best approach is to simply tell them some of what you have to offer if they commit to a scheduled, first phone conversation. Being nice, as commendable as that is, will probably not work when deployed as a stand-alone strategy (but it's a phenomenal and obvious sales support tool).

STRATI-TACTICAL NINE

Messaging for Voicemail

You should avoid trying to sell your product on the message you leave on voicemail. Instead remember to employ tactical way-point thinking. What is your product? Your "mini sale"? Whatever (ethically) is going to get a return phone call. Sell that. Sell them a reason to call you back. When leaving voicemail, think of your actual product (what you're eventually selling financially) as sales support to your real time product (which is the call back). It's the call back commitment you seek. When you speak about product features or outcomes, it should only be done as sales support to persuade them to call you back or accept your future call.

To pique curiosity in the message you can use something like an "I have an idea for you" approach. What this does is makes the DM wonder what it is you've got. What did you notice? What do you know? Is it worth calling you back to find out? When you get these questions posed in their minds, that is the opposite of standardized thoughts of deletion by default.

UTILIZING:
PIQUED CURIOSITY &
PERSONAL
CONNECTION

Fig 9.1:
General Example Message for Voicemail
Tactical Approach: "I have an idea for you"
Example Industry: commercial efficiency

"Hello Kevin. This is [first name, last name of seller] **with Fictitious Company Corp. After** [reading your website]**, I have an idea for you on how to** [insert idea of value related to your industry]**. My professional focus is** [(*for example*) in corporate efficiency]**. I can share this idea with you in less than three minutes. I'm at 555.555.1234. You can also text me at that number which is again, 555.555.1234."**

54 words (not including parentheticals) with a 17 second delivery time (plus phone #s).

The value you insert within the second set of brackets could be anything relevant to your engagement with their company. You:

- saw their ads.
- watched their company video.
- saw a speech their CEO made.
- met their tech person at a trade show, etc.

The third set of brackets are what you can do to:

- save them money.
- save them time.
- make something more efficient.
- improve their effectiveness in some way.
- improve their experience in some way.

It doesn't need to be epic, it just needs to be solid and hold value worth their time. The fourth set of brackets would be something featuring your area of expertise.

UTILIZING:
PIQUED CURIOSITY
USING A SCENARIO

Fig 9.2:
Example Message for Voicemail
Tactical Approach: "I have an idea for you"
Example Industry: recycling & corporate document destruction

"Hello Kevin. This is [first name, last name of seller] **with Fictitious Secure Recycling Corp. You may have seen our armored trucks out on the roads. We transport sensitive corporate documents slated for destruction the same way banks transfer cash between banks. It's how we get your documents to our shredder. While reading your website, an idea came to me for your company that I'd like to share with you. I'm at 555.555.1234. You can also text me at that number which is again, 555.555.1234."**

72 words (not including parentheticals) with a 23 second delivery time (plus phone #s).

In Fig 9.2, the utilization of the armored trucks imagery produces a customized feeling, but affords you a wide application of the messaging; e.g., you can say that to everyone. It's talking about yourself but the content and message are pointing at the decision makers' documentation. Even better, the use of the armored truck in the scenario also implies that documentation not yet destroyed is valuable in the wrong hands and thus is a liability. You can convey that without using a single word within the message to say it. Obviously this angle would have to be true and accurate. There is likely a special angle within your company that is unique that can be positioned in a similar way. If not, you may be seeking to find or discover this in your development of your Emotive Gatekey, in which case you can then open this Strati-Tactical and generate new messaging.

Just make sure you actually have a couple of good ideas about the result you offer and you've read something on their website. Stay honest. Actually do what you said you did or will do.

SALES SECRET #89:
Storing and Tracking Prerecorded Voicemail Messages

Using various services, plug ins, and/or apps, you can store prerecorded messages within various sales enablement software. You can then deliver the messaging directly and track which messages you've used, for which prospects, and monitor the performance of your messages. You will be able to track which messages resulted in call backs and which messages are underperforming.

You can use light humor in sales situations but you need to have the right personality type to pull it off. There is some inherent risk involved especially with unidirectional voicemail where you will have no feedback. You can't stop if the attempt isn't being received well. If you aren't able to tell a joke (or you hear a funny joke but when you repeat it, few people laugh), then this next approach may not be for you.

In Strati-Tactical #10, the N.E.D.A. development process is laid out in step-by-step format to help you build either voicemail messaging like you see here or the cold call messaging featured there. This Strati-Tactical (#9) is primarily examples of messaging and the next Strati-Tactical (#10) is primarily a how-to exercise. You can adopt voicemail messaging to cold calling. With a little work, you can also modify cold outreach messaging to work on voicemail.

UTILIZING: HUMOR & CURIOSITY

Fig 9.3:
Example Message for Voicemail
Tactical Approach: mild humor
Example Industry: commercial facilities support & supplies

"Hello Ms. Thoreson (head buyer in purchasing)**. This is** [first name, last name of seller] **from Fictitious Industrial Supply Corp. You know those demo people at trade shows that demonstrate all of those cool kitchen gizmos? I'm not quite that fun, but almost, and I'd like to stop out and demonstrate a new cleaning product that just came off of our production line. Even if you already have a supplier, this might be a fun three minutes for you and anyone in your department. I'm at 555.555.1234. You can also text me at that number which is, again, 555.555.1234."**

78 words (not including parentheticals)
with a 24 second delivery time (plus phone #)

You can eliminate the humor and simply insert "The reason for my call is," and place that directly before "I'd like to stop out and demonstrate..." This would also work nicely without the humor.

UTILIZING: INFORMATIVE & CURIOSITY

Fig 9.4:
Example Message for Voicemail
Tactical Approach: follow-up call attempt #1 (second call/ first follow-up)
Example Industry: industrial supplies

"Hello again Ms. Thoreson. This is [first name, last name of seller] **from Fictitious Industrial Supply. I now have a three-minute long virtual demonstration set up for you online. I'll send you an email with a link. You can respond to that email or I'm at 555.555.1234. You can also text me at that number which is again, 555.555.1234."**

54 words (not including parentheticals)
with a 17 second delivery time (plus phone #)

By putting the "again" adjacent to the greeting, you take it out of the pestering and nagging context and place it in the friendly zone with a mild undercurrent of "It's nice to speak with you again." Move it to after your name to hear the difference. "**This is** [first name, last name of seller] **again from Fictitious Industrial Supply Corp....**" Hear how that sounds a little on the naggy side? Even in a bright fresh voice, the syntax places meaning on the second call (the fact that you're "calling again") whereas the former approach places it on the greeting.

Depending on your industry, calling once or twice a week is probably sufficient (same with email). Some advisement out there recommends you call daily. That may be excessive and "pushy."

UTILIZING: INFORMATIVE & CURIOSITY

Fig 9.5:
Example Message for Voicemail
Tactical Approach: follow-up call attempt #2 (third call in total, 2nd follow-up)
Example Industry: industrial supplies

"Hello again Ms. Thoreson. This is [first name, last name of seller] **from Fictitious Industrial Supply. I left you a message last week and sent an email with a link. The reason I'm calling is to let you know I've sent you a new link to a 30 second preview of my online video. You can respond to that email or I'm at 555.555.1234. You can also text me at that number."**

67 words (not including parentheticals) with a 21 second delivery time (plus phone #).

By adding one small component, you get a whole new voicemail. By the third attempt you can reconstruct much of what you've already said in former messages by changing the order of the sentences (but don't be apprehensive about developing new messaging). As you develop messages, they should go on your W.O.W. for review and future use. You can develop messages that sound personalized but have a broad application to an entire sector or sub-section of your lists (industry). When you add even more specificity (customization) to your general messages, that will increase effectiveness for prime accounts you are seeking.

SALES SECRET #90: Offer the Option to Text You Back

Always let people know you can accept text messages (if that's true) **at the number you are leaving. You'll increase your engagement ratio simply because many DMs are less apprehensive to text. For some in business, a phone call can feel almost like a commitment. Texts don't. Texts can be read, ignored, deleted, etc. so the power is returned to the DM.**

You can actually start to build a sort of dialogical story as you add to the messages on your weekly follow-up calls. Make it *all* about them. Sellers sometimes use the phrase "Do me a favor and..." followed by some action to take. While it's important to have a "call-to-action," phrasing it as a favor sets the mind up to perceive you as entitled. The question to ask yourself is, "Why should a busy decision maker do *me* a favor?" Often the request is within the context of a DM not returning sales message #2 that you've left or message #3, or #16, etc. A form of self defeat is, "Do me a favor and let me know one way or the other if you're not interested so I don't have to keep bothering you." You're communicating that you're fatigued and you're trying to protect your own time. Never show how you feel about the process because it's solely an experience for them. Not us. The differences may be subtle but the effects are highly visible.

To drive this point home, that it's about them and needs to be an experience for them (and you should pique their curiosity), let's demonstrate this for ***your*** own mind. Imagine that you hear the next message example left on your personal phone.

SALES SECRET #91: Say Your Phone Number Clearly and Slowly (but not too slowly)

It's also a good idea to say it twice. Remember, they are writing it down if it's not a cell phone that captures the number. If you make them repeat listening to the message, that is annoying. You risk deletion. Going too slow is just as annoying so just speak clearly.

UTILIZING:
THE IMAGINATION
TO PIQUE CURIOSITY

Fig 9.6:
Example Message for B2C Sales Left on Your Personal Voicemail
Tactical Approach: a simple question
Example Industry: travel agency services

"Hi [your name]**. Just wondering if you've ever seen Niagara Falls or the ruins of Greece? This is 'Sandy Jorgenson' with XYZ Travel, and I'd like to hear about what destination you've always wanted to see. I might be able to help you get there. I'm at 555.555.1234. You can also text me at that number which is again, 555.555.1234."**

47 words with a 14 second delivery time
(*not including the phone #*)

What did you see in that message? You saw scenes didn't you? Your ideal destination. A few key mental images of the location. Next you recalled the reason you haven't gone yet. Then you justified the failure to go with the logical reasons you outlined prior to this point. Then you saw the long lines, airports, confusion booking to a foreign or far off land...and then a resolution that "you'll still get there someday." But then you hear your mind whisper, "What if...?" Would it really hurt to just play around with a "What if"? What if the agent *could* do something? The message was about you.

That's a very different mental track than what you thought about while listening to the many standard messages you've personally deleted over the years. Those messages were salesy and were all about the seller. Fig. 9.6 is all about you. ***Do you feel the difference?***

Voicemail Diction/Transcription Services
Some corporations use voicemail diction services to convert their voicemail messages to text and then those messages are then sent to decision makers' email accounts or as a text message to their smart phone. Decision makers can often just touch the number you spoke (which was converted to text) **to dial you back. Make sure you speak clearly and avoid rushing** (or the number won't translate to text).

Fig 9.7:
Example General B2B with Specialized Skills
Tactical Approach: stressors on their desk
Example Industry: corporate

"Hello [Mr. Collyard]**. This is** [seller's first and last name] **from Fictional Corp. You're busy and likely have an industrial sized pile of work on your desk—which is why I'm calling. My background is in** [industrial efficiency processes, Six Sigma and lean manufacturing]**, I have a process you might want to take a look at that can take work right off of your desk. Efficiently. I'm even efficient in my communication so you can expect it to only require three minutes when you call back. I'm at 555.555.1234. You can also text me at that number which is again, 555.555.1234."**

85 words (without the phone number) with a 26 second delivery time.

Fig 9.7 isn't epic but it's engaging, different, relevant and piques curiosity because it gets the DM thinking about "what they were already thinking about." The real "twist" on that message is it's not a distraction and lets them get right back to work doing what they were already doing (working on the pile on their desk). The new development being, they have a sales professional's offer roaming around in their mind as they assess and reassess the pile of work. All while thinking, "*Why wouldn't I want to at least see if they have a way of reducing this? It's three minutes. I'll spend longer than that waiting for the copy machine.*"

SALES SECRET #92:
Enhancing Voicemail

An advanced-level message strategy is to use voicemail as an ad impression to enhance persuasive efforts being made in other mediums and channels. For example, a social media campaign that benefits from a delivered vocal message that would help connect a face (social) **to a voice** (voicemail message) **to help convey a personality** (your speaking style)**. Video can accomplish this as well, but voicemail is like a "push notification" whereas most video situations require the viewer to select and click on a video. Voicemail is something checked daily.**

UTILIZING:
TRUST BY ASSOCIATION

Fig 9.8:
Example General B2B Testimonials
Tactical Approach: associative trust
Example Industry: corporate

"Hello Dan. This is [first name, last name of seller] **with XYZ Information Tech. We've handled** (solved) **the** [technology requirements] **for** [large corporation #1], **and** [large corporation #2]. **I would like to share with you a unique way of approaching your technology structure similar to how we set them up to succeed. I'd like to highlight this for you in a four minute phone call so we can both see if a future video call or meeting makes sense. I'm at 555.555.1234. You can also text me at that number which is again, 555.555.1234."**

87 words (without the phone number) with a 28 second delivery time.

This approach of using your other clients as a testimonial can work well when you are approaching large companies or working a list by industry.

UTILIZING:
WE CAN IMPROVE YOUR
EXISTING...

Fig 9.9:
Example Message for B2B
Tactical Approach: "What's in it for you..."
Example Industry: information technology & web

"Hello Maggie. This is [first name, last name of seller] **with XYZ123 Information Tech. I took a look at a few of your pay-per-click ads online. Someone has done a very nice job with the set up. I did see a missed opportunity common to most campaigns though, which is why I'm calling. We manage or improve existing pay-per-click campaigns. I can explain in a few minutes, how you can improve your advertising. I'm at 555.555.1234. You can also text me at that number which is again, 555.555.1234."**

86 words (without the phone number) with a 26 second delivery time

The compliment about the setup helps to disarm potential apprehension. The message conveys that the seller isn't necessarily trying to replace a vendor but augment a result. A follow-up message to Maggie could be:

APPROACH: FOLLOW-UP MESSAGE

Fig 9.10:
Example Message for B2B
Tactical Approach: "What's in it for you..."
Sample Industry: information technology & web

"Hello again Maggie. This is [first name, last name of seller] **with XYZ123 Information Tech. I called last week with an improvement idea for your pay-per-click campaign. I took another look at your ads and have found an additional idea I'd like to share. I'll try again early next week to connect. In the meantime I'm at 555.555.1234."**

52 words (without the phone number) with a 16 second delivery time.

This is a building block approach to messaging that can be effective and it keeps your messages fresh and non-naggy. You can keep adding a small bit of value with each message, or swap out value for different approaches. Their curiosity may result in a call back.

SALES SECRET #93 (and example message):
The Fix for Repeated Call Attempt Cliché: "Touching Base"

Instead of "just touching base" (ugh, cringe) **as your reason for calling when you leave your second, third, and future calls on voicemail, try this instead. "Hello again 'Doug,' this is** [your name] **from** [your company]**. I called last Monday. I'm hoping to reach you in the coming weeks so I can share the quick idea I mentioned I have for you." You can literally leave that same message repeatedly once a week. You've given yourself permission to with the phrase, "I'm hoping to reach you in the coming weeks." When you call back in week 4? You're still trying to reach them in the coming weeks. You aren't "touching base" and you aren't being annoying or pitching and re-pitching long drawn-out messages. It's short and to the point. The VM does its job by simply helping them remain aware of you...while subtly saying, "I'm going to keep trying to reach you." The "coming weeks" approach sounds less eager and not needy. It sounds casual and patient.**

APPROACH: PERSONALIZATION & CURIOSITY

Fig 9.11:
Example Message for Personalization
Tactical Approach: "You can leverage your success. I can help."
Sample Industry: engineering

"Hi Carol. This is [first name, last name of seller] **from Fictitious Marketing Inc. I was just on your website and noticed that you recently received the Conduit of Excellence MP478 Engineering Award** (fictitious award title). **The reason I'm calling is to let you know that a client of mine won that several years ago and using the award's credentials we helped them increase their market. I'm a marketer and I'd like to explain how that was done and what you too could think about doing. I'm at 555.555.1234. You can also text me at that number which is again, 555.555.1234."**

91 words (without the phone number) with a 29 second delivery time.

This is likely an award that the corporation is proud of (in this fictitious scenario) and most companies like to get multiple uses out of each success. Look for information you can use to personalize messaging by researching corporations within your various lists. Adjust the investment of time according to the potential payoff or list the prospect resides on [*see chapter 23*]. Anytime a message is personalized and relevant, you're potentially accessing a potential advantage.

SALES SECRET #94:
Pique Curiosity to Get a Return Phone Call

You must make the DM curious to know more about how you can save them time, money, or make a process easier. If you're leaving them wanting a bit more, they are more likely to call you back.

When the messaging is about the decision maker and includes relevance, even if they begin reflexively starting to move toward the delete or message skip buttons, they often realize they are actually skipping information relevant to them and stay on for the remainder. Personalization and using messaging that sounds different is very effective.

It may be easier to start with message development for voicemail as the time, scope, and purpose are all limited. The confines force organized thinking that will translate to more concise messaging components.

APPROACH: TAKING ON NEW CLIENTS

Fig 9.12:
Example General Message for Corporate
Tactical Approach: I think I can help
Sample Industry: corporate, financial

"Hi Dave. This is [first name, last name of seller]**. I know you're busy. We both are, so I'll be brief. I'm a** [financial advisor] **with** [Fictitious Finance Corp]**. The reason I'm calling is I'm looking to advise a new client about** [finance] **in the** [transportation] **industry. I've been following your products for awhile and because I only want to advise companies like yours with stellar customer service, I'd like a few minutes to share a way I think I can help you** [with finance]**. I'm at 555.555.1234**

84 words (without the phone number) with a 26 second delivery time.

This message (reworded slightly), is also effective for cold calls. Acknowledging their busy schedule shows some empathy and mentioning you'll be brief relaxes their defenses a bit. Starting with voicemail messaging can help you learn **how to create dialogue for cold calls.**

During cold calling,
but especially when you engage
their voicemail and follow up calls, avoid
cliché statements (touching base, circling back, etc.).
Clichés make you sound like a salesy reppy rep.

STRATI-TACTICAL
TEN

How to Create Dialogue for Cold Calls

Just mentioning the words "cold calling" can intensify the pulse rate of many sales professionals. The phrase is actually cold outreach when you consider that the attempts to contact decision makers can be on the phone, social, email, video, virtual, or instant message. Any form of cold outreach will always share many of the same challenges but in this Strati-Tactical we are focusing on the phone. There are other desired outcomes but the majority in sales are cold calling in an attempt to set a first meeting, video call, scheduled longer phone call, or some kind of access for such things as a facility survey or observation of something.

Requirements for Success

Cold calling is seeking a scheduled commitment from a decision maker who is capable of allowing the sale to advance past that first scheduled meeting. Ideally, this DM can eventually make a purchasing decision or provide direct access to the key decision maker who can. To accomplish this you will need to directly connect to a decision maker, engage their mind, elicit a response from them, and secure a commitment such as the scheduled meeting.

The first component to understand in cold calling is your product. You are not selling your product, you are selling a scheduled meeting. That *is* your product. Even when you speak about your physical product, you are trying to support the sale of the first commitment. These four areas: connection, engagement, response, and commitment are going to be pivotal.

SALES SECRET #95:
Use Your Phone's Recorder to Practice

You can use your smart phone's recorder app to practice. Speak your written verbiage you are proposing to use as your sales messages for the DMs' voicemails. Record and re-record over and over until it sounds like a fresh message with no glitches that is engaging and positive. Be upbeat but not overly so.

Connection: You must contact new decision makers or reconnect with existing customers. They must receive your call, listen to your message on their voicemail, read your email, accept your connection request or otherwise be exposed to whatever attempt you make to connect. ***If you don't connect, your sale will not advance.***

Engagement: They must mentally engage with what you are saying or your message. It must pique their curiosity with something at least slightly intriguing. If your verbiage and delivery style don't connect mentally with relevance or something intriguing, they will not engage. ***Without engagement, your sale will not advance.***

Response: They must respond or take action in some way and that can be as benign and passive as just staying on the phone listening long enough for you to explain your value that is worth their time. Their response could also be as interactive as sharing information or returning your call. ***If they don't respond, your sale will not advance.***

Commitment: Driving the clarity of purpose for that first contact with a decision maker is securing the next commitment. That may be a 30 minute in-person meeting, a 20 minute video or phone call, or a facility survey. ***You must secure that first commitment or your sale will not advance.***

These four are important because when cold calling in any communication medium, you are not selling your physical product or service, you're selling a first commitment. You may end up discussing the result you are offering that your product will provide, but you are not selling that product. It's all about that next commitment.

Scope of Your Ideation and Development Endeavor

There's a big difference between earning someone's trust (meaning they fully trust you) and just earning enough trust to agree to a 30-minute meeting, video call, or follow-up phone call. You just need to earn enough trust for that to happen. The same is true of emotional want and logical support. You don't need a large volume of persuasive appeals to get meetings while cold calling. You need just enough so they want to commit to that first 30-minute meeting and can rationalize scheduling it with you because they trust what you're saying will lead to value worth their time.

The risk is fairly low (a half hour of their time). So when you pique curiosity that eludes to at least a tangible knowledge payoff for meeting with you in video, virtual, or in person, they also see the risk/reward ratio as distinctly in their favor—but only if you frame it that way for them, which is why you have a career. That persuasion is selling.

Asking for the Commitment (Scheduling a Meeting)

You can ask for a short meeting during that first cold call and get it scheduled (or whatever commitment it is you are seeking). You also don't need epic sales closes to secure and schedule committed meetings.

You are asking for the Financial Sale (paid for with 30 minutes of their time) on a mini sale and the component sales are all required to close as well. The threshold to be met, however, is much lower on the component sales for a mini sale like that first commitment you seek. The way you ask for the sale can be straightforward. Keep it simple. The following examples assume we are dropping into a conversation midstream.

Fig 10.1 "Jump on a Video Call" to Ask For the Meeting:

"...to explain that more in depth, what do you think of jumping on a video call for 30 minutes later this week? My schedule is pretty open on Thursday and Friday, would either of those work for you?"

Fig 10.2 "Schedule Handy?" to Ask to Schedule a Meeting:

"...if you have your schedule handy, we should schedule a 30-minute meeting or video call for later this week or early next week. I have time on Tuesday afternoon or Wednesday morning. Would either of those work for you?"

Fig 10.3 "Learn More" Approach to Asking for the Meeting:

"...it seems like there is more for both of us to learn about your operational challenges and potential advantages I might be able to illuminate for you. Would you like to schedule a 30-minute video call so we can see if there are potential benefits for you? I have time on Thursday afternoon or Friday morning. Would either of those work for you?"

Fig 10.4 "Work Session" to Ask to Schedule a Collaborative

".....what do you think of getting together for a collaborative work session or a video call to explore this further? I have time on Monday afternoon, anytime Tuesday, or Wednesday morning. Would any of those work for you?"

If you've piqued their curiosity, resistance to meeting isn't formidable (and often not even there). It's usually a small commitment—and if they see you as a consultative resource, it's an offer for them rather than a favor for you. Cold calling is not "simple" or "easy" but it's also not as hard as some of the frequently given advice may make it out to be.

Requirements to Satisfy the Mental Gate Keepers (MGKs)

There are eight basic requirements to satiate the mental gate keepers (MGKs) that form mental question gates when you're calling.

The Eight Gates of the MGKs

1. "Who are you?"
2. "Why are you calling?
3. "What do you want?"
4. "Why should I care?"
5. "Why should I stay on the phone with you?"
6. "How does it help me?"
7. "Do I trust you, or at least trust what you're saying?"
8. "What will be my result if I agree to your request?"

That sounds like a lot of requirements to meet but many of these are derived from transitory emotions and fleeting thoughts that subside almost as soon as the requirements are met. Once met, the gate opens and the MGK allows passage of your information, requests, and suggestions. Once all gates open (or enough of them open to override apprehensions of the remaining), the decision maker will agree to that first commitment to continue talking to you, schedule a meeting, set up a video call, participate in a video call, or engage your next request. To accomplish any of that you'll need to build messaging.

Building Messaging

You have to get the list of eight requirements fulfilled within your verbiage either by implication or explicitly saying the information. To make this easier and ensure you have solid and effective messaging, prepare ahead of time using the same N.E.D.A. process (Nested Element Development Approach) used when we created your 15 Second Segue [*see chapter 11*]. First we need to associate the list of eight gates with the components of your cold call (in the left and right columns of Fig 10.4.) so that we're working with actual components and not just requirements. What you'll see on the coming pages is a progression of messaging being built step-by-step from Fig 10.4 through Fig 10.8 using N.E.D.A.

Tips on Cold Calling

1. **Read chapters 31 and 32 of this book for motivation.**
2. **Read the "utility box"** (like this one) **in this Strati-Tactical entitled, "Use Two Office Phones and Practice."**
3. **Relax. That's easier said than done. So what you can and should do is practice ad nauseam** (see #2 above). **When you are absolutely sick of practicing and want to quit, you're ready for more practice.**
4. **Getting on the phones will be a relief. You'll actually look forward to it** (so you can quit practicing) **and will want to apply your new proficiency.**

Fig 10.4 Cold Calling Requirements (left column) **Converted to N.E.D.A. List** (right column)

8 Gates of the MGKs	Convert Them to Elements
These are the 8 questions the mental gatekeepers (MGKs) will ask and need answers to.	These are the elements that correlate with the questions in the left column that you'll use to build your cold call verbiage.
∇	∇
"Who are you?"	**Your greeting/Who you are/Where you're from/What company...**
"Why are you calling?	**The reason for my call is...**
"What do you want?"	**I want to ask/share/tell/show...**
"Why should I care?"	**Intrigue hook and/or an Emotive Gatekey** (to pique curiosity)...
"Why should I stay on the phone with you?"	**I have value worth your time...**
"How does it help me?"	**You'll benefit because...**
"Do I trust you, or at least trust what you're saying?"	**The way I'll earn trust is...**
"What will be my result if I agree to your request?"	**Their result for taking the action you suggest...**

It will be the N.E.D.A. list (Nested Element Development Approach) that you'll be using for development of your cold call conversation (messaging). Fig 10.5 provides you with a way to expand, reword, and reorder the elements as you modify your messaging to get it closer to how you think it should flow. This work can serve two purposes because it will produce messaging for real time cold call conversations as well as messaging you can use for their voicemail [*see Strati-Tactical #9*].

Fig 10.5 Your N.E.D.A. List
(expanded elements from Fig 10.4)

The following list to utilize N.E.D.A. and create dialogue for cold calls is a simple expansion of the left column of Fig 10.4. You may or may not find you'll use all of these components, but this will serve as a good starting list.

1. **Your greeting.**
2. **Who you are.**
3. **Company you're from.**
4. **Reason for your call.**
5. **Intrigue hook to pique curiosity or an Emotive Gatekey** [see also Strati-Tactical #4].
6. **What's in it for them?**
7. **Benefit #1**____________________ (you may only need or want one benefit, or in some messaging a benefit may not be needed if an Emotive Gatekey has piqued curiosity).
8. **Benefit #2**____________________.
9. **Benefit #3**____________________.
10. **Earn trust** (often achieved by how you deliver messaging).
11. **Their result will be**____________________.
12. **What do you want?**

Using N.E.D.A. you can begin ideation and production of your messaging. You'll probably benefit from working on custom, personalized, cold calling messaging for a client you would really like to sell to (perhaps even from your idyllic prospecting list), [*see also chapter 23*]. This seems counterintuitive as "general" messaging is going to be more difficult. That seems backwards, but think about it. A personalized approach is directed at one (or one industry) type of prospective clients, whereas general broad messaging is directed at many. It's easier to talk to one listener than it is to talk to many. If you had a meeting with a high value KDM, or had to give a speech to the entire corporate senior staff and all management of company where the KDM worked, which would be harder to prepare for? The speech because it targets many. Even if it was the same messaging.

Once you become proficient, or at least comfortable with, your development process, you can move on to creating messaging with an ever-wider target appeal. You can move to the Short List or the Practical List [*see also chapter 23*]. When you populate the N.E.D.A. list, write the information as if you are answering questions. It will be very helpful to have a hard copy (write them down) to work from. It may also help to verbally talk through your answers with a colleague. Then you can denote what was said or use an audio recording.

Fig 10.6 Populating Your N.E.D.A. List
(expanding on Fig 10.5)

---

1. **Your greeting/ Who are you?**
   Hi Cheryl. This is [seller's first and last name] from...
2. **Company you're from**
   Fictitious Compliance Corp.
3. **Reason for your call**
   I thought of XYZ Inc. (Cheryl's company) recently
4. **Intrigue hook to pique curiosity** (test it first on colleagues)
   Your competitor, Made Up Competitor Inc., had a new product release that resulted in some compliance challenges. Getting product off of the assembly line and into the distribution network proved a challenge for retail.
5. **An Emotive Gatekey to pique curiosity** [*see Strati-Tactical #4*]
   You need someone experienced in regulatory compliance which is a rare skill set that requires disciplines in multiple areas.
6. **What's in it for them?**
   XYZ Inc. is about to release a new product under similar circumstances as her competitor.
7. **Benefit #1**
   To avoid stumbling the way Made Up Competitor Inc. did.

8. **Benefit #2**

   You can avoid similar challenges that happened to Made Up Competitor Inc.

9. **Benefit #3**

   I can serve as a compliance expert waiting in the wings—a go to source for questions and ongoing situations as they relate to the product release.

10. **Earn trust**

    Expertise, delivery style, gentle speaking style but clear and concise. I can convey they can trust my information as I connected the dots outside of their company and am calling into their company. That may demonstrate intuition and caring.

11. **Their result will be______________________________**

    Avoiding the same challenges that Made Up Competitor Inc. are now facing. Perhaps a smoother product launch, higher profitability, less distractions on compliance means more focus on distribution, marketing, and sales.

12. **What do you want?**

    I want to set up a 20-minute meeting to talk about protections, prevention and compliance. Ways I can help. My number is 555.555.1234.

After you've populated your N.E.D.A. list with the information you know, you can then eliminate the question-statements, eliminate extraneous information and then work out transition sentences to connect everything as complete sentences. What you'll end up with is something similar to Fig 10.7 [*up next*].

Avoid Confirming Your Appointment

Unless air travel is involved (or an expensive demonstration setup), **avoid "calling to confirm" an appointment. You're just giving them an opportunity to cancel and it looks like you're protecting your own time** (you are)**. That's not a good look. If you show up, or log on and they never arrive, they now sort of "owe you." That's a great position to be in—and rescheduling can be a segue to the next commitment.**

Fig 10.7 Dialogical Messaging
(derived from the work done in Fig 10.6)

DM: **"This is 'Cheryl Grendahl.'"**

SELLER: **"Hi Cheryl. This is** [seller's first and last name] **from Fictitious Compliance Corp. The reason I'm calling is I have a lot of experience in regulatory compliance. I thought of you and XYZ Inc.** (her company) **after your competitor, 'Made Up Competitor Inc.' had some difficulty with their latest product release. Their compliance challenges got me thinking about your upcoming product release. Do you foresee any challenges with your launch?"**

DM: **"Well. We're taking a look at that. Certainly. You can't be too careful...so, um, what exactly does your company do?"**

SELLER: **"Most of our focus is in regulatory consultation in the manufacturing and technical industries. My personal specialization is in regulatory compliance and import/export protections. A second reason I'm calling is that compliance is not very negotiable or flexible. It's more difficult to retroactively comply should you even unknowingly learn you are non-compliant."**

DM: **"And that's what Made Up Competitor Inc. got jammed up over, right?"**

SELLER: **"Yes. But they also had foreign compliance issues which affected their production schedule. Do you source domestically or is importation part of your supply chain?"**

DM: **"Mostly domestic but some import."**

SELLER: **"What are the areas where you suspect you may need to take another look at the regulatory requirements?"**

DM: **"Export. Distribution. Shipping. Import...you know, I wouldn't mind knowing more on all of it."**

SELLER: **"What I'd like to do for you is have a 20-minute video call wherein you can invite others in your organization who would benefit as well."**

DM: **"Okay."**

SELLER: **"I will be offering you a nice overview of what you can expect when distributing domestically and what is likely to occur as you transition to exportation. There are some challenges I can help you avoid with simple information. You'll also have an understanding of what retention of consultancy can offer you, and if that makes sense for your organization or not. Would next week work for you? I have Tuesday and Thursday wide open."**

DM: **"We have a senior staff meeting on Tuesday so let's make it Thursday."**

SELLER: **"Morning or afternoon?"**

DM: **"Morning."**

SELLER: **"How about 9:00?"**

DM: **"That works."** (assume the seller acquires the DM's email address).

SELLER: **"Great. See if you can encourage anyone else who might need to be involved in compliance, attend as well."**

DM: **"I'll do that."**

SELLER: **"I have your email address and will send you an invitation link. Thank you Cheryl. I'll see you next Tuesday. Have a productive day."**

DM: **"You too."**

408 words (without dialogue attribution)
with an interaction time of 2.7 minutes

You can then convert the conversation in Fig 10.7 into a message for voicemail similar to how you did it in Strati-Tactical #9. Within the context of the conversation, the mild fear appeals are understated due to the longer delivery and interaction time. Within a unidirectional message on voicemail in a compressed temporal format, the fear appeal will stand out more readily so if using this type of approach, ensure you don't over play a fear appeal. Mild fear appeals are effective. Intense fear appeals in advertising and sales are often rejected out-of-hand by the human mind.

APPROACH:
MILD FEAR APPEAL—
IMPLIED CONSEQUENCES

Fig 10.8:
Message Example:
Utilizing a Very Mild Fear Appeal to Pique Curiosity

"Hi Cheryl. This is [first name, last name of seller] **with Fictitious Compliance Corp. I thought of you and XYZ Inc.** (her company) **after your competitor, Made Up Competitor Inc. released their new product that resulted in some compliance challenges. I have a lot of experience in regulatory compliance and since you are a similar company to Made Up Competitor Inc. and about to release your own new product next month, you may encounter some of the same challenges. I'm at 555.555.1234. You can also text me at that number which is again, 555.555.1234."**

74 words (without the phone number or parentheticals) with a 23 second delivery time (plus phone number)

It's going to be important to become familiar with your verbiage prior to conversations. Most likely much of it will be what you already know from your industry but placing it into a dialogical format will help you organize the flow. This also assists you in separating out the components because you can look at all of the "SELLER" blocks of dialogue and those are the components you should practice and memorize. You'll see that they fit in many places and are versatile conversational components.

Delivery

We aren't talking about deep critique on the part of the decision makers as it relates to the delivery of your message. It's not speech competition where your every word will be scrutinized. They don't need to think about your offer for a 20-minute meeting or the first commitment any longer than it takes for you to suggest it.

You can and should memorize your messaging and be so familiar with the verbiage that you can deliver it conversationally as if it were extemporaneous. Become very familiar with your messaging so that you can deliver it without prompt cards. If you prefer prompts, you can prepare bulleted lists or cards if you feel you can form cohesive and intelligent sentences just from bullet points.

This notion that cold calling must be difficult, it must be a drudge task you slog through, and it will be rejection-filled, should be met with the question, "Why?" There's no doubt there is a lot of rejection in our industry and you'll never eliminate that, but you can mitigate it with solid work on your persuasive skills, building an effectual tool box, practicing, and being prepared. These Strati-Tacticals will help you prepare and give you an advantage when closing sales.

Use Two Office Phones and Practice

You and a trusted colleague or a seller in a similar industry that you trust should commandeer two offices (or use your home offices), **then utilize two phones, or use two video screens and simulate cold calling each other relentlessly—and simulate sales situations to the point of ad nauseam. Take turns in the roles of GK, DM, and administrative assistant of the CEO vetting you. Then simulate various scenarios that you know you'll encounter. When simulating the DMs and GKs, be nice, be rude, be aloof, try and shut each other down, act interested then switch becoming suddenly uninterested, object, stall the conversation, and/or brush off the seller.**

On the sellers side, come up with responses to what the GKs typically say and have one of you be in each role (seller and GK). **Try and get through to the DM or KDM. What you'll find helpful is to have messaging, dialogue, and phrases that act as interchangeable modular response components that you've pulled from your Wall of Wisdom** [*see also Strati-Tactical #3*]. **Try everything and invest many hours into this and it will almost certainly pay off. Do this until you're absolutely sick of it. Then, do it some more. When you're *really* done, practice some more. When you've reached the absurd levels of practice—do more.**

At the base of each preceding message and dialogical example there is a word count and corresponding time estimate for the message delivery. You won't need to actually speak the message and time it. The following conversion formula is what I've used to write ad copy. It will convert your word count to spoken time. It's not perfect as you may have highly technical words or multisyllabic words in your script that would add a bit of time, but it's usually very close to accurate.

Word Count to Time Conversion:

There is a limit of 96 words in a 30-second radio ad script. When developing messaging for sales you can use that word-to-time ratio as a temporal base measurement. If your messaging is shorter than 96 words, take the total number of words in your verbiage and divide it by 96 to find out the percentage of a 30-second ad spot your script would be. Then multiply that percentage by 30. Like this:

83 words in your message. 83÷96=86%
.86 x 30 = 25.8, round up to 26 (seconds).
An 83 word message will take 26 seconds to deliver.

Double the "96" and the "30" if your verbiage is longer than 96 words but less than 192 (a one-minute radio spot) **and the formula works. Like this:**

147 words in your message. 147÷192=77%
.77 x 60 = 46.2, round up to 47 (seconds).
A 147 word message will take 47 seconds to deliver.

You can scale this formula up to accommodate longer messages.

SECTION 9

CLOSING

"You're in sales? Well then. You don't need a 'haircut'... you need a 'hairdo'. *Just.* Like. Mine. Your head'll look much, much taller. Shall we get started?"

"The myth of the magical sales close is an illusion and sometimes sales will close in spite of the zippy-one-liner, not because of it."

—ImmersiveSelling.com

Chapter 28

The Symphony and the Sale

Very often in transactional sales the buying decision is made at the time of closing. That's occasionally true (but not often) with complex B2B sales. When complex B2B sales are closing, what you do in the sales situations leading up to that close is going to be just as important as anything transpiring in the close itself. Usually a zippy one liner isn't going to compensate for underlying problems within the component sales of the Quad Close. Usually the DMs and KDM already know who they will buy from, what they will buy (and won't buy), for how much, and when.

> **"It's not the length of the one line close that is degrading your sales close, it's the intent.**

When you and the decision makers have set aside a time to go over the final details on the purchase agreement (installation/delivery/etc.)... most of their buying decision has often been finalized within their mind with perhaps a few details and options left to determine. There are also some sales where a couple of vendors are still in the running as you near the close and that "final meeting" is actually a final attempt to differentiate between you and your competitor(s).

Why is that important?

Many sellers are arriving at their sales closing situations pumped full of frequently given advice on "ways to close the sale." This advisement often features "power closes" and "closing statements" that purportedly "work every time!"

They often don't.

Some of them don't work at all. Many of them are unhelpful and actually push your sale back and can even reopen some or all of the component sales that you've already closed. I call these closes "zippy one liners" but there's nothing zippy about them.

SALES SECRET #96:
Avoid Elevating the Sales Close to an Event-Level-Status

Buying is often a natural conclusion to a situation if it's been conducted effectively. When a close is put on a pedestal, sellers get nervous and may talk too much. Buyers' apprehensions may be amplified.

The books, frequently given advice, articles, blogs, videos and the massive volumes of "sales closes" often will work in transactional sales situations only. This is an opinion (mine)—and one that won't be readily agreed with, but the zippy one liners that close transactional sales—almost always backfire in complex B2B sales situations. You've worked hard to position yourself as a consultative resource.

A professional.

A person in the industry leading thought, leading recommendations—at least as it pertains to the DMs and KDM. What follows? A sales closing one liner? Do consultative experts and professionals use gimmicks? Pressure? Hard selling? What does a one-liner close look like from the DMs' and KDMs' perspectives? Whether it's an in-person, video, or virtual close, a zippy one liner may resemble the next analogy.

The Symphony and the Sale

Imagine you have arrived at a symphony concert performance of a world renowned orchestra and are reading the program. Tonight's performance features a guest musician visiting from a foreign country and is known to be one of the world's consummate violinists. You're in for a rare experience only a live performance can deliver. There's no way to actually recreate or totally capture a performance of this caliber on recording equipment even with our most advanced technology. We may come somewhat close, but it's not the same as live and in person.

Tonight's performance is one that will feature one of the most revered and difficult violin solos. There are but about six musicians in the world who can even play it flawlessly and of those, she is often credited with having set the bar.

The orchestra has assembled but the house lights are still up. Each musician has earned their place, and each takes their respective chair. What follows is a quiet cacophony of last minute fine tuning, and music stand adjustments.

The house lights dim and the musicians form themselves into the composure that will be their postures of performance in anticipation of the conductor's arrival...who walks out to applause and then introduces the visiting violinist. The applause resumes enthusiastically as she steps out on stage and assumes her place in the spotlight.

Her first notes cut the pleasant tension that had moments before washed off of the stage's silence and out onto the first few rows...and this is where you somehow were able to be seated. You realize after the first movement that you aren't merely hearing the violin, but are experiencing it.

How does she do that?

Those subnotes that shouldn't be there—but are? You didn't know a human could play like that...and based on the applause neither did

anyone else on your side of the experience. That's what it was. An experience. One that can never be recreated. It's never going to happen just precisely that way ever again. The sound waves have left the air never to return.

Once the performance is over (as per tradition) **she briefly leaves the stage, and then returns. She breaks the edge of the spotlight to rejoin the conductor for that final interaction with the audience as they stand to gift her with an ovation to show their appreciation. The audience expects a quiet and humble bow as a reflection of the reciprocal appreciation.**

That's what's expected, but isn't what she does. Instead, quite pleased with herself, does a football touchdown dance followed by mashup of a 1990's era "stir-stick" club dance move and a half bow, part strut, all followed up by a finale with some kind of an impromptu and unpracticed, "I'm awesome" gesture.

An awkward silence hangs over the room punctuated by a few audible gasps. You turn to others in the audience as they turn toward you, all are wondering, "What just happened?" The performance has been ruined. Absolutely ruined.

That's what you look like in a B2B sales situation after investing so much in a professional performance and follow that up with a zippy one liner sales close you got from some misfocused advice that is "guaranteed to work every time!" Regardless of what the experiences were for the audience in the symphony and the DMs in the sales situations leading up to the sales close—both are ruined. So goes the finale of your consultative sales performance.

If you're in complex B2B sales, technical sales or any form of persuasion that is complex, has multiple decision makers, a committee, or involves large corporations—avoid misfocused advice promoting magic sales closes.

You may be wondering, "Okay, so what about an Emotive Gatekey?" That's similar to a one liner sales close, isn't it? Why wouldn't the same principle apply to a sales close? Why wouldn't that qualify as a "zippy one liner gatekey"? Isn't that the same? That seems logical because you may be observing the "one liner" portion of both components as compared by their length.

However, how much development time did you invest into your Emotive Gatekey? It was a lot of work to customize it for an application to your product's result and industry. How much time did you put into reading that zippy one liner from a book of magic sales closes (for example, "Buy this from me and you'll look like a hero!")? Please don't ever say that. Wasn't the guarantee (works every time!) also just slapped on thoughtlessly?

Your Emotive Gatekey was developed consciously and with intentioned relevance for an effectual outcome. If you put that same effort or intent into a sales close, then the resulting one-liner might be just as effective.

SALES SECRET #97:
Deliver Value Stacking with Statements of Worth

As you're reviewing all that's included (value stacking) **on a purchase agreement/order or contract with a KDM, use this approach with caution. If their perception is that the price is too high, they may be hearing a line-item-explanation for why the price is what it is. If you stack the value, try to tie the line items to very short statements of worth for the major components. Be consultative and relaxed. Also know that value stacking can sometimes be very helpful but in some situations it can backfire.**

It's not the length of the one line close that is degrading your sales close, it's the intent. Key decision makers can sense the "slap it on, and it'll work"-ness of it all. When you have competency with persuasive tooling, your sales situations are founded on fundamentals that support **the first three component sales.**

Economic Curves Ahead

In times of rampant inflation, supply chain disruptions, bear markets, chaos, market uncertainty, lagging consumer confidence, unrest, falling skies, or a natural disaster, the rules of sales pretend to change. What's really happening, however, is everything within the component sales' requirement cores [*see Fig 1.2 in Strati-Tactical #1*] become intensified commensurate with the perceived state of crisis.

People still buy under almost all conditions—and depending on what you sell, if you prepare your tooling and skills to improve relevance you can become a priority result. Their situational awareness may (sometimes) propel your sales, not impede them. People buy emotionally and fear is one of the prime movers of the human mind. You'll need to thread that needle with new perception-changer type tooling.

Reframe their perception using a sales story, an analogy, or new tooling—and then take a look at price. Avoid leading with discounts. If you're getting slammed in this economy, your priorities should be:

- Mind-set
- Strategy
- Preparation and personalization
- Tactical prospecting and research
- Tooling
- Action
- Knowledge (read!)
- Adjustments (only use what's working)
- Advanced search for qualification of leads [*see also Strati-Tactical #7*]
- Accountability

"The sum of the component parts of the Quad Close is Rock Hard Coin."

—ImmersiveSelling.com

CHAPTER 29

The First Three Component Sales

The component sales of the Quad Close can close at any time and often independently of one another. When you are selling in person or remotely and a decision maker comes to a video, virtual, or in-person sales situation your component sales are already being founded. It is upon that foundation that you will need to build your sale.

> "You probably can't buy trust with money, but once you've earned it, trust can be worth stacks of Rock Hard Coin.

This is where we started back in chapter one. We discussed how asking for the Financial Sale will not likely result in a closed sale if the component sales have not. What wasn't covered in chapter one, was how to *recognize* when each component sale has closed.

That will be the primary focus of this chapter but there are three aspects of the component sales you'll need to take a look at. These are specific to the use of the component sales and are not addressing your over-arching sales strategy or methods; e.g., what we are talking about here specifically is related just to the component sales. The three aspects are in the following list.

1. **Strategy: the strategy and tactics you develop to advance and close the component sales.**
2. **Tactics: what you provide** (what you actually do) **to advance each component sale.**
3. **Recognition: how you will recognize when each component sale has closed.**

We'll discuss #1 and #2 briefly here (they've already been covered elsewhere in this book), to synthesize them into context here. Then we will focus on #3 for the remainder of the chapter.

1. Strategy: Your strategy for the component sales will probably involve discovering and predicting what it is the DMs and KDMs are going to need to see for persuasion to occur (the requirement core in Strati-Tacticals #1 and #2 as recorded by you on notecards in Strati-Tactical #3). This is important so that your efforts reflect and fulfill what it is they need and want to see (so persuasion can occur). You can discover this using your past and future experiences in sales (if you're new to sales, you can pay closer attention to your future experiences). Remote selling will yield a narrower spectrum of information but you can move through more sales situations due to the removal of travel time. What you will be taking note of are similar to the examples in Fig. 2.3 [*see also Strati-Tactical #2*] and Fig. 3.1 [*see also Strati-Tactical #3*].

By observing what has gone well, and what hasn't within your sales situations selling remotely or in person, you can take (mental) notes (write them down later) and place them on your Wall of Wisdom (W.O.W.) [*see also Strati-Tactical #3*]. This facilitates a better understanding to determine what the requirement core of the typical decision makers will likely be.

2. Tactics: For each of the first three component sales there are specific tactical advantages you'll want to insert for yourself within sales situations. The component sales will all advance as a result of an effective sales story, analogy, or one of the sales support tools in this book.

What will likely help cinch the component sales is your ability to access the holographic projector within the decision makers' minds and project an image of ownership or a scene featuring their result. They will need to see themselves owning the result you sell. This can be done with words, visuals, analogies or most likely with a sales story [*see section 3*]. When they can see ownership, they can also assess trust, and logic to see how they support the want they feel. It's usually (but not always) going to be the Emotional Sale that leads the other component sales.

3. Recognition: Determining when the component sales have closed (so that you can ask for the Financial Sale), is where intuition, observation, listening and attention to detail will serve you well.

Sales is like a treasure map ripped into four equal squares. Even though the square you can first see is the one with the "X" on it (the Financial Sale), you don't know how to get there. Discovering the other 3 squares of the map is like finding the component sales.

What follows is an exploration of how to recognize when each of the component sales are closing or have closed. This is like placing each square of the map down into its place so you can better see all of your waypoints. We'll start with the Trust Sale and then move on to the Emotional Sale and Logical Sale.

The Trust Sale

Recognizing when the Trust Sale has closed is often easier to detect than the Emotional or Logical Sales. Are the DMs and KDM open with their information? Answering any questions you ask with more information than requested? Have they volunteered any information? Are they making eye contact and are their expressions relaxed?

SALES SECRET #98:
Intuition

If you can tell when a decision maker is untrustworthy (they sometimes are)**, then you can also tell when they can be trusted. This same intuition can also be used to sense how much trust you've likely earned from them. Also be aware that they have the same abilities and can analyze you.**

The decision makers aren't always motivated to hide the fact that they trust you but it isn't a subject that is often directly discussed either. Here are some areas of trust you may encounter that will need to be earned.

The DMs and KDM will probably need to trust:

- **your knowledge.**
- **your judgment in diagnostics for their challenges.**
- **the quality and performance of the product.**
- **that the result you promise will be true.**
- **that you can perform after the sale.**
- **that your actions will match your promises.**
- **that what you say can and will be delivered.**
- **your authority over the sale parameters, price, and deliverables.**
- **the future relevance of your company in your industry.**
- **that there will be future support of the product.**
- **that everything they've divulged will remain confidential.**
- **their business has been accurately assessed by you.**

Next we will take a look at some of the ways to detect trust (these lists are not comprehensive).

The Trust Sale has *probably closed* when:

- **they face you directly in person** (shoulders squared to yours) **while smiling occasionally and actually listening to you.**
- **they ask for your advice or seek out your opinion almost as if you were a hired consultant to share knowledge.**
- **the key decision maker comments** (or nods) **agreeing that you've done what you said you would do for them thus far.**
- **they engage in mannerisms** (that your intuition senses) **that indicate trust has formed. They may seem relaxed and their comments are positive.**
- **you are asked deeper questions about your company.**

- **they confide in you more than is necessary to solve their problem or complete an estimate. They will trust you with information.**
- **decision makers tell you a personal story or add nonessential information** (such as they have to pick their child up from soccer practice later that afternoon). **They may then add additional information** (like what position their child plays).
- **they extend the meeting time by their choice past the scheduled time frame** (even though you made motions to keep to the schedule).
- **they offer some access to their company, information, backstory or anything not available to the general public or even most other vendors.**
- **decision makers refer to you as if you're already a vendor/partner or part of their team. They may use terms like "we" or "us" when referring to you.**

It will sound a bit obvious but often you can assume that if your sales situations are progressing, then the decision makers likely trust you or you wouldn't have made that progress. That also supports the importance of relationships in sales.

SALES SECRET #99:
Becoming a Trusted Sales Advisor (relationship selling)

Being recognized as a consultative resource for your customers will ensure you retain long term accounts and repeat business. At some point you may find that the new sales world is going to belong to those sellers who have the long term sales relationships to help ride out a future crisis.

Ignore all frequently given advice that suggests relationship selling is old school. If it works, why does it matter what school or era it came from? Will you stop and pick up a bunch of quarters off of a public sidewalk? Of course. Even wealthy people like to find small treasures like that. Would you toss a buck fifty back out onto the sidewalk if you discovered the quarters were from 1972, 1980, 1981, 1991, 1993, and 1999? Those quarters are verifiably old school. How much more valuable is a professional relationship?

SALES SECRET #100:
Your Sales Video

One of the most powerful tools of persuasion available to you is a sales video. It's a human-to-human connection that works for you 24/7/365. You can use videos in your LinkedIn profile, your online video channel, and even distribute and promote them with a link in email, DM, or social media. They also support remote selling.

This notion that a sales rep can do whatever it takes to get the next commitment carries a very expensive relational cost if what is done to gain that commitment is not ethical. It may cost a seller the sales close. ***You probably can't buy trust with money, but once you've earned it, trust can be worth stacks of Rock Hard Coin.*** Honest selling is also just the right thing to do.

Of the three component sales, if the Trust Sale fizzles, the decision makers won't waste time with continual or future sales situations. That isn't true of the Emotional and Logical Sales. People will continue to meet while they decide whether or not they want your result or while they search for logical proof and reasons to validate a purchase decision—if they trust you or you and your product. So be honest because it provides more time to close the supporting component sales. Once someone ceases trusting you, or if it was never earned, your sale will probably end up in the weeds. There's not a lot you can do at that point unless it's a misunderstanding (or oversight on your part) that can be remedied with clarification. If the decision makers don't trust you or your company, that's not readily fixable.

Your awareness of the Trust Sale will help you propel your future sales situations forward and experience will increase efficiency when you combine efforts to earn trust with the Emotional Sale.

The Emotional Sale

Recognizing when the Emotional Sale is advancing can be detected often within your conversations. How people speak is just as important as what they say. As in the Trust Sale, if they are asking follow-up questions of you, they are probably interested in what you are discussing. So how do you know when the Emotional Sale might be advancing?

The Emotional Sale is *probably advancing* when:

- **they nod their head in agreement occasionally when you are speaking about the result they will experience.**
- **the decision makers are engaging your social media.**
- **they may have taken some action such as an online form or returned your email and their message was positive.**
- **they've narrowed some choices you've offered and are dialing into a specific direction that includes your result.**
- **the decision makers' questions become more detail-focused.**
- **decision makers may have asked for a proposal or mentioned they'd like some pricing specifics or an estimate.**
- **there's a change in their non verbal communication. The decision maker may relax, lean back, become less rigid and more flexible with granting time for the sales situation.**
- **the decision makers begin making your sales situations a priority and may even let you know they've moved other things around to accommodate your meeting.**
- **they are saying positive statements. For example, something like, "I didn't know it would work that well."**
- **they mention the past, "That would have been really nice to have last year."**
- **they are musing, "Huh. Okay, I could see us using that."**
- **they can be seen repeatedly playing with your business card or contact information.**
- **they glance at the product briefly but multiple times and may be wondering how ownership might be.**

As you see the Emotional Sale advancing you can use your intuition to further your awareness and even gauge how close they may be getting to wanting the result you're offering.

SALES SECRET #101:
Simulate the Change in Their Mind

Simulate the change in their mind first. Describe in positive terms how the change will help their department, company or division. Use a vivid description or a sales story to describe the result you are selling.

Can you tell when someone likes a particular model of vehicle? A dining location suggestion among friends? A particular activity or entertainment venue? The tone is enthusiastic, and their mannerisms are similar to what you might see in sales situations when the Emotional Sale is advancing. The intuition required in sales is the same you would use in social situations to read others—though in professional settings, emotions are often more guarded. Pay close attention and you'll be able to see when someone is into something or not. So how can you tell when the Emotional Sale is actually closed or closing?

The Emotional Sale has *probably closed* when:

- **decision makers repeat some of your own words, indicating they've internalized a new opinion you've shared.**
- **they use emotional terms, phrases and words like, "It'll be nice to get this solved" or "I like what I'm seeing here," or "That's impressive," or "Awesome."**
- **DMs speak in terms of eventualities such as, "I can see this working and I want this to go smoothly."**
- **they speak in terms of trying it on in their mind. They are "situating your result" by simulating it holographically in their imagination.**
- **they nod their head, if even just slightly, when you speak about installation, finalization, ownership, future performance, etc.**
- **they look longer at the product. They may be imagining ownership** (emotional want).

- **they use compliments or expressions of interest such as, "That's cool."**
- **they use a declarative statement such as, "That would fit in with next year's program."**
- **a trigger event occurs and you can tell there is emotional want. An industry changed, a regulatory change happened, damage happened to their equipment, disruptive technology is encroaching, etc.**
- **they are repeatedly touching the product or carrying your marketing collateral around** (a subconscious tell) **even when it's not needed. Any frequently given advice you hear, ever, about marketing materials being "fluff" is all-the-way misfocused. Marketing materials are almost always paramount and integral to sales support. Invest the capital necessary to do this right.**
- **they wonder aloud that they "could really use this** [your result] **when we all work on the next ______________ project** (or whatever your product facilitates)."

Apathy is indicative of disengagement. You know when people are engaged and when they are apathetic in those situations, but how do you know? You are listening to them and their voice inflections, word choices, and tone. That means they are talking about the situation, thing or subject. To gain the same tonal and inflection clues, you'll need to get the decision maker talking about the result you are selling so you can get some feedback.

You can be more assured the Emotional Sale is advancing if you ask a few discovery questions that are open ended. While answering you can watch closely and listen to see if the decision makers seem to be trying on the idea of owning the result your product provides.

Some Open-Ended Discovery Questions That Can Reveal Emotional Want:

- **"How are you feeling overall about the potential result of this solution?"**

- **"I'd like to avoid overlooking anything of particular importance to you. What are some of your priorities for ________________?"** (some of the priorities may be: installation, performance, compatibility, availability, etc).
- **"Assuming you elect to schedule the installation, hypothetically, what would be some of your priorities? What are those things that may be most important to you?"**
- **"If this ____________ were fixed, what areas of business would improve?"**
- **"When we find a solution for your _________ challenge, what will need to happen before you would be able to utilize some of the solutions we've been talking about?"**
- **"How would your team feel about any changes in a few areas we've discussed?"**

The next time you're at a sporting event or any gathering where emotion is on display, take a moment and turn around and study a dozen or so faces. See their expressions? Can you sense which people are happy? Enjoying themselves? Irritable? Content? Frustrated? Hopeful? In a sale you're going to see micro versions of those very same expressions so look closely if possible (don't creep people out but try and study their expressions in a series of passing glances).

SALES SECRET #102:
Video for the Emotional Sale

Using a sales video, especially one imbued with your sales story, contributes directly to the Emotional Sale by bypassing requirements in the mind. People want what they can see and video is visually rich and immersive.

Are you seeing a furrowed brow line? That's confusion and frustration. Eyebrows slightly lifted is interest and perhaps surprise? Are their eyes open slightly wider than normal? Go online and study the hundreds of facial expressions and what they mean. Start loosely monitoring this in your sales situations and you'll probably start noticing flat looks at the onset of your sales situation that slowly morph to expressions of interest (if you're doing well).

The Logical Sale

When you see and hear trust indicators, emotional cues, and logical evidence, these will help you determine when the component sales have closed so you can assess their interest or potential aversion (to change).

It's a challenge to sell a high value product, an expensive upgrade, complicated new purchase, long term lease, major overhaul, large scale installation, significant replacement, large format service agreement, or big improvement...based solely on the logical reasons to change. Change aversion is resistance to buying, which requires effort. In many sales, that effort is similar to what will need to be invested in the acceptance of a continued problem left unsolved (should they not buy). Resisting buying, and adopting change often utilize similar mental processes. Due to this, logical appeals should intersperse the other two component sales to help them along, but you may find the bulk of the logical reasons to buy can come after they want the solution. They are looking for logical rationalization to support their decisions.

The Logical Sale is *probably advancing* when:

- **they nod their head** (if even just slightly) **when you speak about installation, finalization, ownership, future performance, etc.**
- **the decision makers may ask another person for their opinion** (because they are seeking validation to buy).
- **they begin asking questions related specifically to usage or ownership as they mentally confirm reasons to buy.**
- **they use revealing statements of eventuality with a tone of rationalization, "When we get ours, we can have any color we want right?"**
- **you are asked about a window of time** (such as how long something will be available or at a specific price, how long installation typically takes, delivery, etc.).

When you hear logical support for some of the appeals you've already made in a sale, they may be trying out the reasoning within their mind. You may hear this spoken or hear it within questions, or just musings (such as thinking out loud).

The Logical Sale has *probably closed* when:

- **their speech pattern may pick up in tempo as their mind has adopted some momentum. Their thoughts are now attaching themselves to logical reason. These are excuses to buy and ways to support it all.**
- **the decision makers begin talking about price differently than former questions that were merely gaining a scope-of-budget. These newer advanced questions and statements will have a tone of eventuality and may begin hinting at discounts or deliverables, financing, or extended warranties.**
- **they ask risk aversion questions such as, "What is the length of the warranty you offer?" or "If I need to adjust these options just prior to delivery, is that possible?"**
- **the KDM asks you to repeat something like financing options or warranty specifics** (reaffirmation of something they liked or are reassuring themselves about).
- **the decision makers begin taking measurements, seeking installation parameters, or seeing if your result will fit.**
- **you hear rationalization statements such as, "It's the last one. We'll have to get it," or "It has an economy our other system never had," or "We're the first to get this disruptive technology. It just came out," or "The lift capacity is 50% more than what I had. I'm doing more work now so I had to upgrade."**
- **you hear rationalization statements that have ramification implication imbued within them such as, "Our lease will be up soon, so this may be the right time to do this," or "We're a growing company and needed to upgrade."**
- **declaratives are used such as, "We can definitely find a budget for this. We could find a way to make it work."**

You've probably noticed that others in your life whose beliefs are on a different location on the political spectrum as yours are, will not readily accept logic, proof and facts you advance. This is because they don't (politically) trust those who are distant from their position. They also don't emotionally want to concede any part of their position.

SALES SECRET #103:
Prevent GDMs (genie decision makers)

Ask who the KDMs are or will be. If you have an internal champion within, they may tell you. Because your sale is in their minds, the longer it takes to identify the true decision makers, the longer it will take to get the foundations set for the three component sales and you run a higher risk of encountering GDMs.

By easing the decision makers into developing a level of comfort in adopting change, you are achieving the component pieces required to facilitate your endeavor to ask for **the Financial Sale.**

Team Selling

Once you've identified the types of pitfalls in your sales situations that require extra attention, you can work with colleagues to shore up areas where you aren't excelling. Your Wall of Wisdom is an effective sales support tool to facilitate cooperative team preparation. Interacting with a W.O.W. is also a form of practice that facilitates in-person, video, and virtual selling from a team sales approach.

Ensure you don't compete, or talk over one another. It's going to be cohesive and more effective if you've all read the same materials or are on the same approach glide scope in persuasion, so work from the Wall of Wisdom. If your styles mesh and compliment one another you can approach larger sales with a team approach.

Ignore the advice that recommends you avoid team selling. Selling with a team can often yield a larger commission for all involved than anyone could have earned individually. This is true especially on large complex accounts with longer sales cycles. It's also more impressive if you arrive with a few experts (sales professionals that are colleagues) to counter balance the KDM's team that may attend. Unless you are incredibly competent, it can sometimes be a psychological disadvantage to be alone when there are many on the other side of the table.

Conduct mock sales situations and become comfortable with hand-offs and lateral passes within the situation so things feel natural and coordinated. Practice. Then practice some more. Take turns simulating the role of DMs/KDMs so it feels realistic.

"Can you visualize yourself closing the sale? If not, then how will you persuade the key decision makers to see themselves buying?"

—ImmersiveSelling.com

Chapter 30

The Financial Sale

There is a deep emotional reward within the minds of sellers when sales close. Few emotions surpass the elation experienced when you close a sale that you're proud of. You're going to seek out that experience again. Once closed, a new business relationship opens and you'll be continuing to improve others' lives.

Your chances of closing increase when you are not overly anxious. People can sense when you need a sale to close and that can actually increase their apprehension. You've helped others by being a consultative resource, so continue that approach and speak in a relaxed tone. You will want to remain available and helpful, but not pushy.

> "A great pre-close question is asking, 'You may be wondering what's involved in finalizing the paperwork?'

When you arrive at the metaphoric radio tower on the horizon by plotting and following a series of tactical way-points that you plotted and followed, you see your own potential more accurately. You also realize that you have a way to replicate Rock Hard Coin if you ask for the sale. You see that your income is unlimited and no one but you is telling you what you can and cannot earn. You have your own future success to build and it's a liberating realization. You just need to ensure you can ask for the sale.

When selling within complex sales involving consensus buying committees, everything leading up to the close is involved, often difficult, and requires being on top of your game. That's where most of the complexity is because those are the component sales that need to be closed—and that's a challenge. The Financial Sale is often far less encumbered and is just a natural conclusion to a sequential progression of interactions.

Closing the Financial Sale is far more dependent upon what you've accomplished in the sales situations leading up to the close, than anything you'll be doing within the actual sales close. Often the DMs and KDM have decided what they're going to do and aside from some finishing details and paperwork with a few signatures and payment arrangements, there isn't a lot left to hem and haw about.

You may be thinking, "Not in my sales experience. My sales closes are brutal. I have to grind them out. The DMs have to be pulled over the line and often there are objections to handle and major decisions to be made before the Financial Sale can even be discussed. So. What about that situation? That doesn't sound easy, does it?" To which I would say, "You're right. I agree. But you just described the end process of one or more component sales. You aren't in the Financial Sale, you're closing component sales, and as stated previously, that's a challenge." Just because you call a situation a "sales close" doesn't mean it is. You already know what I'm going to say next. **It only matters what's in their mind.** When their mind is at the Financial Sales close, then, and only then, are you closing.

I like straight-forward closed-ended questions that get to the point. When I'm almost certain the component sales are closed I'll simply ask, "Are you thinking about solving this challenge now?" Another simple approach is to ask, "Should we proceed so you can have this result for your company?" These are closed-ended questions, which ultimately describes every closing question. At the time of the close you are almost always seeking a "yes" or "no" answer.

These closing questions aren't of course one-size-fits-all. The definitions of B2B sales incorporates a wide range of sales situations such as: corporate sales, complex selling, consensus buying committee, virtual sales situations, video sales situations, one-to-one, team selling, RFP/sealed bids, contract negotiation, and various proposal methods. You can look through all of sales and even when the sales close is itself an entire process and not necessarily a single question or event, the translative result to you as the seller is the same: it's going to come down to a "yes" or "no" response.

Most of the time the answer for how to close more sales is not in "how you ask" or "what you say." The answer to "how to close more sales" is found in the foundational work and construction process of building the sale through a series of engagements that seek and secure commitments.

Sometimes the decision to buy presents itself before an actual "closing sales situation" is scheduled. Much of the time, however, the close is a scheduled sales situation.

As you're working through the situational close you may often wonder "how to transition" to the closing question(s). An excellent segue is to ask a simple question as a "pre-close" which gives you several options depending on their answer. ***A great pre-close question is asking, "You may be wondering what's involved in finalizing the paperwork?"*** or "You may be wondering what's involved in owning this solution?" or "You may be wondering what's involved for the actual installation process?" You can use those questions to find ways to include the finalizing steps of your sales process such as: financing, measuring, fitting, assessment-of-needs, etc.

SALES SECRET #104:
Pre-close Question

By asking a pre-close question, you haven't yet committed to the final question so if you receive an apathetic answer to the pre-close, you know you'll need to revisit one or more of the component sales.

The reason for this pre-close question is if the KDM nods or shrugs positively, you can proceed and go through explaining the process (whatever that is). This provides you with just a little more time to gauge their reactions to the finalization run-through so they can ask any final questions and you can discover any lingering objections.

It often helps to have something to reference while you describe what will occur or what they can expect as you go through the paperwork/finalization process with them. If they seem distracted or preoccupied with some detail, then this approach allows you to back up and re-engage whatever they may be hung up on.

SALES SECRET #105:
Cost, Price, Result, Investment

When seeking out the price or seeing it, the decision makers will see the price as a cost if they haven't seen the result. If they've seen the result in their own mind through discussions with you, they will see the Financial Sale as an investment.

Use discovery questions to learn what they are thinking. Then you can reintroduce the run-up to the sales close. If they do nod and seem agreeable, that's a strong indicator that the first three component sales of the Quad Close have closed. After going through that with the KDM and/or DMs or the consensus buying committee, you can then just ask, "Does this look good to you? Would you like to proceed?" or "This looks complete, would you like to finalize this and schedule your delivery?" or "What do you think? **slight pause** Would you like to go through the paperwork and finalize this?"

SALES SECRET #106:
The "Slow No" and Serial Sales Situations

Sometimes you'll encounter a decision maker who "likes to meet" or finds it challenging to say "no." When this DM gets paired with a seller apprehensive about asking for the sale, repeat meetings may ensue. When nothing is accomplished, and the sale doesn't advance, this may be an unprofitable "slow no." It's okay to move on from these serial sales situations.

These are all variants of the same question that's asking for the sale. You can also interpret the questions into a conversational approach. You can talk around the subject for awhile and work in some of the same finalizations just mentioned. Once you've asked the question, such as, "Would you like to finalize this paperwork?" remain silent and let them think. Be quiet and listen. This approach will convey confidence. A primary source of confidence in asking for the sale is going to come from your **enthusiastic belief.**

SECTION 10

ENTHUSIASTIC BELIEF

Ten Primary Challenges You'll Face in the Future

1. Lack of Engagement — many DMs don't care until persuaded to [*see chapter 2*].

2. Lack of New Sales Opportunities — sales professionals who avoid prospecting are suffering from P.A.S.S. [*see facing page of chapter 22*].

3. Change Aversion — making a case for DMs and KDMs to change and buy your result will require an understanding of, and use of, the Quad Close [*see chapters 1 and 29*].

4. Commoditization — video and virtual selling have a downside in that your human dimensions are reduced to an often small, flat screen and you may be seen as just an app [*see chapters 13, 14, and 26*].

5. Differentiation — discernment between you and competitors by the DMs and KDM [*see chapter 9*].

6. Price/Inflation — inattention to the Quad Close may result in price objections [*see Strati-Tactical #8 and chapter 21*]. During inflation your price should be attended to (if only in your mind) almost like a separate topic. As a last resort you may find you have to engage in discounting, but don't lead with that crutch.

7. Closing/Achieving Quota — the challenge of achieving quota can lead to suffering from P.A.S.S. [*see facing page of chapter 22*].

8. B2B Complex Sales — there are more moving parts in a sale with multiple DMs and consensus buying committees. Analogies can give you an advantage [*see Strati-Tactical #5 and all of section 2*].

9. Technology — it has a way of requiring compliance to change and adoption of unfamiliar processes. Even when adopted, many will underutilize its power, such as the vast potential of advanced search functions using social selling [*see Strati-Tactical #7*].

10. The Buying Cycle Is Changing (again) — Both buyers and sellers will be influenced and guided by AI. The B2B market place will likely encroach upon sellers' markets [*This entire book will reframe your perception and give you new tools*].

"There's regret...and then there's wisdom-driven-regret."

—ImmersiveSelling.com

Chapter 31

The Eighty-Year-Old-You

"Cold calling" or "cold outreach" aren't subjects in sales. They are answers. Answers to the questions, "How do I improve my sales numbers and exceed quota?" and "How do I accumulate a bigger pile of Rock Hard Coin to achieve the goals I *really* want in life?"

> **It's extremely unlikely you will find immense success while on a low phone diet.**

There's only one perspective that should matter when considering the answers to these questions that will affect the rest of your sales career. One opinion from one person—the most important person you will ever talk to. Except you can't talk to this person—but you can listen as this person talks to you. This person and the one opinion that matters above all others is the eighty-year-old-you.

What your opinion is when you look back from that perspective to now—and then forward again is the ***only*** assessment you should consider for guidance of your sales career. Long after retiring, you and those you love will endure or enjoy whatever conditions the right-now-you set in motion. Your efforts to secure and generate new business, or lack thereof, will be what that version-of-you will have to live with. The eighty-year-old-you will be looking back to now and so you owe it to that person to read this.

You don't have to believe it, use it, or implement it, but you should give the eighty-year-old-you a chance to do something about that past that you can change now. Remember, there are "two pasts"...you can change only one of them. Right now is tomorrow's past that you can change. The past that becomes tomorrow, once passed, cannot be changed.

What the eighty-year-old-you will know then, that you could know right now, is that some of the advice you'll hear and receive is misguided or misfocused. The people and sources of discouragement aren't going to be full stakeholders in your future retirement. Some advice is solid. Some of it will mislead you. So how do you discern between the two? Use your intuition. That little voice inside. How many times in your life have you looked back and said, "I knew I shouldn't have done that," or "I knew that was the wrong way. Why did I do that?" You can sense when someone is covertly toxic and they make "their way" the easier path, but where will they be when you're 80 years old? Will they be accountable? Offering an apology for misleading you? ***You* need to listen to *you*.**

SALES SECRET #107:
Leads!

Prospecting for leads will likely drive revenue. Your revenue. Your Rock Hard Coin. There's a notion that closing is the more important activity...and while that is crucial, it's impossible to close what hasn't been prospected.

You can probably remember in your youth somewhere a neighborhood kid took a dare or made a bad decision based on peer pressure. Goaded on, they then sustained some form of permanent damage they had to live with for the rest of their life. Where are those peers now? Helping that kid-now-turned-adult? Doubtful. They aren't helping that person with the many life challenges that stemmed from the negative result.

No one in your career is going to stand responsible for any discouragement they offered, especially if you take the advice. Worse, if and when you ever do engage in a follow-up discussion about their ill-advice and after you've discovered their unhelpful motive and intent, they usually respond simply with, "That never happened." They won't own it anyway, so why take the advice now?

So how much Rock Hard Coin does that later-on-you ***actually*** have? You need to (literally, for real) sit down and project that forward. Don't hide from past procrastination. Avoid brushing shortcomings under the rug. You may not want to take a look at the truth right now but later you're going to really wish you had. You'll have no choice but to take a look at it then.

Later you're going to realize that, when looking back to now, the primary activities that would have made the difference in your career are prospecting and closing.

The eighty-year-old-you is going to be unencumbered with something you may be grappling with at this time (the truth) and that is that Rock Hard Coin comes from a strong commitment to prospecting. You'll know that then even if you refuse to believe that now. Just because you've heard something repeated to the point of ad nauseam, (the phone is dead!) doesn't make it more true (the phone is a very effective sales prospecting tool). So if you don't want to cold call, and you want to avoid doing the work social media prospecting requires, then you are reducing your own result (smaller sack of Rock Hard Coin). ***It's extremely unlikely you will find immense success while on a low phone diet.***

If you're on that diet, you may want to reconsider your approach because you have some very real challenges facing you [*see facing page at the beginning of this chapter*]. Those challenges all stand in your way of getting more Rock Hard Coin...and they are addressed in this book. But who is really standing in your way? The answer to that question is another question: "Will the eighty-year-old-you have the same answer as the you-of-today?" If the answer is "no" then who do you think is right? You or you? Probably you. You're right. So listen to you especially when you know the goals you seek are going to require you discover **enthusiastic belief and the crash monster.**

A selfie addiction may still find a way, even after the phone battery dies.

It may help to read the quote at the top of the next page while imagining you are hearing a deep, echoic, movie preview voice...

"In a sales world where only closing matters...using one lone pen...only one seller [that's you] can convert a purchase agreement into Rock. Hard. Coin."—ImmersiveSelling.com

Chapter 32

Enthusiastic Belief & the Crash Monster

Have you noticed motivation seems to wane even after a motivational event? Regardless of how motivated you are on a Friday afternoon to "do better next week!" those best-of-intentions seem to form a weekend patina by Monday. The Friday afternoon mental "rah-rah" is really just the mind's compensation for falling short of our potential when looking back on the week—by self-assuring with a promise to do better *next* week.

> **At the core of the decisions, actions, and habits of highly effective sales professionals, is an unwavering enthusiastic belief that they will succeed.**

We all do this and assure ourselves we will prospect more...actually get serious about cold calling...find new leads...improve social selling...catch up on LinkedIn...advance our sales. But the weekend patina on those Friday proclamations by Monday morning really tarnish our best intentions to hit the ground running and, "Become a prospecting machine!"

Monday usually arrives metaphorically in a stress-packed oversized shipping crate. The day gets unboxed and immediately starts symbolically spewing "S-shaped" packing/shipping barnacles all over your calendar and schedule. The Monday problems blow around the office like those packing/shipping barnacles until the pink static-charged things find something to stick to on your schedule, and they always do (and why are they pink?). At some point mid-morning you may give up on trying to keep them contained and just go hide in your CRM.

SALES SECRET #108:
Monday Is an Action Verb

Treat your Monday like it's an action verb and don't get stuck on a screen, or a CRM for the whole day. Get up and move, call a KDM... or twenty of them (or 30, or even 50)**. Work on your tight list of prospects. For you, Monday is an action verb.**

By Tuesday afternoon your frenemy at the watercooler and the gatekeepers on social and the phone have you demotivated and ready for Wednesday. By Wednesday mid-morning you learn an account that looked promising has become less so. Now you're fighting the inevitable motivational crash you can sense is on its way. We've all been there and we all know what comes next. You may have even gotten a head start on creating your motivational crash site (why wait?) and are already bending paper clips back and forth *snap*. You stack up the U-shaped shrapnel from the now-broken paper clips and keep them out of sight in an attempt to conceal the motivational crash site. Others take their crash to some quiet place where they can just meditate in misery. Some go online because you know, there's nothing to do there, right?

Thursday involves your internal mental investigator trying to figure out what happened, why, and who's at fault so that by Friday you have something, some place, or someone to blame because after all...you have that Friday afternoon treaty to re-declare. Again. "Next week I'll get on it. Next week I'll be a prospecting machine!"

Weekend patina on the promise...

Monday—"S-shaped" packing barnacles spilling forth from metaphoric crates

Tuesday—frenemy and the GK rejection

Wednesday—deciding on the best type of crash for that week

Thursday— investigate motivational crash site and find fault

Friday—blame, fib, re-declare treaty
Weekend patina on the promise...
Monday—"S-shaped" packing barnacles spilling forth from crates
Tuesday—frenemy and the GK rejection

and on and on your career goes...

There's going to come a morning when you're finally going to actually decide to stop crashing. One of the ways to stop crashing is to prospect. There are few sellers who will implement this as a solution however. Very few in sales could declare themselves at full capacity in their prospecting efforts. Everyone could prospect more.

Everyone.

Perhaps the greatest human equalizer is time. The time that you have in your life is a resource. Consider the cliche' statement, "food for thought." What is that really saying? There are multiple meanings there but the one often missed is that "time is food." But that won't be apparent until you see someone or something actually eating it.

Where can you see this (seemingly weird) event? That Wednesday morning bending paper clips? Yes. Putzing on the internet or entering data into the CRM or feigning a sales report? Yes. Yes. Yes. These are the motivational crash sites where the time-feedings have taken place. You see the crumbs, shrapnel, remnants, pieces and evidence, but what was feeding there? What caused the crash? What's going on now?

SALES SECRET #109:
Enthusiastic Belief

There are many excellent decisions made by high performers in sales and you can attribute the success to any one or all of them. ***At the core of the decisions, actions, and habits of highly effective sales professionals, is an unwavering enthusiastic belief that they will succeed.***

Look closer, and out of the wreckage of the motivational crash site emerges what I call the "crash monster." The crash monster survives by chewing up your time. It literally eats time. Your time. The more it eats, the more it wants. Its insatiable appetite is sociopathic and uncaring. The crash monster doesn't care about you (even though you're the host for this parasitic creature of self defeat), the crash monster cares about eating time and motivation.

SALES SECRET #110:
Your Invisible Toolkit Is Visible

Various industries have professionals that carry their tools in kits, briefcases or bags. Your career in sales requires a tool kit that is carried in your mind. It's obvious when a technician in another industry has a tool deficiency because you can see they are missing a kit. It's just as obvious to savvy decision makers when a seller is tool deficient. Even though the seller thinks their deficiency is hidden, the DMs know when you've arrived without tools.

The crash monster is very real and it doesn't just hide under your bed and climb on your back on your way to brushing your teeth in the morning. No one around you is likely going to see your crash monster because it stays well hidden. It eats your time and motivation in private. We may even look busy as the monster feeds on our day like an app processing away in the background. The crash monster eats apps for breakfast.

It steals its stealth from you, using shame, doubt, fear, and regret as a ghillie suit for camouflage. Just like the military ghillie suits that utilize materials from the immediate jungle environment (a fern stuffed in the back of the collar, some leaves up front, some mud on the arms, grass on the helmet) the crash monster's ghillie suit uses the office environment. Emails, non-emergency customer service during prime prospecting hours, the internet, cleaning our desks, defendable trips to the water cooler, and superfluous data entry into the CRM. If you work from home it's laundry, cleaning, personal calls, the internet, etc.

For ultra concealment, it has a secret agent type code name too, which changes à la chameleon style. It does this so it can even hide from you so you don't recognize it when you encounter it days after it gets going eating your motivation and time. It can disguise itself by using the alias names "procrastination" or "side work" or "data entry" or even longer names like, "someone-must-pick-up-the-V.I.P.-from-the-airport-so-get-someone-in-sales-to-go-do-it." The crash monster raises a very hairy hand and volunteers every time. Anything smart enough to use an entire sentence as a name? That's a formidable opponent.

The longer it stays hidden from you or disguised as another name, the more time and motivation it gets to eat. So you need to call the motivational crash monster out and assign it a name. Call it what it is so you recognize it when it gets hungry (never feed it...ever). Calling it by name puts a stage spotlight right on that furry frenemy so name your monster. May I suggest, "Crash?" It's very fitting and you'll easily identify it.

You may think that's a bit over-the-top huh? We're at the end of a business sales book playing with some kind of puppet monster? See that right there? That's what it does? It's trying to steal stealth. And what are the four tricks it uses to stay in stealth mode? Crash uses shame, doubt, fear, and regret. My Crash? It's whispering in my ear to *"Make a cool acronym out of those four. Maybe add a fifth? It would be good for the readers. You can help people..."* blah blah blah.

That's my whole point (See? You aren't getting an acronym). Crash doesn't care what kind of time or in what form your time is wrapped in. Crash can use scheduling software or time tracking apps like a tortilla and make a time-track-burrito-wrap. Even methods of accountability are known and easily defeated by Crash. The monster is just that good at being bad. Crash knows everything you know. Everything. It can read your mind because that's where it lives. It can open up memories like a kitchen cabinet and assemble a nice regret sandwich with two slices of shame, a thick piece of fear, and a side of doubt.

You'll sit and watch Crash eat digital clocks right off the wall. Your wrist watch? Num num. The clock on your laptop? It'll eat that too. Analog time for breakfast, digital for lunch, borrowed time for dinner. That's right. The crash monster even makes promises for the Tomorrow-You. Things you could get done today get slid until tomorrow to make more time to feed Crash right now.

Crash is just as smart as you are because, well, look where it lives. And tomorrow? You'll be so disappointed in the Yester-You for letting Crash eat your time that you'll have a stern talk with Crash. Try and get it under control. It laughs, and spits the four things there's no acronym for, right back in your face (shame, doubt, fear, and regret).

SALES SECRET #111:
Decide to Decide

Decisions are hard to make and even harder to maintain a commitment to. When your decision to win fades, you need a different strategy. You can decide to decide.

You've seen that old school scene in movies where the person who lost their job and should be out prospecting for a new one? Their crash monster has them feeding pigeons in the park. This is the 2020s and 2030s version of that. You can now do all of that pigeon feeding right online. How convenient, huh? Crash loves internet time. It's a favorite meat and potatoes, um, pixels and click-bait mainstay meal.

SALES SECRET #112:
Task Momentum

Not everyone likes to clean. But have you ever been house cleaning and find after some time you can't stop cleaning? You don't even want to? That momentum gave you a very clean space. Sales prospecting can go the same way. So stand up, walk to your work station and start on the smallest, easiest task you can find. When you're done, plan an easy task for the next day. This gives you task momentum.

Yester-You, Today-You, and Tomorrow-You all need to get in agreement that Crash needs a cage. You can't get rid of it. That's impossible. It's one of this monster's demotivational super powers. One bad day. One trigger. Some bad news. An argument. A GK hanging up on you...anything can summon Crash and rouse it from its covert slumber. Once it starts eating motivation and time again, it fuels up and gets energized...aaaaand you don't. Crash won't stop until it's consumed it all.

But it can be caged so that you can keep track of the thing. There's only one material you can make the cage out of, however. It should not be made from metal, for that is not strong enough. That is an extrinsic material (you know, all that real world stuff?). This monster can only be contained with an intrinsic material. That requires mettle. Mettle is stronger than metal.

Mettle is mined from deep within the mind. It is smelted in the forges of experience and wisdom and combined with your future dream mettle to create an alloy called enthusiastic belief. It's referred to (okay, now it is) as "EB" on the "Periodic Table of the Elements of the Mind." A cage made from EB is the only one capable of holding the crash monster. Fortunately for us, the cage made from EB alloys can be built instantaneously (as can anything else you want in your mind). Then, all you have to do is get motivated (Crash takes a nap when you're motivated) and then without waking it, simply pick up the "fur ball" (it's actually a huge monster) and toss it into the cage constructed of solid 48 carat EB and lock the door. Who cares if it wakes up, whines, moans, growls, snarls... whatever. When in the cage it can't eat your time. So don't let it out.

SALES SECRET #113:
Selling in a Down Economy

The worse the economic conditions are, the more you should invest in personalization. You'll go slower in volume but you'll be more effective and gain more incremental commitments. Don't let the "down" economy affect your enthusiastic belief.

You hold the keys to the cage and that monster will stay caged unless you decide to let Crash out. It can't break out or escape. The only way it can get out is if you open the cage door and let Crash have a five course meal. You already know what happens. A "Crash course in eating" ensues.

No one can sabotage the cage and no one else has a key. It's mind-ID'd and an internal key...there's only one, and you have it. People IRL (in real life) can tell when Crash is locked up too. So they'll walk up and try and rouse the thing. Try and rattle your cage and get you to go look—afraid Crash is going to escape—but it's a ruse. A lie. You'll recognize cage rattling as watercooler talk...bragging, rumors, demotivational statements, attacks, belittling, condescension, anger, disgust, and haughtiness. See these for what they are. Cage rattling perpetrated by toxic people to get you to go look at the cage. Let Crash out. Just for a snack. After some time you'll see Crash looking gaunt and hungry. Starving for a nice juicy work-time steak, medium rare with a side of literal seconds. Do not open the cage. Do not feed it. Keep the key hidden. Yes, you and Crash had a few good times together. But it's a monster. That was all trauma-bonding and Crash is trying to get you to reminisce. It just wants out and will say or do anything to achieve that end.

Let Crash slobber on the bars all it wants. Don't even get near the cage. It can reach out through the bars, you know? Imagine it gets tossed into a soundproof room like those recording studio windowed-off rooms. At least you won't have to listen to the wails and moans.

SALES SECRET #114: Acknowledging the Motivational Crash Monster

The real cost of feeding the motivational crash monster is atrocious. Once you cage it using enthusiastic belief, you get paid for succeeding at that.

"Time is money," ~*Ben Franklin* (he probably met Crash too). Crash was in a solid cage made of EB when he said that but he did the math. So have I. So should you. Because that's what Crash is actually eating. Your Rock Hard Coin.

Sure, you'll find new business when you get Crash back in its cage, but those accounts that would have been found with the time that it ate? It's a very real opportunity cost. You would not, absolutely would not take Rock Hard Coin out of your real bank account and feed it to Crash...well, some people actually do just that, but you're in sales and you know better. Even if you have, you're building a cage right now.

Once you realize that feeding the crash monster your time and motivation, is actually feeding it Rock Hard Coin, you have to ask yourself what are you getting out of the deal (feeding Crash)? The pure joy of aversion to prospecting is expensive. You are the source of power for that cage made from enthusiastic belief. It's mobile. It's unlimited. It can't be exhausted—even when you are physically spent. True, deep, enthusiastic belief is there waiting for you when you've rested—piles of the stuff. It's mined all night long when you sleep. You can even bury Crash's cage in the stuff if that helps keep it quiet (or muffled). Even when you slip and fall in your sales career, just knowing that you'll win when you get back up, is very motivating.

Enthusiastic belief is at the core of every great achievement humans have ever endeavored. It stands in the face of naysayers and negativity. It rolls right over toxic sludge from envy and spite. When unhelpful people (usually driven by envy) offer resistance to your goals, they concentrate their efforts on your mind, self image and confidence. Why? Because your plan and mental opinion of what you're doing and how you feel about it determines whether Crash is awake or sleeping (remember the monster naps when you're motivated because there's nothing to do).

Your emotional commitment to what you're doing is where they attack, so that's how you know that's your power source. That's where they hit. Every time. Because if they can nail you there, it rattles the cage and you let Crash out to eat. Misery loves company and guess who doesn't even have a cage made of EB? Toxic people. Ignore them because ***their*** Crash is feasting. Gorging itself even on others' time. The toxic people know this. Invest heavily in shoring up your enthusiastic belief with an emotional commitment to maintain it. That decision will protect your decision to believe.

SALES SECRET #115:
Enthusiastic Belief as a Propellant

What keeps you going is enthusiastic belief...far more than verbal motivation or sayings, or quips, phrases, memes or even peoples' positive words (although those are all very helpful too)**. So just believe you can. Just believe you will. Rock Hard Coin will probably follow.**

You can have the same deep advantage as the top performers in sales who all have EB cages and their crash monsters are locked up. You can have that right now. Just believe. Once you make that decision, your mind will align all of the variables you need in your career to win.

Down deep in your mind you need to develop non-negotiable enthusiastic belief that you will close sales...because that gives you hope. Hope is belief. Belief, in its truest form is faith that something will be or won't be, in the absence of proof. When you see this work for yourself you'll have proof it can work, and will again. Should you feel this comes true, ***please recommend this book to others*** you know would benefit from it. The truth is, much of this book will help anyone, even those who aren't in sales. If you know someone who needs motivation, clarity in life, or would like to persuade others, denote which chapters they should read when you recommend this book to them.

SALES SECRET #116:
Ask for a Referral or Introduction (it's worth repeating)

A DM's email or call to one of their colleagues on your behalf will greatly increase your chances of closing another sale. Or ask if they know anyone who could benefit from the result you offer, then get the contact info.

What you've read here encourages belief. The enthusiastic belief, however, comes from within ***you***. You must believe in your abilities. You must believe you can do it. Thank You for reading this book. Lock up Crash, and I truly hope you earn more Rock Hard Coin as ***your*** new result.

Sincerely,

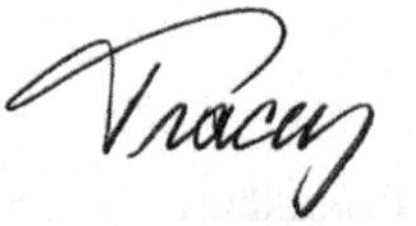

IMMERSIVE
SELLING

ImmersiveSelling.com

Tracey Preston Cook
Sales Coach | Business Strategist |
Analogy & Sales Tool Developer

tracey@immersiveselling.com
LinkedIn.com/in/traceyprestoncook
@ImmersiveSales

Font name: Adobe® Caslon Pro:
Foundry: Adobe®
© Copyright: Adobe® 2012
Release Date: 2012
Used for all text, body text, section title pages e.g., "section 1", and words, "Sales Secrets" on cover
Original Fontographer for "Caslon": William Caslon (1692-1766)
Font designer/fontographer that redesigned Caslon into the current font: "Adobe® Caslon Pro": Carol Twombly (Twombly's 2012 font is the licensed version used in this book). A special thanks goes out to Carol for what you've given the world of design.
Font license purchased by: Tracey Preston Cook/Immersive Publications on December 7, 2020 from MyFonts Inc. Order Number: M11906629

Font name: Corporate Western 22*:
© Copyright 2022
Foundry: Immersive Publications
© Copyright: Tracey Preston Cook
Release Date: 2021
Used for all chapter title pages and strati-tactical title pages.
Font designer/fontographer: Tracey Preston Cook
Font license purchased: (license is self issued) in December 2021. At this time it is not available for purchase and is protected by copyright.

Font name: Illustrationary*:
© Copyright 2022
Foundry: Immersive Publications
© Copyright: Tracey Preston Cook
Release Date: 2021
Used for cover text "You Don't Know" and illustrations in the Strati-Tacticals
Font designer/fontographer: Tracey Preston Cook
Font license purchased: (license is self-issued) in December 2021. At this time it is not available for purchase and is protected by copyright.

*The unauthorized use of Corporate Western 22 and Illustrationary are strictly prohibited without prior written permission. Lifting the fonts from this book and converting them to scalable vector graphics (or any other file format) and then porting the files to a font pack for resale is prohibited and doing so will be detected in the marketplace.

Made in United States
Orlando, FL
04 November 2026

90202236R00184